For my good frie...
whose warm ways and
openness all enjoy.

David

Bodily Expressions in Psychotherapy

Bodily Expressions in Psychotherapy

DAVID A. STEERE, Ph.D.

Professor of Pastoral Care and Counseling
Louisville Presbyterian Theological Seminary

BRUNNER/MAZEL, *Publishers* • NEW YORK

Library of Congress Cataloging in Publication Data

Steere, David A., 1931–
  Bodily expressions in psychotherapy.

  Includes bibliographical references and index.
  1. Psychotherapy patients.   2. Nonverbal communication (Psychology)   I. Title.   [DNLM: 1. Kinesics.
2. Psychotherapy.   WM 420 S814b]
RC469.S69   1983   616.89′14   82-19748
ISBN 0-87630-322-X

Published by
BRUNNER/MAZEL, INC.
19 Union Square West
New York, N.Y. 10003

Acknowledgments

I am grateful to a number of persons who have shared in this work. There are my graduate students here at Louisville Presbyterian Theological Seminary who caught my interest, particularly Christopher Schooley, Jack Cushman, Dan Kirkbride, Don Stokes, and Myrl Moore who were involved in developing and carrying through the first stages of research. Bob and Mary Goulding have been profoundly influential, and I particularly appreciate Mary's encouragement upon reading the manuscript. I am indebted to the careful editing by Chuck Leach and Sarah Brown who did much to make it clear and readable. Nor could I imagine presenting this material without the sensitive artistry of M. Jen Wessler who drew the figures, and Ollie Hofmann's willing hand on the diagrams and tables. Martha Pickering's work in preparing the manuscript with her careful attention to consistency and detail was invaluable, along with the help of Dot Matthews and Patti Eastman from time to time. I am also grateful to my family—to Margaret, my wife, and to Elizabeth, Andrew and Tevis, my children, and to my mother, Marjorie Steere, for their interest and support. And finally, I am grateful to the persons who appear as subjects in this study. Their willingness to become co-discoverers with me in this fascinating field of nonverbal behavior made them more my teachers than my clients.

Contents

List of Illustrations

Introduction

This book is about the bodily movements people make in psychotherapy. It is based upon a decade of observation dating back to the early 1970s
when I began studying videotapes of subjects in individual and group therapy
with my graduate students. There followed from this a number of techniques
which were readily transposed into clinical practice. There also followed a
wealth of information which I offer as a guide to anyone who is interested in developing the ability to work with this fascinating channel of human expression.

In this study, bodily movements are examined as concrete expressions of
specific ego states which belong to a person's repertoire of behaviors. Eric Berne
was the first to identify Parent, Adult, and Child ego states among patients in
group psychotherapy.[1] Although he spoke of these ego states as psychic organs, he was largely concerned with their functional displays in consistent patterns of thinking, feeling, and acting. They were "phenomenological realities"
which any person can be taught to observe in five minutes. The behavioral diagnosis of an ego state included an observation of postures, gestures, and mannerisms. My own work began with efforts to identify specific bodily behaviors
that were part of an enduring system of ego states which persist within the individual as he or she transacts with the world around.

KINESICS

Terms like "nonverbal communication" and "body language" are frequently
employed to describe studies in this field. Something in me resists them because they suggest that movements we make can be reduced to "messages"
which we encode and decode. We do not have bodies, we *are* bodies. Each

person is some*body*. This is consonant with the Judeo-Christian tradition in which the individual is always regarded as a psychosomatic whole. It is expressed in the wisdom of the people of the land and their poets who know the heart "leaps for joy" or "breaks with sorrow." We are no more the words we speak than we are the tingling in our spine. We are no more our ideas than we are our pulse rate or our blood pressure or the way we sit, stand, and gesture.

All our learning as human beings is initially based upon our sensory experience. Piaget observed that our first thinking is in the formation of sensorimotor schemes.[2] Movement is thought—grasping, touching, tasting, crawling, walking. Our eyes widen with alarm, narrow with suspicion, beam with delight. Our legs kick with joy or thrash with a temper tantrum. The bodily expressions that dot our language possess the concrete, symbolic character of thinking in the preoperational period, which for Piaget follows upon our initial sensorimotor thinking. "He kicked hell out of him and ran" may quite concretely describe a physical event, or symbolically describe a short interchange in which the subject accused someone pointedly of an embarrassing indiscretion and then quickly withdrew, excusing himself.

More recently, studies in neurolinguistic programming by Bandler and Grinder suggest all thought is based upon sensory experience.[3] Through an examination of speech (surface structure), the deeper structure of experience governing thought becomes evident. Predicates in an individual's sentences reveal the mental representational system employed to think. If the individual's primary representational system is *auditory,* words and sounds are important. Verbs are auditory: "I hear you"; "Just listen to me"; "That sounds right." Words are etched in profound significance: "She said she hated me." Being heard, listened to, and told are important. If the person's primary representational system is *visual,* thought is in mental images formed from experience. The predicates contain visual verbs: "I see that"; "Let's get this clear"; "I want to focus my thoughts." The visual person thinks in pictures, wants to *see* things clearly, and benefits by being shown. If a *kinesthetic* representational system is primary, the individual thinks in terms of bodily sensations, feelings, and actions. The verbs are kinesthetic: "That feels right"; "I sensed something"; "He makes me sick to my stomach." Since we all learn of the world through our sensory experience, we are all capable of thought in each representational system —auditory, visual, and kinesthetic, even olefactory and gustatory. Language is but one means to represent this experience to others in common verbal symbols.

Within this context, I choose to regard the bodily movements people make within psychotherapy as part of their thought process. Particular movements represent the deeper structures of their sensory experience as human beings. And this *being* we have as humans is more basic than any set of messages we exchange in "nonverbal communication." We gesture not only "in order to . . ." but also "because of . . . " and we are always dealing with a larger life process than mere communicational exchange. The elegant patterns in which we move our bodies are like a poem which should not be reduced to mean this or that but permitted to *be* an expression of many meanings.

I prefer the term *kinesics,* which Birdwhistell chose, to denote the study of basic units of body movement within the process of human interaction.[4] No doubt we are all interested in what common meanings we can attach to a certain movement, posture, or gesture. But we are dealing with something more than a special language, like our spoken one, that may receive definitions in something comparable to a dictionary, as Nierenberg and Calero suggest in their recent work, *How to Read a Person Like a Book.*[5] Birdwhistell is careful to note that the study of kinesics involves more than the mere classification of messages delivered at different levels. It involves understanding the person himself or herself, that person's own history and background, cultural and ethnic origin, and everything else that individual brings into the specific context at hand.

RESEARCH

There are four discernible phases of research in this work. The first phase began in the fall of 1969 with the formation of five weekly treatment groups which have continued without interruption since. These groups became a center for training and research for a number of graduate students in the Doctor of Ministry program at Louisville Presbyterian Theological Seminary, where I am Professor of Pastoral Care and Counseling.

Phase 1 was exploratory. Students learning transactional analysis were concentrating on identifying Parent, Adult, and Child ego states, using the customary means of behavioral diagnosis: voice, tone, mannerisms, postures, gestures, etc. One of the students, Myrl Moore, experimented with rapid-sequence photography, coordinating visual still pictures with time notations on audiotape.[6] Two others, Dan Kirkbride and Don Stokes, devised an ingenious means to quantify a person's bodily behavior in various ego states.[7] A plastic overlay was affixed to the viewing screen on video replays of subjects, providing a quarter-inch grid around an x and y axis, which enabled them to plot each basic posture assumed by the subject and record each identified movement of head, trunk, and appendages through measurement of its extent. Jack Cushman and Christopher Schooley studied the movement of two clients in psychotherapy using the same procedure.[8]

Phase 2 was an empirical study of subjects in group psychotherapy conducted in 1973. The specific bodily movements of 16 members of two weekly treatment groups were recorded on videotape over a three-month period. Christopher Schooley focused his attention on postures and gestures associated with
psychological games (repetitive transactional sequences which end in a payoff
with familiar bad feelings).[9] Kirkbride and Stokes studied changes in patterns of
movement within the ego states of each subject as a measure of psychological
change.[10] Interpretive sessions were held with all subjects afterward to explore
treatment advantages available through the findings. This phase refined the
technical apparatus from which the clinical applications of this work are derived. Chapter 3 offers a summation of the findings in these first two phases. It
contains materials from unpublished papers presented to the summer confer-
ence of the International Transactional Analysis Association in 1972 and 1973.

The third phase was that of clinical application. During Phase 3, over 600 clients were observed in their bodily behaviors in individual and group treatment.
Sketches of basic postures, specific movements, and sequences of bodily behavior were recorded regularly as part of note-taking following sessions. At different periods, a camera was kept in the treatment room and used to photograph particular bodily positions of clients. The materials included in the chapters on Interventions, Bodily Duplicity, and Signal Behaviors were developed.
One notable difference stands out between the video research and the clinical
phases. The bodily behavior of clients was much more striking and dramatic in
the absence of cameras and a research climate.

During the past four years, my clinical research entered a fourth phase of correlating bodily behavior and the client's life script. Berne coined the term "script"
to denote a life plan maintained in one's Child ego state outside of Adult awareness.[11] It is based upon a series of decisions made in childhood, reinforced by
parents and the primary family group, and justified by subsequent events. The
script, as the term suggests, functions like a "part to portray" in life through dramatic exchanges with others from first curtain to last. Berne noted that specific
bodily behaviors could serve as "script signs" including characteristic postures,
gestures, mannerisms, tics, symptoms, and the like. He believed they often revealed the patients going through their life story in a few minutes or seconds in a
way that might otherwise demand laborious months or years to dig out. "Un-
fortunately," he added, "there is no rule to pass on about how to know when
this is happening."[12]

The latter chapters of this book are devoted to classifying script signs and
some appropriate rules for the therapist in spotting them. The task was a difficult one and a source of much delay in completing this work. In the process, I
was forced to abandon the notion that there is one predominant *script sign* for

each person. Instead, there is a whole system of behaviors which are *in script*, the most notable (to us) of which we may call *the* script sign. Once perceived, however, this gives way to another and to another, serving only as a point of entry into the world of an individual's archaic Child experience, well preserved and embellished across the years. The good therapist knows what to look for, never what he or she will find.

As will become apparent, there is a line of continuity between the earlier phases of research by videotape and the latter phases of clinical observation. Yet the two methods are radically different. They represent two entirely different research strategies as discussed by Harper, Wiens, and Matarazzo.[13] The latter is in accord with the *structural* approach which is observational-descriptive, nonexperimental, and nonstatistical in nature. This is opposed to the experimental *external variable* approach which in principle governed the earlier phase. The difference, as Birdwhistell noted, is between the British tradition of observing an ongoing process, and American empiricism with its experimental designs to isolate variables between subjects and control groups.[14]

My own research role in the clinical phases is best described as that of "participant-observer" in the tradition of Harry Stack Sullivan, for I am witness to events in which I participate.[15] The majority of these events appear to defy exact reproduction in the experimental or laboratory setting. I have never seen a photograph or a videotape record which accurately reflects the full, visible impact of another person's bodily presence. For this reason and to protect the anonymity of my clients, I have employed Jenelyn Wessler to sketch all the visual representations. She has worked entirely from photographs and clinical notes to render a more lifelike portrayal of such materials. Her touch is sensitive and profoundly accurate.

Debate about the substance and validity of clinical research will continue as long as the experimentalist insists on airtight designs and the clinician lacks enthusiasm for the tedium of detail. The findings related here are offered in the confidence that any practicing psychotherapist who attunes vision to what goes on in treatment can corroborate them. The work is not exhaustive. It is sufficiently thorough to permit a therapist to approach clients with a working set of perceptual tools and some familiarity with what is important to look for.

Readers who are familiar with transactional analysis will find these materials organized around the major tasks of structural analysis (addressing the internal dialogue between ego states), transactional (and game) analysis (addressing signal behaviors in exchanges with others), and script analysis (addressing the formative scenes that govern an individual's sense of destiny). Readers who are not will find the same materials easily adaptable to their own frame of reference. For their benefit, I have written Chapter 2 to provide sufficient definition of terms to enlist understanding without extensive technical discussion. I also have in mind the growing numbers of persons beyond the helping professions who elect to listen in on our conversations in order to broaden their perspective on life. This group includes our clients who are entitled to as much information about what we do as possible. My aim is to present this work in a fashion that will leave none who are interested behind.

REFERENCE NOTES

1. Berne, E. Ego states in psychotherapy. *American Journal of Psychotherapy,* 1957, 2:293–309.
2. Piaget, J. *The Origins of Intelligence in Children.* New York: International Universities Press, 1952.
3. Bandler, R., & Grinder, J. *Frogs into Princes.* Moab, Utah: Real People Press, 1979, pp. 5–78, contains a good summation of representational systems and accessing cues. See also Bandler, R., & Grinder, J. *The Structure of Magic,* II. Palo Alto: Science and Behavior Books, 1976.
4. Birdwhistell, R. L. *Kinesics and Context.* Philadelphia: University of Pennsylvania Press, 1970.
5. Nierenberg, G. I., & Calero, H. H. *How to Read a Person Like a Book.* New York: Cornerstone Library, 1971.
6. Moore, M. Nonverbal communication as a diagnostic and therapeutic tool. Unpublished Masters Research Project, Louisville Presbyterian Seminary, 1972.
7. Kirkbride, D. L., & Stokes, D. T. A Multi-representational analysis of body movement. Doctor of Ministry Research Project, Louisville Presbyterian Seminary, 1975.
8. Schooley, C. G., & Cushman, J. Body research. Unpublished manuscript, Louisville Presbyterian Seminary, 1972.
9. Schooley, C. G. Games, injunctions and bodily behavior: An investigation into the movement of individuals in a psychotherapy group. Doctor of Ministry Research Project, Louisville Presbyterian Seminary, 1973.
10. Kirkbride, D. L., & Stokes, D. T. Op. cit.
11. Berne, E. *What Do You Say After You Say Hello?* New York: Grove Press, 1971, p. 418.
12. Ibid., p. 346.
13. Harper, R. G., Wiens, A. N., & Matarazzo, J. D. *Nonverbal Communication: The State of the Art.* New York: John Wiley & Sons, 1978.
14. Birdwhistell, R. L. Op. cit., p. 18.
15. Sullivan, H. S. *The Psychiatric Interview.* New York: W. W. Norton, 1954, pp. 3–25.

Bodily Expressions in Psychotherapy

1

The field of kinesics

In Shakespeare's famous play, Hamlet wishes to determine whether the king is guilty of assassinating his father. He arranges for a group of players to put on a skit depicting the suspected treachery before the court. Then he and his friend, Horatio, station themselves where they can observe the king's bodily reactions, with Hamlet's instructions:

> I prithee, when thou seest that act afoot,
> Even with the very comment of thy soul
> Observe mine uncle; if his occulted guilt
> Do not itself unkennel . . . .[1]

It is a matter of time until anyone doing psychotherapy becomes interested in the field of kinesics. "No mortal can keep a secret," Freud once wrote. "If his lips are silent, he chatters with his fingertips; betrayal oozes out of him at every pore."[2] Freud regularly made clinical notes of such "symptomatic actions," believing them to be invaluable in orienting the physician to new or unfamiliar conditions with patients.[3] To the keen observer, they often betray everything, occasionally even more than one wants to know. Freud wryly added that he could not maintain he always made friends with those to whom he told the meaning of their actions. But he remained fascinated by movement and gesture, noting that the person who attends to them "sometimes feels like King Solomon who, according to the Oriental legend, understood the language of animals."[4]

3

BACKGROUND

My own interest in kinesics goes back almost two decades to a period of training in psychotherapy with psychiatrist Warren Cox, then Director of the Louisville Area Mental Health Center. For an 18-month period, he did continuous case supervision of my treatment of a young woman, much of which was videotaped. We watched my uneasy shifting when she blinked her eyelids, the way we leaned back from each other to avoid certain issues, or leaned forward to engage each other. My formal interest began there.

When I think about it, my natural interest goes back much farther, perhaps to the way I watched a teacher in grade school to see if she was aware of notes we scribbled and passed to one another. At least, it dates back to a conversation I had as a sophomore in college with one of the best linebackers I have seen. "Honey," as we called him, played behind me on defense and had an uncanny knack of knowing exactly where our opponents were going to run the next play. When he pointed a stubby finger or jumped in next to one of us, we made a lower charge and looked up immediately to find the ball carrier.

"How do you know so often?" I asked.

"I feel it," he said. "You have to watch the lean of the backfield."

Try as we would when watching films, we could never see the "lean" that Honey spotted from his perch behind the line. The opposing backfield always looked straight and in proper stance. Nor could I ever read that quiet confluence of muscle and balance that Honey saw weekly across from us. My position as a down lineman forbade this. But I did learn to follow the eyes of backs as they broke huddle to spot that irresistible, last-second glance at the point where they were headed.

A Holistic Approach

My own background and training as a Presbyterian minister lent itself to a holistic approach as a pastoral counselor. In 1876, George M. Beard presented a paper entitled "The Influence of the Mind in the Causation and Cure of Disease and the Potency of Definite Expectation" before the Second Annual Meeting of the American Neurological Association in New York. In it, the famous neurologist maintained that disease might appear and disappear without the influence of any other agency than some kind of emotion. So new and startling was the presentation that William A. Hammond remarked during the discussion if the doctrine advanced by Beard were to be accepted, he would feel like throwing his diploma away and joining the theologians.[5]

Beard's paper was a precursor of a holistic approach in medicine and psychiatry which viewed the person as a psychosomatic whole, denoting the constant and inseparable interaction between *psyche* (mind) and *soma* (body). Theologian Daniel Day Williams described the implications in terms of the "principle of linkage" in which "every part of man's experience as God's creature is seen as linked with every other part."[6] Emergent holism fits the ancient Hebrew-Christian view of man as a psychosomatic whole. As Cyril C. Richardson wrote,

> Against the Greek disparagement of the body, the Christian affirmed its resurrection, and thought of salvation in terms of the healing of the *whole* person—body, mind, and spirit. Salvation meant the recovery of wholeness or holiness, for these words (and their Greek counterparts) are originally identical in meaning and derived from the same roots.[7]

"Salvation is basically and essentially healing," observed theologian Paul Tillich, "the establishment of a whole that was broken, disrupted, disintegrated."[8] Although few physicians have thrown away their diplomas from medical schools to study theology, we have entered a new era of cooperation among the helping professions with concern for the whole person. Health for Karl Menninger consists in the capacity of the organism to maintain *the vital balance* necessary under the continual stress of life to pursue its purposes.[9] The point of illness, somatic or psychic, is analogous to the "Plimsoll mark" which indicates how heavily a ship may be safely loaded, yet retain enough surplus buoyancy to withstand the added stress of storms. More recently, oncologist Carl Simonton has worked with cancer patients to assume responsibility for their immune system and fight the disease through stress reduction, regular meditation, and exercise, emphasizing the role of therapists as models for healthy living.[10]

In a holistic approach we are what we do in our bodies, just as much as we are what we think in our minds. With the "principle of linkage," we stand to learn fully as much through paying attention to kinesics as to conversation. For Dr. Hammond's benefit, I have chosen to write this book in interdisciplinary terms, not just for pastoral counselors, so that people with many different kinds of diplomas on their walls can take what benefits it offers.

Transactional Analysis

I began my teaching in a theological seminary as an eclectic among psychological schools, feeling it my duty not to prejudice students toward any given system. I have since decided that an eclectic is someone who takes the best from a number of theories and throws it away. Professional education involves teaching people to practice, and that means learning to do something well, not to discuss the relative merits of differing approaches. Since that time, I have taught transactional analysis.

Transactional analysis is a system of social psychiatry which begins with the task of analyzing or figuring out what goes on in transactions or exchanges between people. It has certain pragmatic assumptions, like any helping theory. One is the assumption that if therapists establish an "I'm OK—You're OK" position with clients, they get on with the task of change. However, OKness is one of the most misunderstood concepts among outsiders. It has nothing to do with moral perfection or psychic flawlessness. It has to do with responsibility, with treating others as capable of making responses, as people who are neither bad nor helpless, but "card-carrying members of the human race," as Berne often put it. The position "I'm OK—You're OK" is a transactional stance which the therapist enters into in good faith with the next client because of its pragmatic effectiveness with the last. Berne thinks he discovered it. I think a similar leap of faith was undertaken in the Christian community by accepting the Pauline doctrine of "justification by faith," that in spite of all the trouble in the world, we can live and act toward each other as though our existence before God is justified or all right.

The same principle of OKness is operative for the clinician who adopts transactional analysis as a primary frame of reference. One need not define oneself in a "school" as over and against others. It is OK to learn from those in behavior modification; they talk about patterns of reinforcement; we talk about patterns of stroking. It is OK to learn from those in the psychoanalytic school; they offer a wealth of developmental theory helpful in understanding the formation of ego states. It is OK to learn from the Gestalt therapists; they explore "top dog—underdog" dialogues in the individual which invariably involve what we describe as intrapsychic dialogues between ego states. It is OK to learn from the family therapists; the talk about an ongoing system of communication that produces an identified patient; we talk about an ongoing game process in the same family unit.

We can trace Berne's interest in identifying ego states through his early papers on intuition.[11] He became fascinated with how we know things intuitively, beneath logical awareness, without knowing how we know them. This led him to patterns of awareness early in life and, eventually, to observing a Child ego state among adults. This also led him to an immediate interest in bodily movements. One of his first explanations for the accuracy of intuitive judgments clinicians make was that they were based on unverbalized processes and observations, "performed 'automatically' because the kinesthetic image has become integrated with personality to such an extent that conscious awareness of how it is done is no longer required."[12]

In 1945, Berne was an army psychiatrist conducting 40-90 second psychiatric interviews with about 25,000 soldiers. He chose to brighten the routine by periods of intuiting the occupations of his subjects, recording each guess. He had his greatest success with farmers and mechanics, guessing farmers as high as 74 percent of the time. Further study of these two groups revealed some properties upon which successful intuitions were based. Among the farmers there was what Berne called "the farmer's eye sign." After a few seconds, their faces froze into a stolid expression, and their eyes shifted to the left to stare out of the window. By way of contrast, "the mechanic's eye sign" met the examiner's gaze by looking straight into his eyes with an expression of lively curiosity, but without challenge.[13]

The same stringent process of observation led Berne later to identify three distinct types of ego states among his clients: Parent, Adult, and Child, each with its own voice, vocabulary, postures, mannerisms, and gestures. Further refinement yielded five ego states functionally (see Figure 1). We can observe two kinds of Parent ego states, critical and nurturing. Critical Parent ego states are concerned with judgments and values, right and wrong, with what ought and ought not to be. Nurturing Parent ego states provide caring, concern, warmth, and protection. Likewise, we can see two types of Child ego states, adapted and natural. The adapted Child is modifying behavior under Parental influence, either compliantly or precociously. The natural Child provides color and creativity to the personality and is observed in those moments when we are uninhibited, intuitive, and spontaneous. Adult ego states process data accurately, give and receive information, and make decisions free from distractions.

The discovery of a sixth type of ego state in our locale bears mention, if not diagramming. It is the TA-Jackass ego state observed in certain individuals with newly acquired knowledge, who move among friends and associates dispensing it unsolicited ("That's your Parent," or "Who hooked your Not-OK Child?"). Upon inquiry, we find the TA-Jackass is not unlike the Psychoanalytic-Jackass ("You're repressing something," or "Aaaaaahhh . . ., Freudian slip!"), or the Behavior-Mod-Jackass ("You're reinforcing negative behavior"). Though irritating, this ego state is not terribly destructive, unless brandished like a weapon, and may prove a necessary phase of learning.

Bioenergetic Analysis

In the late 1960s, a series of workshops with Alexander Lowen and Stan Keleman in bioenergetic analysis carried me deep into awareness of my own bodily processes. They introduced me to the work of Wilhelm Reich and the concept of "character armor" residing in the actual structure of the body.[14] I became convinced that the way people breathe and move (and reach, stand, walk, or

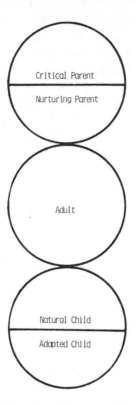

Figure   1. A functional diagram of the ego states

kick) is the product of muscular-skeletal development which, in turn, is the product of all our developmental experience. Although my attention here is on specific bodily behaviors in traditional therapy groups where people sit in chairs, the undergirding awareness of basic posture, stance, freedom of energy flow and movement, together with a sense of where the bodily blocks to this process are, has never been out of the background of my thinking. We are our bodies, as well as our thoughts, and sometimes more so.

Gestalt Therapy

My experiences in Gestalt therapy during the same period were equally formative. Fritz Perls' techniques for exploring the "awareness continuum" persistently focus attention upon assuming responsibility for everything we are doing bodily.[15] Our stomachs do not hurt, and our heads do not ache, and our fingers do not tap the chair. We become the pain in our stomachs or our headaches or the tap that is in our fingers, owning all that we are right now in this moment. Parts of us that emerge in bodily activity are majestically expressive of that which another part seeks to override or avoid or deny, constituting a royal road to the unfinished business of our present lives. Many of the techniques which I present are based upon Perls' fundamental principle of ownership of all that we are in a given moment. We "lose our mind in order to come to our senses" by permitting ourselves to "become" that troublesome part rather than to "talk about it" as something detached from us.

Psychodrama

A year of work with a psychodrama group in 1969 provided another piece in the background of this work. The concept of "acting" became for me a total experience for the first time. I had always avoided school plays, feeling I was a "poor actor." And I was. In psychodrama I learned to assume roles, permitting movement and feeling to flow and become one, realizing for the first time that people can act their way into new ways of feeling. Mirroring the postures, gestures, mannerisms, expressions, and intonations of other persons created new awareness of where another person really was, body to body, not head to head. Seeing myself mirrored in the same fashion placed me in touch with my own bodily presence in situations which had heretofore completely escaped my own cognitive processes. Such understandings are kinesthetic in character and defy simple descriptions through the auditory channel of words. I owe to psychodrama the notion of making an immediate change through moving and acting differently, allowing attendant shifts in responsiveness, affect, and cognition to follow.

Family Therapy

Finally, a number of training experiences with Virginia Satir and others in family therapy focused my attention upon the communication system created in the family unit.[16] Nowhere is the pattern of nonverbal behaviors that continually monitor, regulate, and alter relationships more evident. I became convinced that the "identified patient" or the person labeled as "sick" is so because of the role he or she plays in maintaining balance or homeostasis in the family system. Something analogous to the "double bind," in which the child is given a series of commands in direct conflict with each other in a situation from which there is no escape, is present in the injunctive structure that forms each life script.[17]

Gregory Bateson's concept of "metacommunication" as those behaviors which serve to instruct about or alter the ongoing communicational process opened the door to the most prolific studies of kinesics in our time.[18] Bateson's collaboration with Birdwhistell and others at Stanford in the late 1950s yielded a frame of reference which stripped this present work of any naive assumptions concerning its comprehensiveness. Birdwhistell estimates that upwards of 10,000 pieces of physiological data per second are observable to the serious student of kinesics.[19] Moreover, simplistic assumptions that a given posture or gesture means this thing or that ignore the best evidence that all bodily behavior acquires its meaning within the specific context of its use. Not only must we understand the person, culture, sex, ethnic background, social class, personal style, and regional idioms informing specific bodily movements, but we must also know the situation and the mood in order to place a pattern of movement in context. We cannot have isolated meaningful gestures.[20]

                                              OVERVIEW

We can date the rise of modern studies in kinesics from Charles Darwin's *The Expression of Emotions in Man and Animals*.[21] His classic descriptions of everything from head and limb movements among animals to the facial and bodily expressions of suffering, grief, joy, tenderness, reflection, anger, and fear in people launched a period of inquiry in such diverse fields as choreography, drama, psychoanalysis, and child development. An overview of these efforts will permit us to place this work within their context.

Developmental Patterns

One body of research focuses attention on the process of normal maturation in motor reflexes, locomotion, and coordination. Ames identified the psychomotor tempo with which the child manipulates objects as one that can be measured with great consistency over time and across varied activities.[22] Escalona and Heider accurately predicted the activity level, expressive behavior, and motor coordination from infancy to age six.[23] The Gesell studies revealed a persistence of energy output, motor demeanor, emotional expressiveness, and readiness for smiling over the first five years.[24] Allport and Vernon correlated such consistent patterns of movement with the subject's personality around clusters of variables that included expansiveness and emphasis.[25] In short, a number of developmental studies lead us to posit a natural, innate rhythm of movement present in each individual. This persists across time and can serve as one indicator of the person's personality.

Tension

Another type of study relates muscular and postural tensions to the personality. It appears that all emotional and mental activity is accompanied by specific neuromuscular patterns.[26] Duffy showed the muscle tension increased in one hand among subjects who became excited while doing key press exercises with the other.[27] Electromyographic recordings of muscle activity reveal increased tension in the forearms among subjects in psychotherapy dealing with their anger, increased tension in their legs when dealing with sexual conflicts.[28] Schizophrenic and neurotic children have been observed to evidence abnormalities in breathing and muscle tension.[29] Malmo has shown evidence from electromyographic recordings of a clear relationship between increased muscle tension and psychological stress, even that specific reactions in body parts are associated with somatic complaints.[30] Both the tension studies and the studies of developmental patterns add to the holistic "principle of linkage" in which whatever happens in the mind is evidenced by accompanying processes in the body, and vice versa.

Emotional Expression

Another group of studies pursued Darwin's interest in facial and bodily movements which convey the range of human emotions.[31] Most concentrate on the recognition of facial expressions by naive observers, using films or photographs, with or without a knowledge of the context. Schlosberg, for example, identified three descriptive dimensions for facial expressions which have been widely used: attention-rejection; pleasant-unpleasant; sleep-tension.[3:] Hanawalt found the lower part of the face to be better for judging happy expressions, the upper for surprise or fear.[33] A major issue in these studies is whether facial expressions are natural or learned or can be determined apart from context. Some advance evidence to show there are invariable meanings to certain expressions.[34] Others indicate most facial expressions are learned, and observers cannot agree on their meaning unless they know the context in which they occur.[35] The weight of the evidence in more recent, cross-cultural studies of kinesics is toward the latter view.[36] I have not found these studies particularly helpful to the clinician since they are largely concerned with codifying patterns of expression which are easily interpreted within their context in the treatment room.

Structural-Analytic Studies

Another set of studies is structural and analytic in character. Here, concern is with ways in which an individual's developmental history shapes contemporary movements. Early studies by Rene Spitz identified restricted motility patterns among institutionalized children, together with stereotyped movements and the inability to locomote freely.[37] Gerard related tics to earlier trauma and inhibited aggression.[38] Other studies point to hyperactivity among both animals and children as a result of periodic movement restraint.[39] We have already mentioned the school of bioenergetic analysis represented by Wilhelm Reich, Alexander Lowen, Stan Keleman, and others.[40] In their work we witness one of the more thorough efforts to identify specific muscular attitudes, pathological breathing patterns, and dead or immobile areas of the body. A series of exercises involving stress positions, breathing, and such activities as reaching, kicking, screaming, and striking are designed to effect regression and catharsis around earlier periods of supresed emotion in the person's development. Ida Rolf's techniques of "structural integration" are based upon a similar premise that different postures and chronic displacement of body parts represent "scars" of emotional and physical trauma, although she employs radically different techniques of physical manipulation as treatment.[41]

Seymour Fisher is an important member of the structural-analytic group in his assumption that *landmarks* exist in the body schema through which life experiences are coded as patterns of body movement and survive as circuits of sequenced behaviors.[42] These landmarks reiterate in actual muscle tone what has become important to the individual. Fisher found that the "body images" people possess tend to reveal significant trends in their life. For example, people with a high awareness of bodily boundaries tend to have a high number of skin and striated musculature ailments, as opposed to a low number of physical illnesses such as heart and intestinal ailments, which are more frequent among those possessing a low sense of boundary.[43] Other trends accompany "right awareness" (apparent heterosexual orientation) and "left awareness" (creative expression of the self) or "front-back awareness" (the greater the attention to the back, the greater the anxiety about impulses and the tendency to avoid positive expressions).[44] Fisher has demonstrated experimentally that differences in Galvanic Skin Response exist between left and right hands among his subjects in concert with such awareness.[45]

Among the psychoanalysts, Felix Deutsch has produced the most careful

analysis of bodily movements and gestures. Deutsch insisted that no adult muscular expression is free from its early ties.[46] He kept careful records of "posturo-
grams" during analytic sessions, noting positions of the limbs, postures of the
body on the couch, and specific gestures in relation to his patients' verbal
themes. He was able to identify movements in anticipation of thoughts or impulses which were highly specific in symbolic meaning. Like Reich, he noted
breathing patterns and movement patterns in the chest and abdomen. Postural
attitudes, he felt, became integrated as characteristic acts which are expressive
and consistent with one another. Their integration or lack of it provides the key
to the individual's functioning successfully in society.

Movement Analysis

Closely related, yet originating in an entirely different setting, is the approach
of movement analysis. Rudolph Laban, a European choreographer, developed
a system of movement notation (Labanotation) for dance and later extended it
to study drama, mime, work skills, culture, and personality.[47] Effort-shape
analysis, as it was termed, recorded the spatial pattern of specific movements
together with their rhythm and accent in something analogous to a musical
score. There have been other systems of movement notation by such persons
as Morris, Mosher, and the Russian choreographer Stepanov, but Laban's received the widest application to the diagnosis and treatment of psychological
problems.[48] Labanotation has been used to derive a "movement style" for each
member of a treatment group, to assess managers and executives in British industry, and to diagnose and interpret movement in specific areas of the body
during dance therapy.[49] North provides an impressive record of movement
analysis with school children, correlating findings with psychological tests and
developing specific suggestions for movement therapy growing from them.[50]
Both the structural-analytic school and the movement analysis school assume
that human beings reveal their personality through the accumulation and vari-
ety of their movements. Our bodily behaviors are more than an aspect of language or communication. They are landmarks in the building process of human development in which many and varied operations are compounded as
an expression of our inner being.

Nonverbal Communication

We have already mentioned that the most extensive studies of movement
behavior over the past two decades are in the field of nonverbal communication. Harper, Wiens, and Matarazzo offer an excellent review of research focus-

ing on nonverbal phenomena "that are most important in the structuring and occurrence of interpersonal communication and the moment-to-moment regulation of interaction."[51] They organize the literature into five topic areas:

1) paralinguistic phenomena which include nonlanguage sounds (moans, yells, etc.) and nonwords such as "uh-huh" and such variables as pitch, tempo, intensity, and range;

2) facial expression;

3) kinesics, which they define as all discriminable bodily movements, excluding facial expression and eye movements;

4) visual behavior; and

5) proxemics or how we structure, use, and are affected by space in our interactions with others.

Obviously a large number of bodily movements are kinesic markers synchronized to various units of verbal speech. For example, a drop of the eyes, the head, or the hands often indicates the end of a statement. This will be discussed in Chapter 6 on Signal Behaviors.

Specific patterns of gesturing and posturing have clear roots in the cultural context where they are developed and used. Efron has shown that with cultural assimilation, body movements of Italians and Jews begin to resemble each other in "hybrid gestures."[52] Similar changes occur when persons move upwards socially and economically. Scheflen described the dissatisfaction of a young English woman with the way her American boy friend crossed his legs in a "4-1 pattern," typical among us but offensive to the upper class Britisher who customarily sits with a more proper "scissors-cross." A young Puerto Rican boy who had been taught to sit looking down as a gesture of respect fled in panic from a middle-class American teacher using rapport techniques and trying to force the lad to look her in the face.[53]

Studies in nonverbal communication leave little doubt that a great deal of bodily movement is reciprocal and regulates the interactional pattern between persons. Kinesic reciprocals communicate affiliation, dominance, and submission. They comprise territorial behaviors in stance or seat to include or exclude others. And they evolve with language to become characteristic movements integrated into speaking and listening patterns signaling a range of metacommunication on lexical exchange from involvement to boredom, from assent to doubt, or from initiation to termination.[54] Our friends and intimates learn to "read" this communication well, although usually without awareness of how it

psychotherapy. There we are in the business of changing old rhythms of movement which no longer fit by opening up the freedom to make new ones. The work is fascinating. When we are successful, we can see the difference in the way people begin to move out across the spacious floors of their world toward others and start to "have a ball."

REFERENCE NOTES

1. Shakespeare, W. *The Complete Works of Shakespeare*. Ed. by G. L. Kittredge. Boston: Ginn and Co., 1936, p. 1169.
2. Freud, S. (1905) A case of hysteria. In: A. Strachey (ed.), *The Standard Edition of the Complete Psychological Works of Sigmund Freud*, 7:78. London: Hogarth Press, 1953.
3. Freud, S. The psychopathology of everyday life. In: A. A. Brill (ed.), *The Basic Writings of Sigmund Freud*. New York: The Modern Library, pp. 135-140.
4. Ibid., p. 136.
5. Lewis, N. D. C. American psychiatry from its beginnings to World War II. In: *American Handbook of Psychiatry*, Vol. I. New York: Basic Books, 1959, p. 8.
6. Williams, D. D. *The Minister and the Care of Souls*. New York: Harper and Brothers, 1961, pp. 26-29.
7. Richardson, C. C. Spiritual healing in the light of history. In: S. Doniger (ed.), *Healing: Human and Divine*. New York: Association Press, 1957, p. 207.
8. Tillich, P. The relation of religion and health: Historical considerations and theoretical questions. *The Review of Religion*, 10:351, 1946.
9. Menninger, K. A. *The Vital Balance*. With Mayman, M., & Pruyser, P. New York: Viking Press, 1963.
10. Simonton, O. C., Matthews-Simonton, S., & Creighton, J. *Getting Well Again*. Los Angeles: J. P. Tarcher; New York: distributed by St. Martin's Press, 1978.
11. Berne, E. *Intuition and the Ego States*. San Francisco: Harper and Row, 1977.
12. Ibid., pp. 1, 2.
13. Ibid., pp. 7-15.
14. Reich, W. *Character Analysis*. New York: Orgone Institute Press, 1949. See Reich, W. *The Function of the Orgasm*. New York: Orgone Institute Press, 1942. Lowen, A. *Physical Dynamics of Character Structure*. New York & London: Grune & Stratton, 1958.
15. Perls, F. S. *Gestalt Therapy Verbatim*. Lafayette, CA: Real People Press, 1969.
16. Satir, V. *Conjoint Family Therapy*. Palo Alto: Science & Behavior Books, 1964. Satir, V. *Peoplemaking*. Palo Alto: Science & Behavior Books, 1972. The literature in the field of family therapy is now extensive. The best overview is found in Gurman, A. S., & Kniskern, D. P. (eds.). *Handbook of Family Therapy*. New York: Brunner/Mazel, 1981.
17 A good, recent discussion of theory surrounding the "double bind" is found in Berger, M. M. (ed.) *Beyond the Double Bind: Communication and Family Systems, Theories, and Techniques with Schizophrenics*. New York: Brunner/Mazel, 1978.
18. See Scheflen, A. E. *How Behavior Means*. New York: Gordon & Breach, 1973, pp. 3-6, for a brief description of early studies in the field.
19. Birdwhistell, R. L. *Kinesics and Context*. Philadelphia: University of Pennsylvania Press, 1970, p. 3.
20. Ibid., pp. 65-84.
21. Darwin, C. *The Expression of Emotions in Man and Animals*. New York: Philosophical Library, 1955.
22. Ames, L. B. The constancy of psycho-motor tempo in individual infants. *Journal of Genetic Psychology*, 57:445-450, 1940.

23. Escalona, S., & Heider, G. M. *Prediction and Outcome: A Study in Child Development.* New York: Basic Books, 1959.
24. Gesell, A., & Ames, L. B. Early evidences of individuality in the human infant. *Scientific Monthly, 45*:217-226, 1937.
25. Allport, G. W., & Vernon, P. E. *Studies in Expressive Movement.* New York: Hafner Publishing Company, 1967.
26. Jacobsen, E. *Biology of Emotions.* Springfield, IL: Charles C Thomas, 1967. Duffy, E. Level of muscular tension as an aspect of personality. *Journal of General Psychology, 35*:161-171, 1946.
27. Duffy, E. Tensions and emotional factors in reaction. *Genetic Monographs, 7*:1-79, 1930.
28. Malmo, R. B., Smith, A. A., & Kohlmeyer, W. A. Motor manifestation of conflict in interview: a case study. *Journal of Abnormal and Social Psychology, 52*:268-271, 1956.
29. Duffy, E. *Activation and Behavior.* London: John Wiley & Sons, 1962.
30. Malmo, R. B., Shagass, C., & Davis, F. H. Symptom specificity and bodily reactions during psychiatric interview. *Psychosomatic Medicine, 12*:362-376, 1950.
31. More recently, recognition studies have been taken over as an integral part of kinesics where facial expressions are studied cross-culturally as communication signals or cues. See Ekman, P., & Friesen, W. V. Constants across cultures in the face and emotion. *Journal of Personality and Social Psychology, 17*:124-129, 1971.
32. Schlosberg, H. Three dimensions of emotion. *Psychological Review, 61*:81-88, 1954.
33. Hanawalt, N. G. The role of the upper and the lower parts of the face as a basis for judging facial expressions: II, in posed expressions and "candid camera" pictures. *Journal of General Psychology, 31*:23-36, 1944.
34. Frijda, N. H. The understanding of facial expression of emotion. *Acta Psychologica, 9*:294-362, 1953.
35. Landis, C. The interpretation of facial expression of emotion. *Journal of General Psychology, 2*:59-72, 1929.
36. Birdwhistell, R. L. *Kinesics and Context.* Philadelphia: University of Pennsylvania Press, 1970.
37. Spitz, R. A. Hospitalism: An inquiry into the genesis of psychiatric conditions in early childhood. *Psychoanalytic Study of the Child, 1*:53-74, 1945. Spitz, R. A. Hospitalism: A follow-up report on investigation described in volume I, 1945. *Psychoanalytic Study of the Child, 2*:113-117, 1946.
38. Gerard, M. W. The psychogenic tic in ego development. *Psychoanalytic Study of the Child, 2*: 133-162, 1946.
39. Levy, D. M. On the problem of movement restraint: Tics, stereotyped movements, hyperactivity. *American Journal of Orthopsychiatry, 14*:644-671, 1944.
40. In addition to Reich, W., *Character Analysis,* Reich, W., *The Function of the Orgasm,* Lowen, A., *Physical Dynamics of Character Structure,* see Lowen, A. *Betrayal of the Body.* New York: The Macmillan Co., 1967, and Keleman, S. *Your Body Speaks Its Mind.* New York: Simon and Schuster, 1975.
41. Rolf, I. P. Structural integration: Gravity, an unexplored factor in a more human use of human beings. *Systematics, I*:66-83, 1963.
42. Fisher, S. *Body Experience in Fantasy and Behavior.* New York: Meredith Corporation, 1970.
43. Ibid., pp. 167-234.
44. Ibid., pp. 321-406, 453-474.
45. Fisher, S. Right-left gradients in body image, body reactivity, and perception. *Genetic Psychology Monographs, 12*:197-228, 1960.
46. Deutsch, F. N. Analysis of postural behavior. *Psychoanalytic Quarterly, 16*:195-213, 1947.
47. Laban, R. *The Mastery of Movement.* L. Ullman (ed.), 1950. London: Macdonald & Evans, 2nd ed., rev., 1960. Laban, R., & Lawrence, F. C. *Effort.* London: Macdonald & Evans, 1947. New York: International Publications Service, 1971.

48. Morris, M. *The Notation of Movement*. London: Kegan Paul, Trench, Trubner & Co., 1928. Mosher, J. A. *The Essentials of Effective Gesture*. New York: The Macmillan Company, 1916. Stepanov, V. I. *Alphabet of Movements of the Human Body*. Lister, R. (Tr.), French ed., 1892. Cambridge: Golden Head Press, 1958. Brooklyn, N.Y.: Dance Horizons, 1969.
49. Laban, R. *Principles of Dance and Movement Notation*. London: Macdonald & Evans, 1956.
50. North, M. *Personality Assessment Through Movement*. Boston: Plays, Inc., 1975.
51. Harper, R. G., Wiens, A. N., & Matarazzo, J. D. *Nonverbal Communication: The State of the Art*. New York: John Wiley & Sons, 1978.
52. Efron, D. *Gesture and Environment*. New York: King's Crown Press, 1941.
53. Scheflen, A. E. *Body Language and Social Order*. Englewood Cliffs, N.J.: Prentice Hall, 1972.
54. Ibid.
55. See ibid., pp. 77-81, for a discussion of transcontextual acts.

2

Movement behavior
in psychotherapy

There are three different ways to address movement behaviors in psychotherapy:

1) We may view them as expressing something *internal* to the client. This intrapsychic focus in transactional analysis is termed *structural analysis*. Specific bodily movements may be explored for what they reveal about the internal dialogue going on among a person's ego states.

2) We can also examine movement behaviors as *external signals* from the standpoint of what they communicate nonverbally to others. This is the concern of *transactional analysis proper*, where specific exchanges between persons are analyzed for their manifest and latent content. Signal behaviors also punctuate the moves of psychological games at the ulterior level and involve us in *game analysis*.

3) Finally, we can focus our attention on movement behavior as a key to *formative experiences* in the individual's growth and development. In transactional analysis, this is the concern of *script analysis*. Here movement can be seen to embody characteristic responses to formative scenes in life. The manner in which these experiences govern current strivings with a sense of destiny becomes accessible through exploring these movements in the context in which they occur.

Of course, the above classes of movement behavior are not mutually exclusive. In fact, each is but one vantage point from which to view the same individual's inseparable life process. My aim in this chapter is to present some of the clinical advantages of doing so. There are other purposes, too. I want to introduce readers unfamiliar with transactional analysis to some of its basic conceptual tools. Also, these three perspectives on bodily movement need presentation at this point because the rest of the book is organized around them.

At the time of this writing, I had just seen three persons the day before, actually four, since the last hour was spent with a couple. It was the day I spend seeing individuals for intake, group preparation, and follow-up. For a number of reasons I want to begin with these three hours. First, the reality of our work is fresh and vivid. Second is a long-standing desire that clinicians write in terms of the everyday and commonplace, rather than of memorable cases. Finally, as good fortune would have it, each hour contains a good, clinical example of one of these three ways to address movement behavior in psychotherapy.

STRUCTURAL ANALYSIS

Structural analysis involves identifying with the client what is going on in the significant ego states surrounding the problem that occasions treatment. We can count on being met with some form of internal conflict. One part of the person wants to change, another does not. Otherwise, the desired change would have already been accomplished. The transactional analyst looks for this intrapsychic conflict within specific ego states that are vested with opposing interests. Structural analysis explores these opposing trends between the client's repertoire of Parent, Adult, and Child ego states. The clinician can usually see this duplicity in the client's body long before it is granted clear, verbal expression.

Kenneth's Machinations

Kenneth came at 2:00 P.M. He is a well-dressed, dark-haired, 41-year-old investment broker with considerable self-acquired wealth. As with all clients discussed, his name and significant facts about him are altered to prevent identification. I had seen Kenneth three times last year while he ended a marriage of 21 years with divorce and much professed guilt. Now his girl friend of the past two years was pressing him for emotional involvement. Emotional involvement—that was the one thing I had never sensed with him. I glanced over the records of a psychiatrist who saw Kenneth for eight individual sessions a decade ago, together with the psychological evaluation he requested at that time: "emotionally detached"; "the most salient feature is this man's lack of involvement with anyone"; "a fascinating, but inaccessible individual." We both knew the same person.

Kenneth wanted emotional involvement but somehow resisted committing himself to work on it, fearful he would "lose his drive." He never appeared troubled, unless he talked about his women or his family (two daughters, one of whom was psychotic). Even then, he began in his Adult ego state as though he were discussing a business problem. He is one of those clients I have to interrupt in order to be able to talk, which was one clue that something other than Adult was present. Another clue was the slow shift over to the right and away as he continued to speak, the curtailment of eye contact, and the emergence of rapid, chopping movements from a noticeably rigid right arm (see Figure 2). His left hand occasionally joined with his right in movement but with a striking lack of coordination for an old athlete. I interrupted to call attention to what he was doing bodily. "You mean my machinations?" he replied, in knowing familiarity with what he so aptly named them.

Kenneth's machinations revealed more than anything else going on. They are an excellent illustration of how bodily duplicity emerges beneath social level discourse to reveal the presence of another ego state with energy to resist the professed desire for change. I am confident the student of nonverbal communication could synchronize them with point units of conversation. I am sure a movement analyst would record their effort and shape as repetitive and distinct. From my own work, the cock of the head sideways, the occasional upward glances, and the hand movements outward with palm up, predominantly from one side, are all characteristic of a Child ego state. The important point was to encourage Kenneth to get in touch with what these bodily movements express so we could both find out for sure.

Diagnosing Ego States

Skills in diagnosing ego states are the most fundamental ones employed in transactional analysis. Berne sets forth four means to do so, which form the basis for structural analysis.[1]

1) The *behavioral diagnosis* is made in terms of the particular demeanors, gestures, voices, vocabularies, and other characteristics directly observable to the therapist. My own behavioral diagnosis was based upon Kenneth's postures, gaze behavior, and movements, not upon his voice which sounded Adult.

Figure   2. Kenneth's machinations

2) A *social* or *operational* diagnosis is made in terms of the responses one elicits from others with this behavior. In this instance, the therapist was aware of a fleeting impulse to "correct" Kenneth, to tell him to stop talking so much. My own Parental response served to confirm the behavioral diagnosis of Kenneth's adapted Child.

3) The *historical diagnosis* corroborates the first two when the client can recall scenes from prior life associated with the same behaviors. Here the repetition of a specific posture, movement, or gesture can often help the client recall other instances of doing the same thing. "This is the way I move when I'm trying to talk to my girl friend," Kenneth observed, "I struggle for a while, like with my wife, then I just give up and say, 'Fuck it.' "

With encouragement ("Keep moving like that awhile and tell me what comes to mind"), the clinician can often add to the historical diagnosis. I spent about 10 minutes doing so with Kenneth. First, he associated his "machinations" with memories of being an awkward, skinny high school kid who worked hard on academics, fought his way on the basketball court, and lived a social life restricted by shyness. Then the machinations led him to thoughts about being eight years old, withdrawing from the family, reading a lot in his room, and resolving to become a successful businessman like his father. This was followed with memories of being punished by grandmother and mother who provided him with daily reminders of how inhuman and nonfeeling men were, like father who was gone all the time. The two women had good cause for such an attitude since grandmother's husband left before mother's birth, insisting grandmother get an abortion. Kenneth's machinations took on the character of a struggle of long standing around members of the opposite sex from whom he always seemed to have to get away.

Structurally, Berne referred to the Child ego state as the *archeopsyche* because it served as a repository of past experiences.[2] He termed the Parent the *extereopsyche* because of its origin in the incorporation of behavior patterns from actual parental figures.

4) A *phenomenological diagnosis* validates the other three when the client can reexperience the intensity of archaic feelings transposed into the present. For example, Kenneth could have exclaimed, "I'm so scared, I feel like I'm five years old and cornered by Grandma." Such a momentary regression so excludes the other ego states that Kenneth would actually have felt five emotionally, but his strong Adult control precluded this. With other clients, such momentary regressions permit a phenomenological diagnosis.

Occasionally, a full regression can be quite dramatic. Randolph, a competent but proper lawyer who avoided being close to people, dreamed about an early scene when he was four. Father had left to live with another woman downtown. Mother was at work and siblings at school, while Randy was left with an erratic assortment of baby-sitters. His only remaining friend was a small dog named Scotty. He remembers sitting by a tub in the yard, calling Scotty at the top of his lungs, only to watch his pet run off and never return. As he recounted the incident, a flood of tears, accompanied by the rising wail of a small boy's voice, came forth so authentic to his age of four that he stopped abruptly to exclaim, "My God! I'm four years old!" The voice defied subsequent reproduction by conscious effort, but the emotional impact of an early decision never again to be so vulnerable remained.

Clinically, structural analysis constitutes such an exploration of specific ego states that the client brings to treatment. Beneath Kenneth's Adult profession of desire for emotional involvement, movements characteristic of him since he was a small child emerged to dominate the process. We are forced to deal over and over again with this adapted Child ego state and its resistance to desired change. And structural analysis takes shape as the task of figuring out with clients how they go about not getting what they say they want.

Psychic Energy and Executive Power

For those unfamiliar with transactional analysis, the concepts of psychic energy and executive power are important for understanding changes from one ego state to another.[3] Berne employed the term *cathexis* to denote an investment of psychic energy in a given ego state. There are three states of *cathexis:* bound, unbound, and free. *Bound cathexis* exists in an inactive ego state where energy is only potential and unexpressed, as in Kenneth's Parent ego state which was not active during the process. *Unbound cathexis* exists as kinetic energy released in motion or emotion when an ego state suddenly becomes active. *Free cathexis* exists in the ego state of chosen investment where the person is conscious of electing thought, feeling, or movement. The ego state in which free cathexis is predominant is perceived as "the self."

Executive power or control of the organism resides in the ego state with the greatest investment of active energy (unbound plus free). When Kenneth began to talk, free cathexis was in his Adult. With the rising emotional content of the conversation, unbound cathexis increased in his Child to the point where it effected a shift of executive power to this ego state. This normally happened without awareness for Kenneth who still maintained free cathexis in his Adult,

regarding himself as objective and desirous of emotional involvement. On occasion, he proceeded to shift free cathexis into his Child ego state, saying,
"Fuck it," and leaving (see Figure 3).

The aim of structural analysis is social control. Recognition, on Kenneth's
part, of the emergence of unbound energy in his adapted Child when the situation requires emotional involvement can create options. He has increased opportunity to maintain executive power in his Adult or to consciously shift
energy to another ego state more of his choosing. He may experience himself
as a person (free cathexis, Adult) who continues a conversation while aware of
mild discomfort or anxiety (unbound cathexis, adapted Child). Or he may elect
to express his anxious feelings and experience himself as a person who has

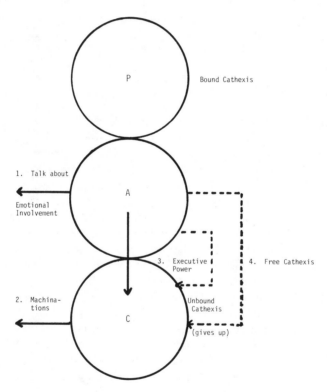

Figure 3. Kenneth shifting psychic energy from the Adult ego state in four steps

chosen to abandon himself to spontaneous expressions of emotion in the moment (free cathexis, natural Child). More frequently, interim measures like showing concern and understanding from a less threatening ego state (free cathexis, nurturing Parent) in such situations provide a more suitable means of social control.

TRANSACTIONAL AND GAME ANALYSIS

Transactional analysis proper concerns itself with an examination of social units of interchange between persons. Bodily movements addressed from this perspective constitute *signal behaviors* which regulate interaction. Signal behaviors are characteristic postures, movements, and gestures which elicit common responses from others. In contrast to bodily duplicity which normally goes unnoticed, signal behaviors are more easily sensed and "read" by friends and acquaintances. Their repetition is contingent upon the reactions they evoke. Their presence serves as a sign that something familiar is about to happen. The moves of every psychological game are punctuated by kinesic markers which reveal the ulterior alliance carefully disguised from awareness at the level of social exchange.

Leonard's Postures

Leonard, whom I saw at 4:00 P.M. with his wife, Marge, is one of those clients whom I find difficult to write up. He had been in group for six months following a preparatory weekend. His contract for change was to "stop getting put down." Although he had held a number of responsible positions, he had lost several and failed to advance in others. He and his wife existed on the brink of carrying their marriage into the courtroom to end it legally. Often their children intervened by telephone calls and visits to keep them together. Nothing was changing for Leonard in his treatment or in his life.

The occasion for seeing Leonard and Marge together was a telephone call just prior to his last group meeting. Leonard was on the phone, saying Marge objected to his being gone another night this week. Then he passed the phone to Marge, who stated her opposition in person. For better or for worse, I agreed to see them together, given the fact that Marge had terminated her treatment at a local mental health center which had referred Leonard initially after a year and a half of unsuccessful marital counseling.

I watched Leonard out of the corner of my eye, as he entered the room and sat back quietly, as if to signal he would await his turn. I made mental notes of his posture. I had charted it and photographed it before during his work in group (see Figure 4). He sat back in his chair, his trunk shifted slightly to his right, his left arm and left leg crossed over right arm and right leg. His only movement was an occasional twist or flick of his foot.

As if on cue, Marge took over the session, inundating Leonard with accusations. He was "thoughtless and uninvolved with the family," "a tyrant who brought her from a happy home to this foreign city, adding insult to injury by having an affair soon after their arrival," and "planning to leave her alone and destitute after using up her youthful and attractive years." She sat on the edge of her chair and persisted in stating her case, oblivious to my interventions, regardless of how astute, until I told her she was right and asked her how she felt. "Like a bitch," she replied, "Unattractive, unwanted, and unloved."

With this, Marge shifted back in her chair and took a tissue to her moist eyes. This proved a signal for Leonard to shift into a second posture, one with which I was equally familiar (see Figure 5). His body was thrust forward, elbows on thighs, preserving a very slight tilt of the torso to his right. His hands were folded and intermittently separated to permit movements predominantly from his right to accentuate the counter-accusations which constituted his case. Marge was "chronically unhappy, in spite of everything he tried to do," "she was never warm and affectionate or understanding," and she "constantly accused him of falsehoods so gross it would take hours to set the record straight."

Ulterior Transactions

Ulterior transactions contain a covert message at the psychological level beneath the overt message sent at the social level. In Leonard's case, the session began with appropriate greeting rituals and an overt profession of intent to resolve conflicts with his wife. His initial posture signaled something else unspoken from his Child ego state to the effect: "You go first, I'll sit back and have my say later." His wife accepted the invitation. This kind of phenomenon led Berne to postulate the third law of communication: the behavioral outcome of an ulterior transaction is determined at the psychological level, not the social level.[4] In this case, it certainly proved true. Instead of resolving conflicts, each partner, proceeded by tacit, though undeclared, agreement to have their "say," quite oblivious to the professed task of problem-solving.

Leonard's postures provide a good example of how bodily movements can become signal behaviors regulating the flow of interaction at the ulterior level. They repeatedly indicate to others how he is going to relate to them and, conversely, how they are invited to respond. Leonard returned to Posture 1 at the

Figure 4. Leonard: Basic Posture 1

Figure   5. Leonard: Basic Posture 2

conclusion of his "defense speech" as if to rest his case. This precipitated rebuttal and another attack from his wife. Notable for our purposes is how Leonard's postures characteristically signaled others around him to respond in familiar ways. In group notes, Posture 1 was recorded as a posture which he normally assumed when "put down." He had previously characterized his feelings in it as "depressed," "isolated," "misunderstood," yet, at times, "comfortable." It customarily followed a sequence of transactions in which he engaged others from Posture 2 with the forward lean. Often in Posture 2 he gave advice in hopes of being regarded as important or engaged in futile efforts to "straighten out someone's thinking." Also previously noted was Leonard's uncanny ability to say exactly the wrong thing at the right time, or vice versa, causing others either to ignore what he said or reject it outright. This invariably led to a shift back to Posture 1 in resignation.

Psychological Games

Signal behaviors provide the ulterior stance from which psychological games are played. A game is an ongoing series of transactions which are both ulterior and complementary, progressing to a well-defined payoff that is predictable.[5] By definition, games are played outside of Adult awareness, so they have the deceptive quality of a mutual agreement, unspoken or unacknowledged, that somehow subverts the "intended" process into a dramatic switch in roles, producing a familiar negative outcome. Once the clinician learns the client's moves, the outcome can be predicted. If not, either there is no game, or we have missed the signals.

The game Leonard and Marge played was a three-handed game called "Courtroom," the aim of which is to engage in alternating transactions of accusation and defense before a third party, who is invited to be judge and render a verdict. The ongoing series of moves is best shown in transactional diagrams depicting the ulterior, complementary structure of the exchanges (see Figure 6). Specific moves in the game are marked by the signal behaviors we have been discussing. For Leonard, Posture 1 signaled his readiness to listen to the accusing Parent ego state of his wife, like a small boy sitting still while someone else tells his or her side. In Posture 2 he shifted energy to his Parent ego state to present defense and counter-accusations.

The switch in roles which accompanies games is best viewed in terms of Karpman's drama triangle which depicts changes in any direction around the basic roles of *persecutor, rescuer,* and *victim* (see Figure 7).[6] Each partner alternates *persecutor* and *victim* roles during the phases of prosecution and de-

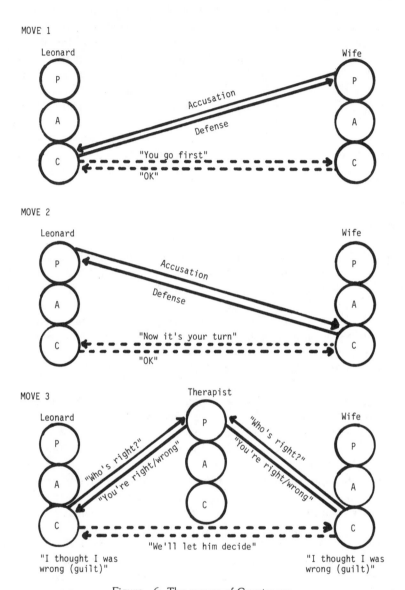

Figure   6. The moves of Courtroom

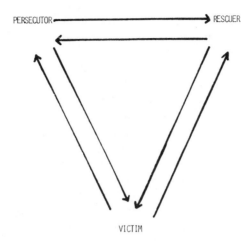

Figure 7. Karpman's drama triangle

fense in Courtroom. The hapless therapist is awarded the *rescuer* role through being invited, by common agreement at the ulterior level, to decide between them. The childhood prototype is one of brother and sister running to mother to settle a squabble. The final switch for both players, however, is from *persecutor* to *victim*. This was observed in Leonard's final shift back to Posture 1, signaling his resumption of the victim role with attendant feelings of futility, guilt, and resignation. Even momentary achievement of a favorable ruling fails to dispel the underlying payoff of guilt at having one's wrongdoing exposed, as represented in Marge's response ("I feel like a bitch, unattractive, unwanted, and unloved").

Primary and Secondary Games

Leonard's postural records are valuable to understanding psychological games because they reveal a line of continuity between three different games he played. The same sequence of shifts signaled moves in each one of them. And they provide us with the occasion to distinguish between *primary* or *core games* and *relatives* or *secondary games* which support them.

1) In group treatment, Posture 2 accompanied Leonard's efforts to "help out" from a rescuer role in his nurturing Parent ego state, with a return to

Posture 1 and withdrawal as a victim when his efforts were rejected. Although these signals appeared to accompany a classical version of ITHY ("I'm only trying to help you"), the customary switch to persecutor in anger toward ungrateful recipients of help was notably absent, or at least fleetingly bypassed in his switch back to rejected victim.

2) On occasions when Leonard recounted some incident of being put down in his working or domestic life, he began leaning forward in Posture 2 while recounting details, only to shift back to Posture 1 when concluding with his failure to succeed. He portrayed his own role as rescuer, always victimized. Of most importance to the clinician in game analysis was the transactional response from others when Leonard assumed the victim stance. It ranged from cold detachment to irritation and disgust. Usually people were left in a disapproving Parent ego state, quietly entrenched in a role of subtle persecution ("Leonard always does this!"). This is the key to determining Leonard's *core game* of "Why does this always happen to me?" (WAHM), which is a version of the life game Berne called "Kick me." Courtroom and ITHY are but *relatives* supporting a repetitive pattern throughout his life of making efforts that not only fail, but also anger others, leaving him feeling unappreciated and unloved.

It is significant that Leonard assumes the same postures to punctuate moves in his primary game (WAHM) and in two secondary games (Courtroom and ITHY) which add a sense of wrongdoing and rejection to his basic payoff of feeling unlovable. The rhythm established in these postures reflects the essential movements of Leonard's life script, which called for repeated periods of striving to please his parents, only to fail in despair of securing their love. Mother's favorite was older brother. Leonard worked hard for her favor, but she repeatedly put him down through brutal comparisons and thoughtless criticism which led him to conclude he was unlovable. Occasionally, father would notice Leonard's unhappiness and offer encouragement for more effort, which was invariably revoked by critical tirades to the effect that Leonard could do nothing right. The constant rhythm of his childhood, striving to please, followed by failure, was preserved in the postures we observed as basic movements of his life-style through which he furthered his script by playing his chosen games.

Advantages and Cure

The key to cure of a primary life game lies in understanding the *advantages* the client gains by playing it.[7] Failure to address them often accounts for sudden reversions to the game process that prove disappointing to therapist and client alike. This is what happened with Leonard. In a weekend workshop, he established awareness of his scripting and decided he could be lovable. This was followed by several months of "honeymoon effect" with his wife, to which they both alluded as the high point of their marriage. It was broken when Marge left with the family to spend the summer at their cottage and Leonard called her in loneliness to confess how hard it was to overcome his temptations to see other women. The violent arguments which ensued had persisted ever since. Cure, which may be defined as abandoment of the game, is contingent upon Leonard finding other means to satisfy the six *advantages* he gains through playing.

1) There is an *internal psychological* advantage that permits the expression of emotional trends in an individual and contributes to psychic stability. In Leonard's case, there was a need to depend and please which was followed by guilt-free expressions of anger in his own defense and self-justified forays to meet his emotional needs outside the marriage. Cure was contingent upon Leonard discovering ways to please himself independently and express appropriate anger when it is occasioned rather than fearfully saving it for release upon occasions that "justify measures of defense."

2) The *external psychological* advantage of the game is found in the avoidance of anxiety-producing situations it affords. Leonard's long-standing fear of his mother underlay his avoidance of close and intimate contact with his wife. The game not only granted him safe distance but afforded "pseudo-intimate" encounters in occasional liaisons with others. Until he learned to replace this with sustained and durable emotional contact with his wife, the pressure to play would continue.

3) The *internal social* advantage lies in the means the game provides for structuring time with intimates. Both at home and at work, Leonard was preoccupied with the next response he would get (pleased? angry? disappointed?). He and Marge always had the latest incident to talk about after they said "hello." In this respect, stopping a game always creates a void. The crisis of not knowing what to do or talk about is tantamount to breaking a relationship, until people learn to structure time with an entirely different repertoire of transactions.

4) An *external social* advantage is found in the use made of the situation in less intimate social contacts. "Ain't it awful?" pastimes about wives and work situations structured "small talk" for Leonard with friends and acquaintances. He was often hard pressed to talk about something else. Cure of the game involves realistic interest in other things.

5) A *biological advantage* to playing the game can be stated in tactile terms as the kind of stroking it provides. Leonard got attention stroking in the form of pats on the back from sympathetic friends, group members, and therapists. He got petulant slaps in the face from his wife and occasional periods of caressing

and making up. He also gained intermittent, passionate embraces from lovers. An elaborate stroking system surrounds every game. Since stroking is as essential to life as air, food, and water, cure of the game is contingent upon replacing its stroke economy with a more satisfying one outside of its moves.

6) The *existential* advantage is seen in the basic life position the game preserves. Leonard was OK because he was constantly trying hard. Others were not OK because they continually "put him down." This was his primary line of defense against feeling "unlovable." Some similar rationale derived from the life script governs every game.

A hard lesson for clinicians to learn is how game processes persist in spite of dramatic redecisions, insights, and emotional experiences. Supporting each life course is a consistent repertoire of movements based upon a recurrent rhythm of archaic ego states. I believe we successfully addressed Leonard's *existential* advantages in the workshop. This, however, is seldom enough until we successfully deal with the other advantages, helping Leonard replace them with substantial alternatives.

SCRIPT ANALYSIS

The third perspective we may take upon movement behaviors in psychotherapy is the formative one. This is the domain of script analysis. Bodily movements serve as *script signs* when they are concrete expressions of those ego states in which the individual's central life conflict is vested. The life script is an unconscious life plan based upon a series of childhood decisions that govern one's sense of destiny.[8] Script signs successfully embody an individual's response to formative scenes which shaped it.

Carol's Wink

Carol's wink, which occurred during our three o'clock hour yesterday, is a good example of a script sign. It is to be distinguished from the type of wink made in full awareness and received as part of a general facial expression signaling jest, camaraderie, flirtation, or the like. Her wink was made outside of any awareness of her role as sender and was rarely noted or acknowledged by receivers. Characteristically, it does not fit whatever else is going on in facial expression, bodily movement, or verbalization (see Figure 8). I have learned to attend winks of this type with clients because of the number of times they accompany subterfuge or self-deception.

Figure   8. Carol's wink

"I really want to (wink) marry Bob," Carol explained, returning to her old doubts as to whether she could remain loving once committed to a lasting relationship in marriage. I had worked with Carol twice over the past two years in extended group sessions, which I conduct from time to time over a weekend. These provide an excellent preparatory experience for entering weekly groups and a powerful focus for decision-making in brief psychotherapy. They also make available to individual treatment in follow-up sessions a range of techniques similar to the one I employed with her. Carol had seen others explore random bodily behavior through conducting a conversation with it ("Become your headache and speak some words to yourself"), a procedure from Gestalt therapy in wide use today. Its success is contingent upon the client's willingness to cathect a Child ego state. Carol was encouraged to surrender logical (Adult) thought control and, changing from one chair to another, play both the wink and her response to it, permitting a dialogue to develop.

Initially, Carol's conversation sounded like an old one between her mother and herself. The wink said, "Don't get married; have a career and stay free of men." Nothing new—for 30 seconds. Then the wink changed in posture and voice. It found fault with her past boy friends. It declared her favored position as the youngest of three daughters, recalling her beauty as opposed to the musical accomplishments and intelligence of sisters one and two. The wink moved on to voice father's sexual frustration with mother, which he had verbalized to Carol during her last visit home. It ended by inviting her back home to be "near." "No!" shouted Carol from her own chair, "I won't!"

Script Formation

Carol's wink provided a glimpse of a series of scenes in the formation of her script. It took on the decided character of her father's voice. It laid bare the emotional impact of a whole series of transactions between her father and herself. Previously, she had dealt with her anger toward him since adolescence and the repetitive arguments which provided the two of them distance, through Uproar. For those unfamiliar with transactional analysis, Uproar is a psychological game in which a father and teenage daughter engage in vicious arguments —often around her sexual conduct with boys—which normally end in both going to their separate bedrooms and slamming the door, underlining security against unacceptable sexual impulses toward each other. Carol had made a conscious decision to let herself care for Bob, despite some deep discomfort which she attributed to her feelings about her father. But she had remained unaware of this aspect of her scripting revealed in dialogue with her wink: namely, the notion she was not to have a man of her own. Instead, she was to have a series of unhappy relationships ending in dissatisfaction, all in service of a fantasy of returning home to be near father.

Script signs such as Carol's wink appear to be specific reproductions of some aspect of bodily behavior accompanying an actual series of exchanges between father and daughter, long since forgotten. The wink itself, which once played an important role, now lingers as an involuntary expression of early imprinting with no apparent relationship to the here and now. Several other winkers have established recall of such early scenes; Carol could not. She could recall the special relationship she had with father when she was a small girl, between ages three to six. In contrast to her older sisters, she was his "beautiful princess." This changed radically in adolescence, when father vigorously disapproved of her boy friends and distanced himself in argumentation.

The Script Matrix

Claude Steiner developed the *script matrix* to depict the structure in which scripting occurs in such formative scenes.[9] It requires what is called second order structural analysis of the Child ego state (see Figure 9). Simply put, the early decision governing script is made with only the information and experience available to the individual at the developmental stage in which it occurs. It represents an early choice by a small child (represented by A_1) to be a certain way, with specific feelings surrounding the circumstances of that choice (C_1), in the face of a particular set of parental demands (P_1). This experience forms one

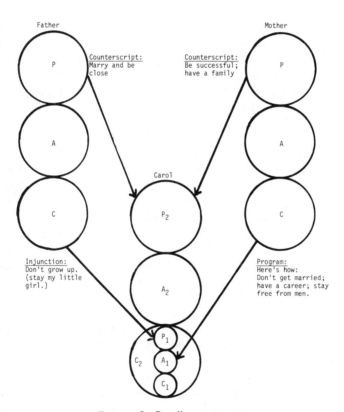

Figure 9. Carol's script matrix

persistently recurring Child ego state (C_2) which functions quite independently of Adult thinking as an entity all its own. When cathected, it organizes contemporary experience according to the protocol of the formative one.

In Carol's case, it appears we are dealing with an early decision to maintain a special relationship with her father (A_1), accompanied by strong fear when she contemplates marriage which would threaten that relationship (C_1), in the face of parental demands not to grow up and live her own life (P_1). This structure persists as one Child ego state (C_2), which imposes a pattern of archaic attitudes quite independent of her current Adult and Parental thoughts. The *script matrix* breaks this process down into three major components which can guide the clinician in working with it: the *injunction*, the *program*, and the *counterscript*.

1) The *injunction* prohibits or limits some striving vital to natural development. It is normally abbreviated as a "verbal message" for sake of clarity, although it is delivered through a whole process of interaction with a small child. I chose to abbreviate Carol's injunction from her father as "Don't grow up." It is drawn from his own Child ego state since it arises from his own particular needs and is not delivered with conscious intent. Since the injunction is nonverbal, visceral, and preoedipal, it manifests itself as deep discomfort whenever she contemplates breaking the tie and establishing a lasting relationship with a man of her own.

2) The *program* constitutes a set of instructions concerning how to obey the injunction within a life plan. Normally the injunction comes from the parent of the opposite sex and the program from the parent of the same sex, although there are many variations. For Carol, the program came from watching mother and listening to her for concepts which fit a pattern of living in accord with her injunction, such as "Don't get married," "Have a career," and "Stay free of men who can spoil your life." Again, verbal abbreviations are given to designate a much broader process of modeling behaviors and attitudes.

3) The *counterscript* is composed of the series of moral precepts about how one should live that is incorporated into the Parent ego state during latency and adolescence. In contrast to the injunction and the program which are delivered without conscious intent, the counterscript is acquired in direct instructions from parents and other proponents of cultural norms. The counter-injunctions, as they are sometimes called for they are often counter to the injunction, are verbal, remembered, and postoedipal. Carol had a clear set of counterscript instructions: "Marry," "Be close," "Be successful in your career," and "Have a family."

The result which we observe clinically is a young woman who has decided she wants to get married, possesses a value system that includes marriage, intimacy, and family, but who experiences deep visceral discomfort in her Child ego state at the prospect of being able to sustain love. The emergent doubt is the result of a childhood decision not to grow up and to stay near father.

Redecisions

Bob and Mary Goulding have emphasized that early childhood decisions are amenable to *redecision* in the client's Child ego state.[10] We may gain an impression of a person's script through information they give in their Adult ego state by the use of checklist questionnaires, history-taking, and talking with that person about how life is going. I reserve the term *script analysis proper* for those times when clients willingly cathect or invest energy in their Child ego state, permitting its archaic patterns of thinking and feeling to emerge in the present. Our impressions of the script must always be checked against what actually comes from the Child spontaneously. Often bodily movements, like Carol's wink, are among the most reliable *entrees* to what has long been denied Adult awareness.

Redecisions become possible at times when the specific ego state in which the script is vested is fully cathected. At such times, there is a sufficient return of the original feelings (C_1) surrounding the formative scenes of the script, so that the intuitive part of the Child (A_1) can engage the parental figure in such a way that the introjected demand (P_1) is reexperienced with force and clarity. In such circumstances, the Child can be free, in effect, to decide, "I don't have to go on doing that for you any more." In Carol's case, the resounding "No, I won't do that!", which she shouted to the figure of her father in the chair, constituted for her a *redecision*. It was in clear response to the injunction, "Don't grow up; return home and stay near."

We will need to say more about life scripts in the later chapters which deal with script signs. This much is sufficient to permit readers to find their way through the materials ahead. By way of summary, bodily movement in psychotherapy has been addressed from the standpoint of *structural analysis*, which is concerned with exploring an individual's *internal dialogue* between specific ego states. The behavioral, social, historical, and phenomenological means of diagnosing them have been discussed. Changes in ego state are the result of cathexis or an investment of psychic energy which is encountered in bound, unbound, and free states. Bodily movement may also be examined as

signal behaviors for what is communicated nonverbally. Signal behaviors constitute ulterior transactions at the psychological level beneath overt messages exchanged at the social level; they also provide kinesic markers to the ongoing
series of moves encountered in psychological games. Some tools for game
analysis have been presented: transactional diagrams of ulterior transactions,
the drama triangle, and the six advantages of a game. In addition, from the
standpoint of *script analysis,* certain movement behavior may be addressed as
script signs which embody a person's responses to formative scenes. The *script
matrix* composed of the *injunction,* the *program,* and the *counterscript* has
been introduced, as well as the process of *redecision* in the Child ego state. We
are now ready to proceed to the first phase of video research.

REFERENCE NOTES

 1. Berne, E. *Transactional Analysis in Psychotherapy.* New York: Grove Press, 1961, pp. 75,
    76.
 2. Ibid., p. 23.
 3. Ibid., pp. 40-42.
 4. Berne, E. *Principles of Group Treatment.* New York: Oxford University Press, 1966, p. 227.
 5. Berne, E. *Games People Play.* New York: Grove Press, 1964, p. 48.
 6. Karpman, S. B. Fairy tales and script drama analysis. *Transactional Analysis Bulletin, 1:*39,
    1968.
 7. See Berne, E. *Games People Play,* pp. 56-58.
 8. Berne, E. *What Do You Say After You Say Hello?* New York: Grove Press, 1971, p. 418.
 9. Steiner, C. Script and counterscript. *Transactional Analysis Bulletin, 5:*133-135, 1966.
10. Goulding, M. M., & Goulding, R. L. *Changing Lives Through Redecision Therapy.* New
    York: Brunner/Mazel, 1979.

3

Body movements
in ego states

Structural analysis is the key to all significant behavioral change in transactional analysis. Once clients are aware of their scripts and games and have made a clear decision not to take their payoffs, they alter their patterns of stroking and time structure through the simple stopping and starting process of changing from one ego state to another. Currently, however, we possess only minimal tools for analyzing Parent, Adult, and Child ego states in ourselves and others.

This chapter describes procedures developed in our graduate training program at Louisville Presbyterian Theological Seminary to identify the bodily expressions of ego states. It contains (1) a synopsis of three independent research projects by graduate students and (2) a series of hypotheses for clinical treatment, based upon the author's work with them.

ISOLATING CHARACTERISTIC POSTURES

For a number of years, we have asked therapists in training to sit like the group members they are presenting on tape, reproducing their gestures to give the clinical seminar a visual picture of their clients. We find they can do so with amazing intuitive recall once they develop minimal skills in identifying ego states.

Myrl Moore conducted the first research project, which was designed to iso-

---

This chapter contains in large part material presented at the summer conferences of the International Transactional Analysis Association at San Francisco in 1972 and 1973. It provides a picture of the origins of this work, together with some of the early clinical implications which seemed immediately evident. Readers disinterested in the technical details of video research may choose to skim the first half.

late visually the characteristic bodily expressions of ego states for each member of a group.[1] An interpersonal-relations group of 12 undergraduate students in Clinical Pastoral Education at Central State Hospital was chosen. Moore obtained permission from the group members to record their interaction in rapid sequence photography, moving around the circle of chairs, taking pictures of each person's transactions. He also tape-recorded the proceedings, noting photos on a time line to permit later comparison of verbal and visual records. The design was to photograph intuitively for four weeks, selecting basic postures characteristic of each member. Moore could then predictably photograph each characteristic posture during the next three weeks. Identical photographs would demonstrate an isolated bodily expression of an ego state which was consistent, predictable, and photographable. Predictive photographs were viewed by a panel of judges, and their descriptions of the basic postures were recorded for comparison with similar descriptions of confirmatory pictures. The ego state was determined for each basic posture by placing it in the verbal context.

Moore demonstrated the following:

1) Between two and five basic postures for participation may be isolated and photographed for each person in a 12-member group.

2) One characteristic posture consistently expresses a Parent ego state, another a Child.

3) Once each posture is identified, its appearance may be predicted with the ego state it characteristically expresses and vice versa; its appearance is a behavioral cue to that ego state.

What Myrl Moore did with photography, most skilled therapists do intuitively, often without perceptual awareness. These intuitions lack a technology or a set of workable tools so that they can be employed consistently. Clinically we find we have little difficulty diagnosing ego states with customary behavioral and social means in their gross or pronounced expression. However, in the subtleties of mundane or routine interchange, even careful examination often leaves us uncertain. The next two research projects were devoted to developing this technology.

MEASURING BODILY BEHAVIOR

Berne initially identified ego states as phenomenological realities present in the process of group treatment ("That looks and sounds like a Parent or a Child talking").[2] The second research project, by Dan Kirkbride and Don Stokes, separated seeing and hearing in order to measure less dramatic, ordinary bodily behavior in ego states.[3] Three individuals were chosen for 15-minute interviews which were videotaped. Once the process was refined, it was repeated with 16 members of two weekly therapy groups conducted by the author. The interview was structured toward casual pastiming by questions about the setting, the subject's family, and the subject's vocation.

For the reader unfamiliar with transactional analysis, pastimes are a series of semi-ritualistic, complementary transactions around a single field of material which serves to confirm roles and stabilize positions while structuring an interval of time; e.g., "General Motors" (comparing cars); "Who won?" (sports); "Have you ever been to . . . ?" (travel); or "PTA" (schools).[4] Pastime interviews were conducted in this vein.

The video and audio tracks were then separated for study by different research teams in order to heighten perception and isolate cues from each channel. The audio team, composed of four graduate-level students trained in transactional analysis, listened to the sound track playing and replaying until they were able to reach a consensus on the ego state expressed in each segment of verbal content. They registered each change from one ego state to another on a time line.

The video team viewed a full-screen picture of the subject taken from 14 feet away. A 10½" × 15" grid overlay was superimposed on the playing screen, dividing the picture into four equal quadrants, each containing squares of one-fourth inch numbered horizontally and lettered vertically. With the center point of the grid set in the person's navel, (1) the subject's body position was accurately plotted in each posture assumed throughout the interview; and (2) each identified movement of the subject's head, arms, and legs was measured in grids or squares representing approximately four inches of actual movement.

A relatively simple mode of recording data was adopted which can easily be repeated by any interested researcher (see Figure 10). Once the subject was seated in the chair, a Basic Posture appeared on the screen. From this Basic Posture the subject made a number of movements with hands, arms, or legs. These were easily quantified by counting the number of grids in each move from the rest position of the Basic Posture to the outward extremity of the move. The exact bodily position for each Basic Posture was recorded on a paper copy of the viewing grid by plotting its key points on the coordinates. Identified Movements were counted in each position until there was a Trunk Shift establishing a new Basic Posture to be graphed and the process repeated.

The number of Identified Movements between Trunk Shifts was termed a Set. Set material was recorded between slash marks (/) which indicated the Trunk Shifts, and Identified Movements were registered in terms of the number

Figure 10. Charting Basic Posture and Identified Movements

of grids for each movement. Recorded head movements for a Set appeared as follows: Head /1 + 2 + 1 + 3/. The Expenditure or total number of grids moved by the head was seven. The Set had four Identified Movements of the head. Descriptions of the movements (tilts forward, backward, right, or left) were recorded on each Basic Posture sheet.

The elementary vocabulary established thus far is as follows:

1) The Mass Distribution (MD) indicates the body's mass and its distribution according to the x-y axis of the quadrants on the viewing grid, determined by plotting points on the bridge of the nose, the breastbone, both shoulders, elbows, hands, navel, genitals, knees, and ankles.

2) A Trunk Shift (TS) marks a postural change, a movement of the spinal cord from one basic postural position to another.

3) A Set (S) denotes a series of Identified Movements bracketed at the beginning and end by a Trunk Shift.

4) An Identified Movement (IM) is an observable movement of arm, leg, or head (a) from a resting position, returning to that position; or (b) from a resting position, going to a new rest position.

5) The Expenditure (E) is the total number of grids per Identified Movement. Hence, a four-grid movement by the right hand has an Expenditure of four, representing movement of approximately 16 inches.

FINDINGS

By design, the pastime interviews provided mundane interaction in which pronounced visual cues to ego states were not present to such an extent that the video team could view a segment of tape and identify the executive ego state in the subject apart from the context. The video team could, however, through charting each Basic Posture and recording its Identified Movements determine when the subject changed from one ego state to another. The video and audio teams agreed on changes in ego states 88.5 percent of the time. Moreover, once the video team learned the precise ego state it was charting, consistent identification of its reappearance was possible through charting the Mass Distribution and checking the established rhythm of Expenditure within its Identified Movements. Five generalized findings may be drawn from these data, tentative though they may be, at this stage of our work.

1) A Trunk Shift that alters the subject's Basic Posture simultaneously accompanies each change in ego state. Not every time a Trunk Shift occurs is there a change in ego state. Some ego states display several Sets, but each time the ego state changes there is a measurable shift in the subject's spinal cord.

2) There appears to be a pattern of Identified Movements within each subject's ego states. More IMs consistently accompany one ego state than another. For example, arm movements showed mean Expenditures (Grids/IM) and IMs for the first three subjects in the Parent ego state as follows:

Subject	IMs	Expenditure
1	2.6	3.9
2	2.7	6.2
3	2.5	4.1

In the Child they were as follows:

Subject	IMs	Expenditure
1	1.8	4.5
2	3.5	6.2
3	1.7	6.1

With the calculation of mean Expenditure for each ego state, the video team was able to predict with a fair degree of accuracy when a change to another ego state would occur. Sets tended to appear at various times with approximately the same Expenditure. Subjects settled into this rhythm only after an initial phase of beginning activity and departed from it with a similar flurry of terminal movement, as indicated in Figure 11. Here Subject 1 evidences for 80 percent of the interview a rather consistent expression of Parental Expenditures approaching a ratio of two to one over the Child. No Adult behavior was detected. The ordinal measurement of IMs does not reflect this tendency in the averages above. If the first and last three minutes were eliminated, the differential between Parent and Child would substantially increase. During the balance of pastiming, eliminating ritual greeting and departing behavior, Identified Movements appear with regular increases and decreases as the subject switches from one ego state to another.

3) Some rhythmic expression of the number of Sets in contrasting ego states also appears. Figure 12 presents Subject 1, evidencing twice the number of Sets present in her Parent behavior as in her Child. This is roughly commensurate with the appraisal of the audio team of judges who recorded her functioning in her Parent 68 percent of the time. We have observed Sets as short as

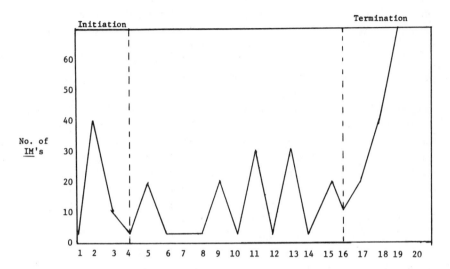

Figure 11. Identified Movements per ego state for Subject 1

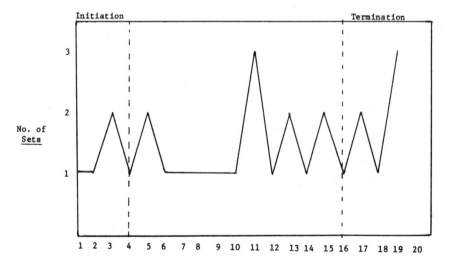

Figure 12. Sets per ego state for Subject 1

three seconds and as long as a minute. Time in and of itself does not dictate the number of Identified Movements or their Expenditure. It does create the possibility for more Sets to form. Within this time, one ego state appears to contain a number of Sets in its expression, while another contains only one.

4) Identified Movements of head, arms, and legs within a given ego state appear with a consistent pattern of choice. For example, a number of IMs in the arms is not accompanied by a corresponding number of moves in head or legs. In an elementary rank correlation of Sets within ego states, no correlation was evident. However, in a second rank correlation between the three appendages (arms, head, legs) and the Parent and Child ego states, a negative correlation appeared, indicating not only that these ego states were not alike, but that they tended toward opposite forms of expression in bodily movement. This suggests that the subjects make their IMs within an ego state, using hand, arm, or head movement in consistent patterns, and they choose distinctly different channels of physiological expression for different ego states.

5) A distinct rhythm of movement in chosen ego states appears in pastimes. Subject 1, a 48-year-old, divorced female with three children, revealed Parent behavior of 191 Expenditures and 18 Sets, far outweighing her Child behavior of 82 Expenditures and seven Sets. This constitutes over twice as many Sets and Expenditures in the Parent as in the Child. Some similar pattern was present in the other subjects, one ego state far outweighing the other.

The content of Subject 1's Parental pastiming centered around nurturing concern for her children. A mixture of "Ain't it awful?" and "Isn't it nice?" themes interwove themselves around a flow of praise and uneasiness for their welfare. Her Child behavior was notably restricted with virtually no free or natural expression in the face of a constantly returning nurturing Parent. The shorter Child Sets were marked by expressions of helplessness and "uselessness," gesturing with palms up and hands flipping outward. Several weeks following the pastime interview, she was fired from her job, having "messed up" a number of assignments of decreasing responsibility, given her by a nurturing employer who finally had to "let her go."

A clinical interpretation of these data suggests we consider her predominant Parental behavior in pastiming as the "second hand" in her major game activity. Her pastiming forms an apt arena for locating nurturing or helping Parental types with whom she can play Schlemiel and ITHY. Schlemiel is a psychological game in which an individual victimizes others by making messes and apologizing, extracting forgiveness by preying upon their propensity to understand. ITHY ("I'm only trying to help you") is a relative which ends in anger when rescuers tire of "helping" and switch roles to persecutor. Her pastiming falls within the realm of counterscript behavior, or what she does in between periods of script accomplishment. The strong Parental behavior evidenced in her termination activity indicates a more pronounced stance within the Parental hand, since the Adult behavior of the interviewer did not permit her to play either of her chosen games.

MOVEMENT AND CHANGE

The apparent rhythm among chosen ego states in pastimes suggests itself as one measure of behavioral change. An individual making significant life changes could be expected to reflect a corresponding change in ego states selected for pastiming. This led to the second phase of research by Kirkbride and Stokes.[5] Pastime interviews were repeated with the 16 subjects in group therapy three months later. This experimental group was compared to a control group of 10 persons not engaged in psychotherapy who underwent the same process over a three-month interval. The hypothesis was that the difference in quantity and pattern of movement in specific ego states will be greater for the experimental group between the two tapings.

This phase of the study was marred by the fact that of the 16 original experimental subjects, only six completed the entire process. Four were dismissed because of failure to make the second taping and six had to be excluded because of equipment failure. Similarly, of the 10 controls, only four completed the testing process. The major mechanical problem was the wearing and distorting of inferior videotapes before the excessive amount of replay required to accurately measure and chart each identifiable body movement. The limited number of subjects upon which complete data was obtained render these findings tentative at best. They do provide, however, so consistent a picture as to merit their discussion.

Change in Overall Movement

There were two measures of change in overall movement: the total number of Identified Movements and the total Expenditure which reflects the extent or magnitude of these moves. The results for Identified Movements are shown in Tables 1 and 2.[6] The difference in the number of Identified Movements for the experimental subjects was almost twice (1.7 times) as great as for the controls. An analysis of variance indicated an average of 10 times more variability among experimentals.[7] This was not true for Expenditures which constitute measurement of the total amount of all movement in terms of grids. This was much greater (18 times) for the control group, which proved a source of be-

Table 1

Total number of Identified Movements by
experimental subjects in the two tapings
and the differences between the two

	T_1	T_2	Differences
X1	266	215	51
X2	203	205	− 2
X3	238	370	− 132
X4	115	161	− 46
X5	36	145	− 109
Y2	734	202	532
Totals	1,592	1,298	304 (51)*

*Number in parentheses reflects average per subject.

Table 2

Total number of Identified Movements by the
control group in the two tapings and the
differences between the two

	T_1	T_2	Difference
N1	461	384	77
N2	333	269	64
N3	232	336	− 104
N4	372	291	81
Totals	1,398	1,280	118 (30)*

*Number in parentheses reflects average per subject.

wilderment to the research team.[8] One possible explanation is that one member of the control group (N4), who showed a difference in Expenditure of 1,678 between tapings, was suspected to be under the influence of drugs at one taping. Even so, there does not appear to be a change in Expenditure commensurate with measured changes in the number of Identified Movements among subjects.

It should be noted that the measurement of Expenditure is the most inaccurate one recorded in these studies. The one-dimensional charting procedures employed are obviously deficient at the point of detecting the magnitude of movements made toward and away from the camera. Even the use of a second camera at a standard distance to the side would not allow for differences in plotting exactly the varying angles of Trunk Shifts and Identified Movements vis-à-vis the viewing screen. The one-dimensional procedures were justified by the assumption that such discrepancies would balance out for comparative purposes with the large number of measurements among subjects. This may not have been the case with so small a control group.

Another assumption undergirding this work is that there is some relationship between the magnitude of a person's movement and the psychic energy that person invests in various ego states. Determining exactly what we are measuring in Expenditure remains a task for much more extensive research. In the back of our minds was the notion that we are measuring some rough equivalent of "mechanical energy" expended in specific, identifiable movement of the body. Potentially this could be correlated with physical energy as constituted in gram-calories and open to some conversion with sophisticated procedures. Thus, changes in movement patterns among ego states can be seen to represent physiological expressions of corresponding shifts in cathexis among a subject's ego states.

Within this context, a more plausible explanation for the failure of overall Expenditure to reflect the changes in the number of Identified Movements among experimentals may be found in Jack Dusay's constancy hypothesis: $(P + A + C)_{mm} = K$.[9] By this formula, he suggests that the amount of psychic energy available for distribution among a person's repertoire of Parent, Adult, and Child ego states is a constant (K), provided we have "mother's milk" $(_{mm})$ which designates the basic biological and social factors necessary to sustain normal life processes (we are not starved, heavily drugged, in a concentration camp, etc.). Consequently, an increased investment of energy in one ego state necessitates a corresponding decrease of energy in another. So changes in the number and the pattern of Identified Movements made by subjects appear to accompany the shifting of psychic energy from one ego state to another. At the same time, we do not witness any corresponding change in the overall extent or quantity of

movement representing the total amount of psychic energy available for investment, which remains a constant (K).

Changes in Specific Ego States

Changes in the pattern of movement among specific ego states was the other
measurement taken in this phase of the research. Each ego state was determined by its recurrent charting in the same Basic Posture and compared with
the records of the audio team, which made the diagnosis on the basis of voice,
tone, and content. Kirkbride and Stokes prepared kinesic graphs for each subject, which presented the total Expenditure of all Identified Movements in each
ego state, alongside of a time graph, which represented the actual percentage
of time each subject spent in each ego state. Among the controls, the pattern of
behavior in specific ego states was uniformly consistent from first taping to second, indicating no appreciable redistribution of movement between them. The
kinesic graphs and the time graphs for Subject N3 in Figure 13 are representative.[10]

Significant changes in the pattern of movement among ego states were registered for all but one of the experimental subjects. Four of the six experimentals
reflected a shift in their pattern of Identified Movements that corresponded to
fulfillment of their change contract in treatment. Subject X5 provides a good
example. He entered therapy to reduce his negative, critical behavior toward
his wife which he poignantly expressed as a desire to "Stop picking at Barb."
His kinesic graph reflects a major reduction of Expenditure in his Parent ego
state (from 76 grids to 2 grids) between the two tapings of his pastime interview
(see Figure 14).[11] Movement was redistributed among Adult and Child ego
states in a corresponding elevation of Expenditures in both. Changes in the
time graph were commensurate, though not identical. The Adult ego state remained the same while more time was spent in his Child and less in his Parent.

A redistribution of concrete movement behavior among ego states is not nec-
essarily accompanied by a corresponding change in their display timewise.
Subject X4 evidenced a strong shift of Expenditure to her Child ego state without a radical change in its duration (see Figure 15).[12] At her first taping, she indicated to the researchers that one of the reasons why she was in therapy was
to learn to enjoy herself and free up her natural Child. Her kinesic graph showed
that her Child evidenced the least number of Expenditures (19 percent) among
her ego states. During the second pastime interview she reported with great delight an increase in activities that were pleasurable. Her kinesic graph indicated
her Child ego state now displayed the greatest amount of movement (53 per-

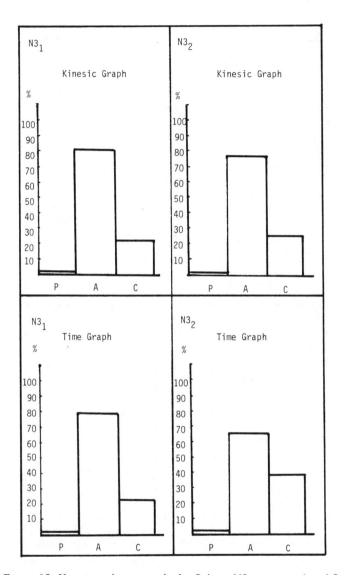

Figure 13. Kinesic and time graphs for Subject N3 at tapings 1 and 2

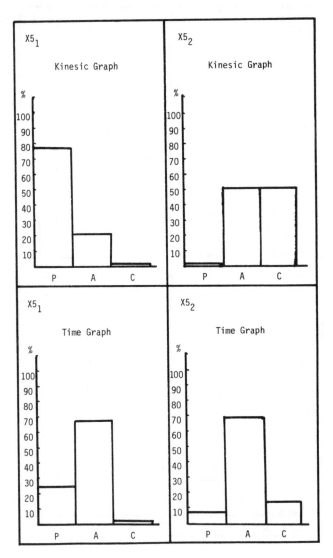

Figure 14. Kinesic and time graphs for Subject X5 at tapings 1 and 2

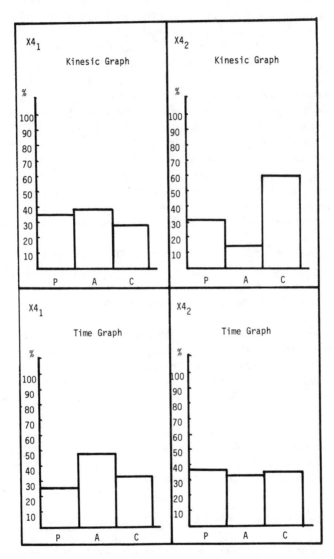

Figure 15. Kinesic and time graphs for Subject X4 at tapings 1 and 2

cent). Time graphs show her Child occupying approximately the same amount of the available time at each taping (31 percent and 33 percent respectively). It is the actual investment of movement in an ego state that tends to reflect the intensity with which that individual experiences it.

The two other experimental subjects displayed patterns of Identified Movements toward chosen ego states which corresponded strikingly to their status in treatment. This was determined at the end of the project when the researchers received status reports from the therapist's notes on the group, together with the third research project, which we shall discuss next, in which Christopher Schooley studied the bodily behavior of the same experimental subjects on videotape during the actual treatment sessions. Subject X2 evidenced a change in her movement behavior similar to the others (see Figure 16).[13] The marked increase in her Parent Expenditures parallels the observation by her therapist that she became more firmly entrenched in arguments with her husband during this initial phase of their treatment. Not all changes in movement behavior indicate what we would regard to be positive behavioral change in terms of goals.

The only experimental subject who evidenced no discernible change in his pattern of movement within ego states was X3. Interestingly enough, this was the subject whom Schooley characterized in group as spending the entire period resisting therapy. He wrote the following summation:

> The Series I test and retest instruments emphasize X3's busyness (sic) and tiredness. The significant change over the test and retest phase appeared to be mock openness toward his wife. His pseudo-compliant attitude upon entering therapy disappeared. In the retest phase, he often folded his arms across his chest and stared at group members, avoiding his wife.[14]

Thus the movement behavior of subjects in pastime interviewing proved a fair measure of their progress in treatment. In contrast to the others, X3 was one of those clients whom we would say "was just not moving."

VIDEO STUDIES OF MOVEMENT DURING PSYCHOTHERAPY

A third research project was conducted by Christopher Schooley analyzing videotapes of subjects in individual and group therapy according to the charting procedures we have described. First, Schooley, assisted by Jack Cushman, studied two subjects in therapy with the author.[15] Each received the standard

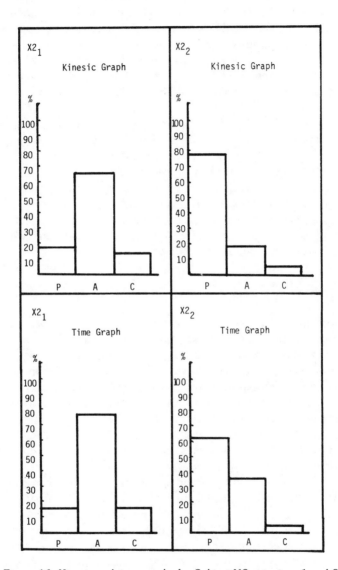

Figure 16. Kinesic and time graphs for Subject X2 at tapings 1 and 2

15-minute pastime interview, followed by examination of each subject's movement during a one-hour session of individual treatment. Then Schooley joined
the cooperative project with Kirkbride and Stokes, studying the movement behavior of the same 16 subjects in their group sessions with the author over a
three-month period.[16] The design was to analyze taped segments of each
member's behavior, made between eight and 12 weeks apart, to see if characteristic postures and movements could be identified as signs of that person's
game and script.

The camera was located behind an L-shaped screen with an opening which
provided some mobility and a minimum of interference by the equipment. An
effort was made to arrange seating to preserve the standard distance from
which charting was done in the pastime interviews. This excluded several
members at each group session from accurate taping. The aim was to film each
subject at a time when that person was actively engaged in working through
some problem with the group. In contrast to the earlier research which separated sight and sound, specific movement behaviors were examined within their
context of verbal transactions with others.

Bodily Duplicity

The most striking feature of bodily expressions in treatment was a duplicity
within Basic Postures when the subject was dealing with personal conflicts. This
duplicity manifested itself as a bodily "split" while the subject was discussing
conflictual behavior. The "split" was either left/right or top/bottom in distribution, one side of which expressed the borrowed or "mimicked" behavior of the
Parent ego state, the other side expressing past or present modes of responding
to it. These splits were graphable in the Mass Distribution diagrams previously
described, revealing a pronounced distribution of the body toward one quadrant and away from the central axis on the viewing grid. This was immediately
evident with the subjects in individual sessions.

Subject 1, Alpha, was a 52-year-old married female who entered treatment
complaining of depression and frigidity. She was a "professional patient" with a
prior history of psychotherapy, including private psychiatric care, pastoral
counseling, family therapy with her two daughters, two transactional analysis
marathons in another setting, and one Gestalt workshop. She was aware of her
scripting to avoid closeness, with a program calling for a series of desertions by
men, beginning with father who died when she was three, stepfather who left
when she was 13, her first husband who had committed suicide 14 years be-

fore, and a succession of other significant males who failed her, including her therapists. A clinical analysis of her "Little Match Girl" script is given below, following the form developed by Berne.[17]

Thesis: The little match girl is driven out to work all her days selling matches because father has died and mother demands it of her. She is conscientious and always tries to be good and help, but no one buys her matches. She becomes cold in the snow because no one lets her in. Finally, trying to warm herself with her own matches, she freezes to death slowly because no one cares.

Clinical Diagnosis: Depressive neurosis.

Fairy Tale: Little Match Girl.

Roles: Helpful Child, Persecuting Mother, and Rescuing Father who fails (leaves).

Switches: Rescuer (advising, nurturing Parent) to Victim (sad Child) to Persecutor (of those who don't care or help).

Parental Precept: Be a good, helpful girl (almost perfect).

Parental Injunction: Don't be close, never be happy, and freeze to death.

Parental Program: If the men had done right, everything would have turned out well.

Position: I'm OK (because I'm trying). They're not OK (because they don't listen or help).

Decision: I'll try hard, stay sad, and maybe he'll rescue me (Santa Claus Fantasy).

Script: Freeze to death.

Antiscript: Straighten others out before it's too late for them (and me).

Sweatshirt: Front—I always try harder; back—and it never works.

Game: IWFY.

Trading Stamps: Depressions

Final Payoff: Lonely old age and death.

Epitaph: She tried harder than anybody and look what it got her.

Antithesis: Goodbye to sad little Alpha and good little Alpha.

Permission: To be close and have fun.

The problem current to Alpha's treatment lay in making her redecisions stick. Her stance as a "professional patient" led to converting all awareness gained in treatment into another "hard try" outside the treatment room.

Videoanalysis with Alpha established three Basic Postures (BP) during therapy. BP-1 concentrated Mass Distribution in the upper left quadrant of the screen (see Figure 17). Her "T-zone" (formed by head, shoulders, and trunk) was tilted four to six inches left of the central axis. Dominant gestures were with the left hand, palm down (making "laying on" movements), or palm in (making chopping motions). Legs were shifted back into the lower left quadrant, with any motion coming from the left foot. The right arm was limp on the lap or arm rest, often with palm up. Verbal material from this posture described what she had accomplished, giving detailed reports of the week, decidedly her maternal Parent, "bringing her little girl for treatment to discover new things to make her do." Complementary transactions with the therapist were Parent to Parent at the ulterior level, as if to say: "What are we going to do about little Alpha? She's so unhappy."

Basic Posture 2 was formed by a Trunk Shift over to the upper right quadrant, leaning slightly forward, tucking her legs back toward the central axis (see Figure 18). Major Identified Movements were with the right hand and arm, ordinarily with the palm up. Verbal material here came from the adapted Child or "Good Little Alpha," who tries hard, constantly looks for commands from any Parent, acknowledges her need, and often utters a characteristic phrase like, "I know I do that, but how can I stop?"

Basic Posture 3 was formed by a Trunk Shift farther back into the upper right quadrant, normally after "Good Little Alpha" had "struggled for a while," proving that no matter how hard she tries, "it's hopeless." This was "Sad Little Alpha," who is normally tearful, bringing her right hand (sometimes made into a fist) to her mouth to cover her speech or holding a balled Kleenex in the air (see Figure 19). The left hand became active in BP-3 only to reach over and stroke the right hand when it rested limply on the lap or chair arm, palm up.

This sequence of behavior was invariably followed by a Trunk Shift back to BP-1, where the same process was reinstituted at a more subtle level three times during a 30-minute segment of tape. The fourth time around, the resumption of BP-1 was accompanied by allegations and doubts surrounding the efficacy of treatment, the hope for change, and, ever so subtly, the competence of the therapist ("If it weren't for you—I'd be better"). At this point, it appeared we had reaped the reward for the therapist Berne described who "watches every movement of every patient at every moment during the session."[18] We had observed Alpha going through her script in condensed form: launching herself into perfectionistic behavior with good precepts and high ex-

Figure 17. Alpha: Basic Posture 1

Figure 18. Alpha: Basic Posture 2

Figure 19. Alpha: Basic Posture 3

pectations; trying hard and struggling only to fail; falling into repeated episodes of sadness; and finally blaming the male who fails to rescue and leaves her alone to be miserable.

Neither Alpha nor the therapist was aware how all-pervasive this cycle of scripted behavior was. The videoanalysis permitted these Basic Postures to be systematically identified in treatment. Alpha was coached to break the cycle and cathect her Adult by placing her feet firmly on the floor, straightening her spinal column against the back of the chair, squaring her head on her shoulders and coming "on straight." This produced an immediate behavior change toward realistic, Adult data processing in therapy. During subsequent sessions, Alpha reported success in employing this procedure at home, breaking her escalation of the cycle that set up her periods of depression at the precise point she "caught" herself in it.

Alpha's behavior roughly corresponds to what Taibi Kahler and Hedges Capers described as the miniscript which is a repetitive sequence of behaviors: "Try hard" (Driver), "Fail" (Stopper), "Be sad" (Pay off), and IWFY (Vengeful Child).[19] Initial hopes that we might establish a similar pattern punctuated by Trunk Shifts among all our subjects were short-lived. Beta, for example, who became our second subject, adopted one single posture repeatedly during the hour as she described her emotional abuse in a long-term affair she sought to end. Her bodily duplicity was top-bottom in distribution, formed in the lower viewing quadrants by crossing her legs and winding her upper instep around her lower ankle, where she remained stationary for sustained periods of time. Berne described this posture as a "script sign," noting its characteristic protection against violation.[20] Instead of the sequential shifts observed in Alpha, Beta firmly assumed one posture and persistently held it as if security depended upon it. Subsequent studies, as we shall see, have revealed many different patterns of postural display accompanying behavior in script.

Movement and Games

In the video studies of group treatment, Schooley had greater success identifying movements related to games than he did specific script signs, which at this stage of our work remained stubbornly elusive. The hypothesis was that an associated set of bodily movements can be identified which correspond to the moves of a psychological game for each subject. A more specific focus was upon an identifiable pattern of movement surrounding the moment of payoff to the game, marking its sudden and dramatic switch in roles. This Schooley was able to isolate for 12 of the 16 subjects upon whom he was able to obtain a full workup.

The subject designated X1 provides a representative example. X1 was a 44-year-old male who entered treatment with his wife, complaining of impotence. His game, which was termed a form of "Kick Me," was accompanied by a distinct sequence of Basic Postures, each with its characteristic pattern of gestures. He would normally begin by talking with the group about his problems in general, assuming Basic Posture 1 (see Figure 20). This was what we came to term a Rest Posture as opposed to a Cathected Posture, because it served to express several ego states. When the predominant number of Identified Movements was made with his left hand and arm, he was in his Child. The verbal content usually involved a series of complaints about the way his wife treated him. On

Figure 20. Subject X1: Basic Posture 1

occasions when X1 moved predominantly with his right hand in this posture, he made chopping motions and became highly critical of the way she acted (Parent). His game could begin in either chosen ego state.

Basic Posture 2 was also formed with a shift of the torso forward and to the left (see Figure 21). It was judged a Cathected Posture because it always expressed X1's adapted Child ego state. It could appear to initiate the game or it could follow Basic Posture 1 as another move in the ongoing series of transactions. From this posture, X1 would address his wife directly, sometimes with a slight whine in his voice, making subtle accusations that she mistreated him

Figure 21. Subject X1: Basic Posture 2

which elicited a rising crescendo of hypercritical responses from her. While he talked or listened in this posture, he engaged in a large amount of head, arm, and hand movement, jingling coins in his right hand, or pulling at his right hand with his left. In the lower left quadrant, his right leg crossed his left and his right foot moved in a circle three times per minute when he spoke. Foot activity similar to this is a characteristic signal behavior of Kick Me players.

At the point where he engaged in overt, angry transactions with his wife, X1 made a Trunk Shift to the right to assume Basic Posture 3 (see Figure 22). His right arm was extended rigidly and was thrust vigorously up and down to punctuate his allegations that she tried to dominate him and rejected him over and over again with her coldness. This was his angry, critical Parent which moved predominantly from his right with accentuated chopping motions, the palm of the hand down or vertical to the floor. At the conclusion of this series of Identified Movements, the right arm fell limp over the back of the chair as if to signal resignation and the inability to carry through what he had begun. This was identified as the characteristic movement behavior, marking his switch from angry persecutor to victim. It normally proved a cue for his wife or someone else to deliver their final counter.

This was followed by a period of sullen withdrawal for X1 to Basic Posture 4, formed by a Trunk Shift back and slightly to the left. It had two alternating expressions (see Figure 23). This was the posture in which the payoff was taken. While in it, he remained adamantly closed to any efforts by others to establish contact with or encourage him.

The advantages of exploring movement behavior surrounding games are obvious. X1's rigid right arm, which suddenly pitched itself limply across the back of his chair, is an obvious key to his symptom of impotence. And it effectively places this symptom within the broader context of the kind of relationship he and his wife have. The same essential movement from "hard/angry" to "limp/helpless" proved characteristic of his response to the whole range of belligerent, ipsisexual exchanges between the two of them. Clinically, if afforded them an opportunity to work on the dynamics surrounding X1's impotence in the group treatment room, as well as in the bedroom. The first step, in either place, is not to take the payoff of resignation as evidenced in the subsequent postures of sullen withdrawal.

SOME HYPOTHESES FOR CLINICAL USE

At this stage, we have little hope of forming a descriptive catalog of Basic Postures or Identified Movements universal to Parent, Adult, or Child ego states. However, once we learn the coherent set of behavior patterns compris-

Figure 22. Subject X1: Basic Posture 3

ing the ego states for one subject, we may observe their unique style of appearance with amazing accuracy and consistency. Within the limited number of subjects we have observed experimentally and clinically, certain trends toward common behaviors in Parent, Adult, and Child ego states are evident which leave us steering a somewhat uncertain course between the Scylla of chaotic dissimilarity and the Charybdis of universal meaning. This state of affairs seems plausible if we take three things into consideration.

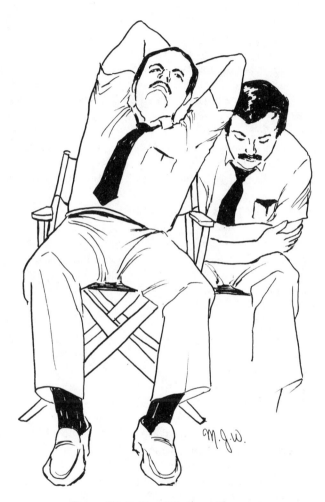

Figure 23. Subject X1: Basic Posture 4

First, there are basic cultural similarities between parents and their parenting patterns. For example, parents often point their finger when telling a child what to do. Children no doubt learn by observation to reproduce these gestures when acting like a parent (Parent displays), as well as learning common postures and movements in response to being rebuked which assist them in their common task of coping with such corrections (Child displays).

Second, basic differences in size, visual angles of interaction, and bodily stance exist between parents and their children, and between children and other children. Hence, different stances and movements may persist in accord with their initial patterns which were learned during times of ego state formation. For example, we often observe people tending to look up in Child ego states, anatomically reproducing the customary visual angles of an earlier age.

Third, each individual learns to make his or her own unique movements in response to a particular developmental history. For example, George was repeatedly swatted on the back of his head when his angry father disciplined him. Now, 20 years later, he flexes his neck muscles and thrusts his head forward slightly when threatened. This Identified Movement is both characteristic of and unique to his own developmental history.

For the clinician, I want to glean from our studies so far a number of observations which may be immediately useful in the processes of psychotherapy. The 15 hypotheses for clinical use below were all developed during this initial stage of research, although they have proven accurate with the larger numbers of persons in the clinical research that followed.

1) Shifts in the spinal cord (Trunk Shifts) are the key to changes from one ego state to another. A full Trunk Shift involves a movement of two to four inches of both head and trunk. For example, rocking forward and backward expresses one continuing ego state (ordinarily Child in search of a nurturing Parent) and not a Trunk Shift, since the spinal column remains stationary and is rocked "as a pole" on the pelvic hinge. Rocking to and fro does not appear to constitute the same psychophysiological state. Side-to-side rocking evidences confusion and disorientation in a small number of clients observed and may signal the presence of psychotic behavior.

2) Changes in ego state may be elicited by encouraging clients to alter their Basic Posture and realign their spinal cord. This phenomenon is evidenced in the "top dog/underdog" dialogues developed between two chairs by the late Fritz Perls.[21] Not only do the two chairs separate the internal dialogue between the ego states, but also the act of physically shifting from one chair to another precipitates differing Basic Postures expressed in each chair. Less labile clients who evidence indistinguishable behavior from each chair may be suffering from

exclusions. For those unfamiliar with transactional analysis, an exclusion is the investment of energy in only one ego state, while energy remains bound in all others.

3) An ego state is a psychophysiological event involving the whole organism. Terms like "body language" or "nonverbal communication" suggest the body is "saying something" through another channel than the mouth. This is only partially true. Parent, Adult, and Child ego states appear as concrete states of being, not simply ways of communicating something which originates elsewhere (as in the head). They constitute our own unique mode of "being in the world" at a particular moment. In all probability, certain aspects of an ego state, such as Basic Posture or stance, are integrated neurologically at the subcortical level.[22] Unwitting therapeutic efforts to deal with ego state changes in terms of "finding something else to say" may bypass the thoroughgoing, all-pervasive organismic system we confront. Methods which get clients up, alter the way they stand and sit, change the way they reach out from their spinal cord to give and get strokes, give them something else to do bodily with their time, and teach them coordination or dance may provide a much more effective treatment regime than a therapy that reduces everything to verbal or lexical terms—simply talking with patients about how they are acting.

4) There are two distinct types of Basic Postures. There are Rest Postures from which we observe multiple patterns of movement expressing not one but a number of different ego states. I term them Rest Postures, because they are frequently chosen for listening or when the individual appears relaxed and relatively disengaged from strong involvement with others. Cathected Postures differ in that they consistently mark the appearance of one and the same ego state to such an extent that their presence merits safe assumptions about how the subject will behave. It is possible for persons, with careful attention to the task, to carry behaviors from one ego state over into an entirely different Cathected Posture. Such acts transgress the customary rhythm of stance and movement so that most individuals report an uneasiness when doing so. Once their attention to the unusual deployment of their bodies has been diverted, they invariably return to a more familiar physical expression of the former ego state, or proceed with different behavior in a new one.

5) Basic Postures for the Parent ego state tend to be formed by tilting the spinal column back or away from the other person and toward one side. Mass Distribution diagrams show the T-zone (formed by head, shoulders, and trunk) tipped decidedly away from the central axis into one of the upper viewing quadrants. In approximately 70 percent of the persons observed, the first Parent ego state evident is formed by a Trunk Shift to the left; in the others, it is to the right. This is the predominant Parent. When a second Parent ego state

appears, it is with a Trunk Shift that places head and shoulders over into the opposite quadrant. The two Parent ego states are radically different. For example, in one subject, Parent 1 tended to be nurturing and "helpfully controlling" with only a mild critical apparatus; Parent 2 expressed itself from the opposing quadrant at times of excitement with blustering, devastating criticism. In a number of clinical instances, we have gained historical confirmation that these distinct behavior patterns are borrowed from each actual parental figure.

6) Angles of the head in the Parent ego state tend toward front/back tilting. In a number of instances, Parental heads can be charted literally "looking down their noses" at the other, physically reproducing the angularity of big people looking down at little people. For this reason, we have tended to discourage floor-sitting by members of a group, which leaves them looking up to others, creating visual angles that stimulate similar postures.

7) Characteristic hand and arm movements in the Parent ego state are frequently arc-like, over from above, with palms down. In many instances, they appear to reproduce the motion of bigger persons reaching down to pat smaller ones on the head, laying something on them (like a benediction), picking them up, or pointing something out definitively (the inevitable finger or penetrating handchop, with palm in). If the T-zone is tilted left, the left hand is predominant; if right, then the right hand leads in movement. The arc-like movements, with palms charted down or in, stand in vivid contrast to Child hand movements which frequently have palms up and movement outward.

8) Basic Postures for the Child ego state are ordinarily formed by Trunk Shifts to the opposing quadrant of Parental activity with the spinal column shifted decisively to the side, forward or backward. Trunk movements from one quadrant to the other frequently measure from six to 18 inches. Alpha's Child behavior, for example, transpired with Mass Distribution in the upper right quadrant, the right hand being predominant for gestural movements. This opposed her maternal Parent, who operated from the upper left quadrant with an ascendant left hand. Such right/left divisions of expression, when placed into the "top dog/underdog" dialogues of Gestalt therapy, consistently produce a scene (or series of scenes) between mother and daughter, which is perpetuated structurally in the current appearance of Parent and Child ego states. Once the right/left division has been established for the client, the ascendancy of one over the other becomes readily apparent in the most subtle expressions of mundane conversation.

9) Head angles in Child ego states tend toward more pronounced degrees of departure from the line of the spinal column. Ernst has done an excellent job of describing the radical tilts up ("Who's up there?"), down, or to one side, noting the "angle" the Child brings to game behavior.[23]

10) Identified Movements of the hands in Child ego states are frequently diagrammed up and out in direction, with the palms up. Physiological models are the infant reaching up for the mother's arms, the open hand reaching for something to be given it, the circular motion of the open hand which often accompanies descriptions of "trying hard," or the outward shrug of the hands so commonly made in our culture with the words, "I don't know." By way of contrast, the Parental finger is delivered with palm down or in. The Child finger is delivered vigorously with palm up.

11) Another form of bodily duplicity commonly charted in Basic Postures is the top/bottom division of activity (upper quadrants versus lower quadrants). One subject who complained of frigidity was animated from the waist up and virtually motionless or "dead" from the waist down. The lower quadrants form a rich center of activity for the Child ego state being denied full expression. The toes turn in to simulate "standing pigeon-toed," or feet come off the floor to be tucked underneath. Foot shuffling and wriggling often accompany Child impulses to leave and run away. Ankle arching and foot flicking, twisting, and circling often signal Child impulses of anger which simulate the act of kicking. In fact, foot kicking and foot shuffling appear frequently as the rough psychomotor equivalents of an archaic impulse toward fight or flight reactions in the face of threat.

12) When denied behavior does find bodily expression, it is often with Identified Movements of pronounced magnitude (Grids/Move) or Expenditure. Exclusions may be accurately identified in this manner. Berne located Mr. Ennat's excluded Child by focusing attention on the occasional thump he gave his thigh, tracing down "adventures during toilet training" through this gesture.[24] The clinical method of exaggerating an Identified Movement which protrudes into the executive rhythm of another ego state often accomplishes effective structural analysis.

13) Adult behavior is marked by a T-zone (head, shoulders, and trunk) aligned in a position approaching straightness with the central vertical axis on the viewing grid or leaning forward from it. The "Ernst phenomenon," which is the practice of "leveling" the head on the shoulders to cathect the Adult, approaches similar procedures we have found to be effective.[25] Squaring away the body to "come on straight" involves a shift in Basic Posture. Placing feet flat on the floor so that bodily activity may be equally distributed in all quadrants aligns both trunk and head along the central axis naturally.

14) Identified Movements of hands and arms in the Adult ego state appear to be equally distributed right and left, with frequent coordination of movement from both sides. One plausible explanation is that the organism is free from the right/left imprinting in Parent and adapted Child ego states and becomes cap-

able of balanced bodily expression in response to the moment. Clinically, it appears the free or natural Child possesses a similar balance and coordination appropriate to a person's age and development. This is in contrast to the kinesics of adapted Child behavior which do not appear to have the same contemporary flow. Thus far, however, we have been unable to study the free Child on the viewing screen, to chart its expression accurately.

15) Analyzing the bodily expressions of ego states may give us a much better reading on subtle contaminations than the verbal or ideational analysis with which many of us have been working. We are struck by the amount of material in therapy where subjects appear to be processing data in their Adult, while assuming their Basic Posture for Parent or Child. Immediate progress is made clinically when the Basic Posture is changed. The same material when processed again with a straight T-zone permits subtle contaminations to be identified in the ego state where they belong.

The greatest contribution of these video studies lies in the training of psychotherapists. Most therapists do not really look at their patients. In fact, it is possible to sit in the treatment room for a lifetime listening to what people say, maintaining appropriate eye contact, and never seeing what others are doing in their bodies. This is probably because most parents teach their children it is impolite to look at other people. They will, however, let their children stare at others on television for hours on end. Once we receive permission to look at our clients on television, the process is easily extended to all kinds of expanded visual awareness in the treatment room. Staring never proves necessary.

The use of videotape in the treatment room is another matter. Our enthusiasm soon gave way to the realization of a number of disadvantages it poses. First, the practice of replay during the treatment hour dominates the process. Relocations and replays are costly timewise, regardless of the efficiency of the video team. Regular use in normal clinical practice is prohibitive economically, both in terms of equipment and trained personnel to operate it. Moreover, continual attention to replays of significant bodily postures and movements distracts from the full range of therapeutic functions in a curative group.

Feedback sessions were conducted with each of the experimental subjects in group treatment. They saw both their pastime interviews and segments of their behavior in group treatment and were appraised by charts and diagrams of their characteristic movement patterns. The aim was to determine the advantages such awareness would provide to their treatment. During these sessions we encountered a performance factor in every Child ranging from 30 minutes to three hours ("Hey, look at me on TV!"). Even with subjects viewing their behavior three weeks later, the desired Adult data processing was impossible. One male sat and cried for 15 minutes, seeing only his awkwardness on the screen. One female tolerated lengthy discussion of various movements while utterly preoccupied with her facial features and how her hair looked, later recalling nothing that was said. We finally abandoned efforts to share research data until subjects had viewed the film in its entirety. Then, we dealt with significant reactions in terms of the client's self-image and appearance to others. For those who wish to address such concerns, video playback provides a medium without peer.

For my own purposes in clinical practice, I am interested in assisting the client to establish awareness of his or her own bodily behaviors in significant ego states, both as a means of self-discovery and as a means of learning to change from one ego state to another. This is best accomplished by a specific set of interventions within the normal processes of group treatment, which render the use of video replay unnecessary. These techniques, which the clinician can employ in any group setting, are the subject of the next chapter.

REFERENCE NOTES

1. Moore, M. Nonverbal communication as a diagnostic and therapeutic tool. Unpublished Masters Research Project, Louisville Presbyterian Seminary, 1972.
2. Berne, E. *Transactional Analysis in Psychotherapy*. New York: Grove Press, 1961, pp. 29-37, 238-244.
3. Kirkbride, D., & Stokes, D. The measurement of body movement. Unpublished Manuscript, Louisville Presbyterian Seminary, 1971; _____ Body analysis: Physiological aspects. Unpublished Manuscript, Louisville Presbyterian Seminary, 1972. _____ Considerations concerning intuitive analysis of body cues. Unpublished Manuscript, Louisville Presbyterian Seminary, 1972; and _____ Experiment on body language: A working paper. Unpublished Manuscript, Louisville Presbyterian Seminary, 1972.
4. Berne, G. *Games People Play*. New York: Grove Press, 1964, pp. 41-47.
5. Kirkbride, D., & Stokes, D. A multi-representational analysis of body movement. Unpublished Doctor of Ministry Research Project, Louisville Presbyterian Seminary, 1975.
6. Ibid., p. 22.
7. Ibid., p. 25.
8. Ibid., p. 23.
9. Dusay, J. M. *Egograms*. New York: Harper & Row, 1977, p. 123.
10. Kirkbride, D., & Stokes, D. A multi-representational analysis of body movement, p. 58.
11. Ibid., p. 67.
12. Ibid., p. 66.
13. Ibid., p. 64.
14. Schooley, C. G. Games, injunctions and bodily behavior. Unpublished Doctor of Ministry Research Project, Louisville Presbyterian Seminary, 1973, p. 68.
15. Schooley, C. G., & Cushman, J. Body research. Unpublished Paper, Louisville Presbyterian Seminary, 1972.
16. Schooley, C. G. Games, injunctions and bodily behavior.
17. Berne, E. *What Do You Say After You Say Hello?* New York: Grove Press, 1971, pp. 215-230.
18. Ibid., p. 346.

19. Kahler, T., & Capers, H. The miniscript. *Transactional Analysis Journal, 4:*26-42, 1974.
20. Berne, E. *What Do You Say After You Say Hello?* pp. 316, 317.
21. Perls, F. S. *Gestalt Therapy Verbatim.* Lafayette, CA: Real People Press, 1969.
22. Grossman, S. *Physiological Psychology.* New York: John Wiley & Sons, 1967, pp. 241, 262, 294, 512-514, 815.
23. Ernst, F. H. Handbook of listening. Mimeographed. Copyrighted, 1971, pp. 7, 35-37.
24. Berne, E. *Transactional Analysis in Psychotherapy,* p. 65.
25. Ernst, F. H. Op. cit., pp. 109-111.

tle ball. I also include in this class postural displays that carry the person away from others to some expression of isolation. One man who exaggerated a posture with his torso thrust forward in the chair completed it by pitching himself helplessly forward onto the floor.

When the Identified Movements are *expansive*, their exaggeration carries them outward from the body toward others. *Completion* involves instructing clients to carry through their movement to the point of tactile expression with some*body*. The end point is discovered through making actual physical contact with someone else in the room. A flick of the foot completes itself as a kick on the shins; an open palm extended forward reaches out to pull another closer; a protrusive chop of the hand becomes a blow to the face.

Whatever the case, cooperative clients who exaggerate a posture or a movement to its end point normally evidence a strong rise of affect heretofore denied or suppressed. The procedure provides heightened experience in the visual mode, as well as the kinesthetic, as an individual acts out bodily to the most pronounced point possible. Incidentally, rules against violence or tissue damage have never proved necessary with such interventions. Any aggressive movements are made tentatively in the surprise of self-discovery. If the desire to slap, hit, or kick surges strong, appropriate measures for expression can be readily structured by the therapist (an open palm held for slapping, pillows and the like for hitting and kicking).

Experimenting

A third set of interventions into the kinesics of an ego state invites the client to experiment with contrasting postures and movement. This is best done by encouraging persons to experiment with the opposite of what they have been doing. If the client has moved entirely from one side of the body, we encourage reversal of this trend by elevating the other and requesting movement expression in that position. Through doing the opposite, we encourage the individual to experience a polar tendency which the first position excludes. Joyce, who made herself "little" through diminutive posturing, was encouraged to do the opposite, making herself as "big" as possible and experiencing that. George, who made contact with a circular, pleading movement with his right hand, was urged to make opposite kinds of movement with his left.

Experimentation with the kinesic opposite often produces a profound change in affect. The satisfaction that a large number of clients experience when doing this suggests that many primary adaptations in the Child ego state mask a contrasting set of feelings beneath. The "polar opposite" is not a logical opposite, but a behavioral one unique to the individual. It appears that if be-

havior A with its attendant feelings is forbidden, then behavior B with its attendant feelings is formed in the Child ego state as an enduring adaptation.
Behavior B has the substitutionary quality of a racket, as described by Fanita
English, in which the individual learns to feel B in place of the original, authentic feeling A.[5] Interventions which interrupt pattern B and invite expressions from pattern A can constitute a powerful basis for immediate change in
the here and now. If Joyce, who is forbidden to feel and act big, is encouraged
to experiment with big, grown-up behaviors immediately upon the awareness
of her "little girl" adaptation, concrete measures for change are introduced into
her treatment at the precise point where old patterns of adaptation in the face of
threat have prevailed.

These interventions, which serve to interrupt kinesic patterns of ego states, I
employ less than two percent of the time in group treatment. Another 20 percent of the time I may switch attention to register the pattern of movements a
person is making. Still another 20 percent of the time I may attend body movements peripherally, while working at another level in order to check the effectiveness of what is transpiring. All techniques are easily integrated into the procedures of a normal therapy group. Berne used to suggest that therapists, on
occasion, shut their eyes to listen fully to what the client is saying.[6] I suggest that
therapists, on occasion, shut their ears to see fully what their clients are doing.

A CASE: LETA

The use of these techniques with Leta can serve to illustrate clinically how
they are incorporated into the normal flow of group therapy. Leta was a
23-year-old nurse who entered treatment because she was failing nurse's training. Her failure came in her last semester after making top grades throughout
her previous studies. She readily passed repeat examinations and was gradu-
ated, when she decided against her previous plan to return to a western state to
care for her alcoholic father upon finishing. She subsequently took a job at a local
hospital, got married, and continued her treatment working on a contract to stop
pleasing people and stand up for herself. Her life was continually beset by repeated calls and visits from her father, who presented a series of dilemmas around
unemployment, lack of funds, sickness, loneliness, and general misery. These
somehow became Leta's responsibility in the economy of their relationship.

In her formative years Leta assumed the maternal, caring role in the family,
because of mother's repeated hospitalizations for psychotic episodes. During
these times, father drank heavily. Leta cooked and cared for her younger sister
and once rescued the family from a house fire which father started in a drunken
stupor. When Leta was 12, the family collapsed and Leta went to live in a foster

home where she continued to "earn her keep," grew beautiful, and felt guilty about deserting her post with father.

Leta's husband complained that her life was not her own. She was always helping others and never accepted anything for herself, which included everything from fun to affection to orgasms. On this particular day, Leta was sharing her distress with the group over another visit from father. Tearfully, she described how miserable he was and how sorry she felt for him, acknowledging that a mixture of guilt and resentment overwhelmed her. Verbal interventions, including a conversation with her father in an empty chair, yielded no change in ego state or movement through her impasse. Leta's Basic Posture revealed a pronounced division of her body between left and right (see Figure 24). Her left side was altogether ascendant and dominant in Identified Movement. The entire right side of her body was limp and recessive.

Attending

The therapist intervened at this point to call attention to Leta's posture:

> Therapist: Leta, I'm struck with your posture. Will you hold it for a moment? (Getting up and walking over.) Everything on this side (pointing to the left) looks ascendant and dominant. This side looks limp and "out of it" (pointing to the right).

A member of the group mirrored Leta's posture, "playing back" to her the arclike gestures with her left hand, which moved down from above to rest with the palm up parallel to the arm of the chair, then returned to perpendicular ascent above her elbow. Leta reproduced these gestures upon encouragement, accepting the invitation to experience herself in the left side of her body.

> Leta: I'm working . . . laboring, uh, trying so hard, to hold things together. I'm back in "the little mother" part of me, hoping Dad will be OK. I'm so tired (tears) of everything. I'm just like mother . . . crying all the time.

Exploring

The therapist then invited Leta to explore her posture. The instruction was to move with her left side, reporting whatever thoughts and feelings accompanied that movement. To do this effectively, Leta had to shift free cathexis to her in-

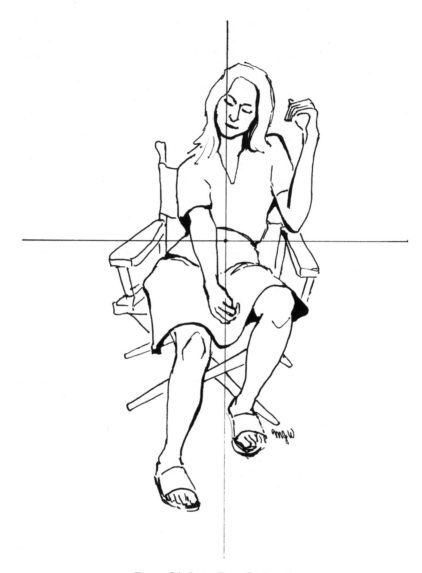

Figure 24. Leta: Basic Posture 1

tuitive Child, often called "the little Professor" who knows, without bothering to know how knowledge comes. Sometimes the process is arrested at this point and confined by the client to Adult exchange about what is happening. If so, the task of exploring ceases and the client talks about the impasse that is being experienced. This is of only limited benefit to Leta in redistributing her energy among her ego states.

> Therapist: Will you move with your left side of your body, making bigger and bigger moves, giving out with feelings and thoughts that come?
> Leta: I am trying so hard . . . (sob), you'll never stop (to father's chair) . . . never understand . . . never know. (Left hand extends outward, palm up, then drops across the arm of the chair.) Some day . . . (sob), some day maybe you will realize how much you've made me suffer.

With her Child ego state fully cathected, Leta was in a position to redecide an early decision to placate her father and suffer in hopes that he would mend his errant ways and change. This was her primary adaptation. More often than not, however, Leta's adapted Child will remain hypercathected, unless we explore with her the side she denied in this major life circumstance. The failure to do so is a common pitfall in redecision work with placating clients who, like Leta, can sense what others want and all-too-readily produce it with no genuine integration. Full measures of exploration called for an invitation to "move into" her right side to experience what was there.

> Therapist: Leta, will you shift awareness over into the right side of your body and experience yourself there?
> Leta: I'm subservient . . . totally relaxed . . . I'm . . . numb, dead, inactive. I don't want anything . . . I don't do anything. I just exist.

Experimentation

Experimentation involves inviting the client to experience the polar opposite of a posture or gesture. In the case of such decided right/left divisions as Leta's, I have found the most successful suggestion is to ask the client to reverse the posture, elevating posture and movement in the opposing quadrants of bodily activity. Effective experimentation is like "trying on something new for size" to see if we like it and want to keep it. The first movements are often tentative but revealing.

> Therapist: Leta, let's reverse this division in your body for a moment and see what you experience. Yeah . . . get your right hand ascendant and let your left be limp in your lap, and extend your left leg out, doubling your right back, and shifting over to the right . . . Good!

Leta reported feeling awkward in her reversed posture (see Figure 25). Her tears disappeared as she began to talk about her father, gesturing with her right hand. Several times she checked her urge to lean or move left. She expressed in a strained voice how tired she was of these scenes with her father, noticing the thin edge of irritation in her tone.

Another group member called attention to her loosely gathered fist elevated on the right. Immediately, Leta tucked her thumb between her first two fingers, a gesture she reported she had often noticed among newborn babies:

> Leta: I know I'm angry, but I didn't realize how frightened I really am . . . uh, it's like I'm in this thumb, suddenly wanting to be encased, surrounded, like some sort of protection . . . almost like getting back inside the womb. That's crazy. I mean, I'm really frightened of him, of all the anger . . . the terrible fights and beatings. (Slowly beginning to thrust her right fist up and down) I'm scared to death of him . . . I'm even scared of you, all of you. I'm scared to think about me. I'm not ready to take him on yet . . . going to need some practice there. But I can refuse to talk to him until I'm ready. And I can do a lot of other things, too.

Redecision becomes possible when one reclaims the denied part of oneself which underlies the adaptation governing present experience. In Leta's case, her angry-assertive right was part of behavior A which was forbidden expression when she was small, upon threat to her survival. Behavior B, which was expressed from her left side, embodied her efforts to placate and suffer until father changed, and constituted her primary adapted Child ego state. Experimentation with the polar opposite becomes the royal road to change in personality and script.

TREATMENT IN OZ

I began this chapter by posing certain practices surrounding childbirth and puberty rites as models for interventions in psychotherapy. I want to end it with a parody for clients like Leta who experience the process successfully. My

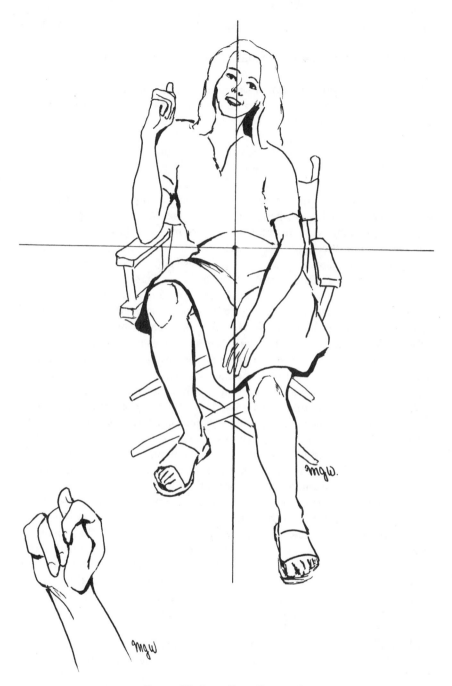

Figure 25. Leta: Basic Posture 2

choice is the Wizard of Oz, which many of us watch annually on television with our children.

Usually, clients enter treatment like a rudely displaced Dorothy wandering around, lost in Oz, and deciding to go see the Wizard. And the opening exchange with their therapist goes something like this for them:

> Therapist: I am the great Oz. What do you want?
> Dorothy: I want to go to Kansas.

What happens next differs according to each wizard's theories about his work. Some already know what is involved in the task: "First, you must kill the Wicked Witch of the West and bring me her broomstick." Others provide a road map with proper directions and set about reinforcing correct turns. If, having been given proper directions, Dorothy still doesn't go, she has a problem. And so does her wizard. Some organize tours from the Emerald City with opportunities to relate to a Scarecrow, a Cowardly Lion, and a Tin Woodsman. I belong among those wizards who believe it is important to figure out with Dorothy what she is doing wandering around Oz, when she really wants to be in Kansas.

What wizards do between the time Dorothy arrives and the time she finally decides to go back to Kansas is a proper concern for their training and technique. This constitutes their paraphernalia as wizards. Some have impressive rooms and accents very different from people in Kansas, which increases Dorothy's faith in their expertise as wizards. This seems important at first. Others have an impressive assortment of lions, witches, and the like which provide valuable social learning for Dorothy when she returns. Still others use this setting to concern themselves with Dorothy's style of getting caught in tornadoes and various other wanderings against her will. Two crucial things must happen, however, at the time she actually does go back to Kansas on her own.

First, there comes a time when Dorothy discovers that the wizard's paraphernalia is really different from the wizard. This discovery may come sooner or later, depending upon how much wizardry Dorothy requires. In the movie, her tiny dog, Toto, pulls the curtain aside exposing the wizard as an ordinary sort of person, just like her. "Why, you're not a wizard at all," observes Dorothy, "you're a very bad man!" At this point, the proper response for the wizard is "No, not at all, I'm a very good man, just a very poor wizard." This happens shortly before Dorothy returns to Kansas, and is usually a rather joyous event once the disillusionment subsides.

Then comes the realization the truth of the matter is that Dorothy can return to Kansas any time she wishes. Actually, she could have done so at any point. All she had to do was click her heels three times and wish. What is important here is that wishing is never enough. Dorothy must also make some different movements in her body which coincide with what she wants.

REFERENCE NOTES

1. Leboyer, F. *Birth Without Violence*. New York: Alfred A. Knopf, 1975.
2. See Eliade, M. *Rites and Symbols of Initiation*. New York: Harper & Row, 1958. Van Gennep, A. *The Rites of Passage*. Chicago: University of Chicago Press, 1960. Turner, V. W. *The Ritual Process*. Chicago: Aldine Publishing Co., 1969.
3. Bandler, R., & Grinder, J. *The Structure of Magic II*. Palo Alto: Science and Behavior Books, 1976.
4. See Perls, F. *Gestalt Therapy Verbatim*. Lafayette, Calif.: Real People Press, 1969.
5. English, F. The substitution factor: Rackets and real feelings (Part I). *Transactional Analysis Journal*, 1:27-32, 1971.
6. Berne, E. *What Do You Say After You Say Hello?* New York: Grove Press, 1971, p. 321.

5

Bodily
duplicity

Bodily duplicity is the hallmark of kinesic behavior when an individual addresses a major life conflict. Contrasting activity in another portion of the body emerges to mark the presence of a second ego state which has long opposed the changes desired in the first. Unbound energy from this ulterior ego state forms an internal impasse which inhibits problem-solving and blocks constructive resolution. Structural analysis of the client's internal conflict becomes necessary in order to create the possibility for change.

The literature of analytic psychology is replete with discussions of ambivalence and resistance. We can count on the presence of both in each person we treat. If all of the client's ego states—Parent, Adult, and Child—concurred about the desired change, it would have been accomplished long ago without benefit of psychotherapy. Ambivalence involves an intrapsychic conflict of interest between two ego states, so that an individual thinks and feels two different ways. Resistance designates the inevitable emergence of energy, both psychic and kinesic, to oppose whatever change clients say they want. We make a strategic mistake whenever we fail to acknowledge and honor the value of such resistance to the client. However debilitating it may be now, it once made supreme sense to the individual as a means to survive and maintain affection.

This chapter presents the seven major types of bodily duplicity encountered in the clinical phase of research. Cases to represent each type are selected from a minimum of five, and normally 10 or more, recorded instances. They appear with such frequency that I am confident any practicing psychotherapist can identify them among clients. My attention will be upon the structural analysis of such duplicity and the interventions of choice in each instance.

96

PROTRUSIONS

Protrusions constitute the first type of duplicity. A protrusion is an interruption of activity in one ego state by another. It is normally marked by an abrupt Trunk Shift to another Basic Posture with a different pattern of Identified Movement. This occurs without any transactional stimulus from someone else to elicit it. Protrusions are observable in persons who characteristically stop themselves from doing something.

Dave

Dave was witnessed on a number of occasions to curtail his activity at points where he became excited, playful, or enthusiastic. At these times he sat erect, talked vigorously, and made extensive bilateral movements, using both hands in concert. This was followed by a sudden Trunk Shift over into the upper right quadrant. An ascendant right hand, palm in, moved downward in an arc to come to rest upon his right thigh (see Figure 26). This new position was accompanied by noticeable sobering and sometimes saddening, as if he had been "shut down" or someone had "put a damper on" his spontaneity.

When the therapist attended this postural shift and encouraged Dave to give expression to the movement with his right arm, Dave immediately spoke the words, "Now don't get carried away." The gruffness of his voice surprised him with its similarity to his father's. An historical diagnosis of this Parent ego state was immediately possible through a flood of memories in which father's stern disapproval continually curtailed his freer moments of fun and excitement.

When a protrusion occurs, the intervention of choice is to attend it immediately, permitting the client to assess its meaning. This normally neutralizes its stopping effect, enabling persons to experiment with reactions more to their own choosing. Most people have learned to take the painful effect of such protrusions for granted and seldom admit them to the light of conscious awareness.

James

Failure to deal with a protrusion will normally permit the therapeutic process to be subverted by an intrapsychic impasse. Often, placing the protruding ego state in an empty chair for dialogue exposes the underlying conflict. James announced at the beginning of group that he wanted "to smooth out something that happened" with his wife. A few moments later, he leaned forward to place

Figure 26. Dave: a protrusion

his hand on his forehead and announce he had such a terrible headache he wasn't sure he was up to working. The protrusion required attention first. Coaxing James to go ahead anyway, as several members of the group wished, would have ignored an internal conflict which had already rendered him ineffectual.

James was encouraged to place his headache in an empty chair and give it words:

Headache: I am hurting you. I am going to split your head wide open.
James: Why? Why do you want to hurt me?
Headache: Because you are utterly selfish and completely thoughtless.
You never consider other people's needs.

In the resulting dialogue, James became entrenched in explanations and apologies to his headache for his behavior. Another member of the group observed that he spoke to it the same way he spoke to his wife. But the headache did not sound like his wife to James. It sounded like his mother. And his headache disappeared upon his explosive direction to get out of his head and stop trying to run his life. This, incidentally, is not unusual for headaches and other symptomatic protrusions of a nonorganic origin. Dealing with this protrusion from his Parent ego state left James free to engage directly in conversation with his wife, abandoning his earlier intention to "smooth everything out."

First-degree Impasses

The Gouldings have distinguished between first-, second-, and third-degree impasses in intrapsychic conflict.[1] Most protrusions we encounter clinically have the character of a first-degree impasse, which involves an internal dialogue between the client's Parent (P_2) and Child (C_2) ego states (see Figure 27). This is markedly different from second-degree impasses which evidence an early decision to obey a script injunction lodged within the Child ego state. We will discuss their kinesics shortly. First-degree impasses are formed by a stalemate between messages in the client's Parent ego state and Child responses to them. The dynamics of procrastination are a good example: The Parent says, "Work hard"; the Child says, "I don't want to."

In protrusions, clients usually experience little difficulty in putting words to movements associated with their Parent ego state. This can be done even when the client has no previous awareness of their presence or significance, let alone their effects upon behavior. These Parent messages form a nucleus of moral precepts for living which serve to drive the Child ego state into varied responses of compliance or rebellion. As such, they are part of the counterscript as discussed in Chapter 2 which, unlike script injunctions, is composed of parental prescriptions which are verbal and memorable ("Work hard," "Always do your best," "Never tell a lie," etc.). This accounts for the ease with which persons identify meanings associated with such movements. Protrusions have the character of kinesic reproductions of the actual Parental displays which accompanied the deliverance of these messages. Dave can verbalize his father's com-

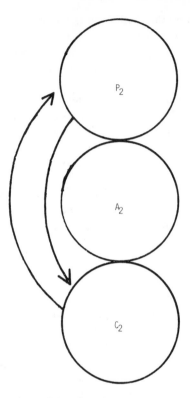

Figure 27. A first-degree impasse

mand, "Now don't get carried away." James can identify the source of such precepts as "Don't be selfish" or "Always consider others" as his maternal Parent.

Most protrusions quietly emerge to curtail Child activity unnoticed by everyone. A common example is the pat on the back that frequently protrudes into a hug between two persons interrupting the pleasurable sensations of physical contact. The patting invariably expresses another ego state than sexually excited Child. The movements are decidedly Parental, maintaining goodwill at the ulterior level of "good boy" or "good girl" transactions, reminiscent of scenes between parent and child which stop at a safe place, far short of incest. This leads to the clinical axiom: A pat on the back means no sex tonight.

Protrusions: An interruption of activity in one ego state by another.

Dynamics: First-degree impasse.

Structural analysis: Internal dialogue between Parent and Child.

Prescription: Attend and establish meaning.

SIMPLE DIVISIONS

Simple divisions of activity between contrasting spheres of the body compose a second type of duplicity commonly encountered in treatment. Decidedly different patterns of posture and movement are visible in each sphere. The division may be between the upper quadrants of bodily behavior and the lower ones (top/bottom) or between one side of the body and the other (right/left). When such kinesic divisions occur, the client's progress in pursuing thought, feeling, or action to any conclusion is arrested.

Eve

Eve provides a clinical example of a top/bottom division. She discussed with the group her application for a graduate fellowship, together with her growing disillusionment with the men in the department. Men were decidedly favored. They dominated women and treated them as "sex objects." From the waist up, Eve was animated and balanced, making coordinated bilateral movements with both hands (see Figure 28). Her behavior was Adult, and her description of exploitive attitudes among professors and fellow students was reasonable and possessed a ring of accuracy.

In the lower quadrants, Eve's buttocks were shoved forward; her legs were tightly crossed in a manner which offered a partly exposed knee and a subtle glimpse of her thigh by permitting an unbuttoned flap of her skirt to fall back conspicuously. Upstairs she mounted rational protests against being regarded as "a pretty face" and "a sex object." Downstairs she presented vibrations which could not go unnoticed by any "red-blooded American boy." Expressing both these behaviors simultaneously is the key to simple divisions.

A male member of Eve's group observed that her knee was so distracting that he could not take seriously what she was saying. This aroused anger in Eve as she recrossed her legs more tightly without bothering to adjust her skirt, which fell even more open. She recounted how she turned herself off to men and pushed them away, even when she liked them initially. Then she related an incident with her father the week before. She had just taken a shower and gone to her room clad only in her housecoat. Her father came in to talk and suddenly placed his hand through the open front upon her bare breast. Shocked and indignant, she moved out of the house, something she had contemplated for some time, sensing he had such feelings toward her. A similar preoccupation

Figure 28. Eve: a simple division, top/bottom

with sexual undertones accompanied all her troubled relationships with men. She could neither relax and enjoy her sexuality as a woman, nor set it aside and engage in open and free exchange unencumbered by its presence. She, too, maintained a constantly divided attention between the two trends of behavior expressed simultaneously in the two halves of her body.

The treatment of choice with simple divisions is to encourage the client to own each sphere of activity fully. Eve's Adult ego state was unaware of the seductive invitations issued by her Child. Exploring this duplicity as it occurs is

consistent reappearance of restraint postures with a conflicted ego state in the course of treatment.

Restraint: Interaction across quadrants of bodily behavior, one part holding another back.

Dynamics: Second-degree impasse.

Structural analysis: Visceral discomfort in the Child at the prospect of disobeying a parental injunction (P_1).

Prescription: Place opposing members in dialogue with one another for redecision therapy.

ATTACHMENT

Attachment is the fourth major type of duplicity encountered at points of impasse. It is evidenced across right/left quadrants with movement largely restricted to the hands which join each other, cling to each other, or stroke each other. The internal conflict results from maintaining an attachment to significant figures in the past. There is a profound reluctance to let go. No movement through the impasse will be made so long as attachment gestures persist.

Joan

Joan had just completed a Plan A divorce. Plan A divorces involve a legal moving-out while the essential game process of the marriage is continued with heightened excitement, accentuated by stroke deprivation in separation and punctuated by an elaborate pony express system provided by children and friends that keeps each party well informed of the other's activities. Plan B divorces involve saying goodbye. Joan complained to the group that her ex-husband was in her home at least four times a week, watching and checking up on her. Her Basic Posture appeared Child. Her torso shifted left, her left hand at her side gesturing with an open palm in outward movements as she expressed her inability to do anything about the situation (see Figure 33). Her right elbow was firmly planted on the arm of the chair in an ascendant or domineering position.

When members of the group questioned why she allowed this, Joan shifted radically right and, with emphatic Parental gestures, described how good a father her ex-husband was—how he picked up the children every other day and put them to bed when he brought them home (see Figure 34). When this ar-

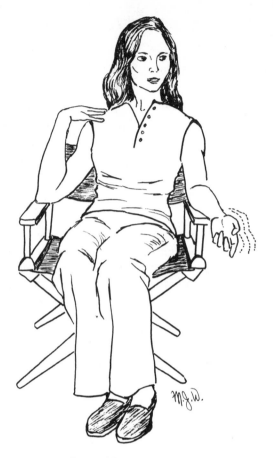

Figure 33. Joan: posture 1

rangement was soundly challenged by several others as a setup to continue to suffer the indignities of his presence around the house, Joan shifted back into the left quadrant and, in resignation, joined her hands together in her lap, insisting this was the way it had to be and that was all there was to it (see Figure 35). The fingers of her left hand clasped those of her right in a clinging fashion.

Attachment postures are characteristic of persons with unresolved dependency upon a parental figure. The tendency is to keep this person around in their heads, if not literally in their lives. Clients who evidence such attachment at the

ulterior level will not take positive action toward remedying their difficulties until they deal with the primary relationship to which they cling. The intervention
of choice is to abandon discussion of the contemporary dilemma to attend and
explore the nature of the attachment itself.

As with restraint, the most effective measure is to create a dialogue between
right and left. Often the two-chair conversation is an appropriate aid in structuring it. Joan's conversation started by talking with her husband and then abrupt-

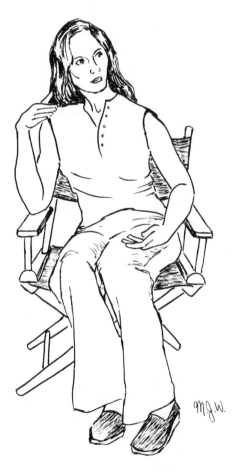

Figure 34. Joan: posture 2

Figure 35. Joan: posture 3, attachment

ly stopped with her accusations that he was suspicious, always watching and intruding upon her relationships with other men. The drama was a familiar one
for her. It was reminiscent of scenes with her father during adolescence, where
his watchful eye constantly spoiled her dating life. She recalled his disapproval
and constant visits during a former marriage. This prompted a conversation
with father which exposed Joan's impasse surrounding his message to stay
away from men, a recurrent issue in which her ex-husband was but another
pawn to perpetuate an original decision never to get close to anyone else.

The Impasse

Attachment postures consistently reveal a second-degree impasse. They are assumed by persons who, like Joan, cling to a significant relationship in the past and avoid full involvement with others in the present. Their kinesics represent the symbolic character of that relationship through recurrent joining of the hands. The script is often based upon an early decision not to grow up or not to be close to anyone else. Another common theme is "I can't change until some-one else does." Sometimes the client has assumed the role of holding the parents' marriage together and fears the family will fall apart if the attachment is broken. In any case, redecision work centers around granting the client permission to abandon the futile task of maintaining the attachment of the past and to get on with new attachments of one's own choosing in the present.

An important subtype among attachment postures is encountered in persons who cling to their relationship with a deceased spouse. Grace provides an excellent example. Her husband had died, after a prolonged and painful hospitalization, two years before she entered treatment. At the age of 51, Grace found herself aimless, with few friends, and unwilling to make the effort to invest herself in anything other than work. Periodically, she suffered a loss of energy and sleep disturbance and was medicated for depression. During her first three hours of individual psychotherapy, her Basic Postures evidenced attachment approximately 80 percent of the time. Her left hand grasped her right, stroked it, caressed it, and enfolded it constantly.

The intervention of choice with such attachments is to assist the client in saying goodbye. Normally, the reason this has not been done is found in the client's history, where a primary attachment to a parent was transferred to the spouse. In Grace's case, there was much unresolved grief surrounding her father's death. Resolution of her current loss was contingent upon Grace cathecting her dependent Child ego state and doing the necessary grief work to divest it of the energy consumed in keeping departed figures around. Breaking the attachment and saying goodbye is accompanied by a flood of genuine grief over the loss. Grief can be distinguished by the clinician from depression or a sadness racket by the waves of affect which come, followed by the experience of relief and satiation. The closure of grief will also be marked by the disappearance of attachment postures.

Attachment: Hands interacting to join, cling to, or stroke one another.

Dynamics: Second-degree impasse.

Structural analysis: Unresolved dependency and/or grief in the Child ego state.

Prescription: Redecision to break the attachment and invest energy in new attachments of one's own choosing.

ENACTMENT

Enactment is a fifth type of bodily duplicity encountered in the treatment room. Enactment designates a range of Identified Movements which convey the feeling state at the point of a client's payoff in game or script. Their distinguishing feature, however, is that they are seldom, if ever, made at the actual point of payoff. Instead, they appear in bodily duplicity as kinesic expressions of an ulterior ego state in anticipation of that payoff. What remains unacknowledged at the social level is quietly enacted in bodily behaviors, while the client normally denies awareness of the intent they express.

Ralph

Ralph's bodily behavior combined both restraint and enactment as he and his wife came for counseling regarding a crisis in their marriage. Ralph had just announced his plans to go away for a week with a woman he met at a recent convention. His wife sat across the room from him, squirming and red-eyed, biting her nails. Ralph spoke in reasonable tones, never fluctuating from his Adult ego state which remained in executive control. Quietly he described in detail the facts surrounding an affair his wife had three years ago. He had known about it all along and said nothing. He had lost a lot of sleep, smoked a lot of cigarettes, but acquiesced to the inevitable. He saw no reason why his wife should now take such rabid exception to his plans, given their history.

As he spoke, Ralph sat erect, making no movements bodily to accompany his steady flow of rationality (see Figure 36). He talked on for some time before the therapist noticed the restraint pattern between left and right in his lap. Ralph's left hand covered a fist made so tightly that his fingernails cut white marks in the palm of his right hand. Precisely at the moment he completed the elaborate vindication of his plans, Ralph's right foot extended itself in a deliberate kicking motion toward his wife. This, his first Identified Movement of any kind, constituted the enactment in his kinesics of a Child ego state completely excluded from his Adult awareness.

All that was contained in his bodily duplicity came as a complete surprise to Ralph when the therapist encouraged him to attend it. This is characteristic of enactment behavior. Ralph was completely out of touch with the fierce satisfaction he quietly took in the accomplishment of a three-year desire to retaliate. Dialogue between the left hand and the right hand revealed strong injunctions

Figure 36. Ralph: enactment

against any display of anger. An exploration of the elegant kick yielded more mileage in terms of the transactional realities underneath his cool exterior than weeks of conversation at the verbal level could have accomplished.

Payoffs and Awareness

By definition, all psychological games are played out of Adult awareness.[8] This gives the payoff its exciting, dramatic, and unexpected quality. Likewise, the irony of outcome in all script activity necessitates its payoff be denied to everyday consciousness. What appears so obvious to others is concealed from self-awareness through no malice or stubbornness. When fundamental expressions of affect and action are forbidden, as in Ralph's case, the elegant and repetitive movements of his Child are literally subversive activities to be denied in his cool, rational Adult.

This fact must be borne in mind if we are to deal successfully with enactment behaviors. The intervention of choice is to attend and explore them on the spot. Attending alone is never sufficient, because the client's Adult ego state will invariably perceive them as alien. Exploration is contingent upon the client's willingness to invest energy in the Child ego state, through exaggeration of the movement and other techniques, permitting a different consciousness of Child intuition to emerge. When successful, exploration establishes awareness in both the Adult and the Child ego states. A client like Ralph is then in a position to elect the first step in extricating himself from the grasp of game and script behavior—choosing not to take his payoff.

Emma

The distinguishing feature of enactment behavior is its separateness from the transactional process at hand, revealing what is internal to the client. The phenomenon constitutes something decidedly more than an ulterior transaction. Often such enactment behavior reveals an internal dialogue involving several ego states and can be discerned only through exploring a series of Identified Movements made during a period of momentary withdrawal. Emma, whose contract was to get close to men, provides a clinical example.

The occasion was an announcement from Ernie, toward whom Emma had developed some feelings of warmth, that he had "fallen in love." Ernie, who seldom expressed his feelings, made the announcement with such exuberance that Emma leaned forward in her chair and exclaimed spontaneously, "Ernie, you're fantastic!" Then, as conversation circled the group, Emma executed a series of movements that were completely out of her awareness. First, she shifted erect in her chair and slightly to the right for a full three-second count.

Then she leaned forward again and straightened her skirt downward. This was followed by a Trunk Shift back into the upper left quadrant where she began to scratch her head.

The entire process would have been lost to posterity had not the therapist noted it and invited her to explore what went on, carefully sculpting her into each posture and encouraging her to experience her movement. In her initial posture, Emma reported feeling warm and excited by Ernie, whom she "liked a great deal" (see Figure 37). The brief shift to the right in Posture 2 brought to mind several Parental messages about not being forward and guarding her feelings around men, lest they "get the wrong idea" (see Figure 38). She reported some flashes of shame in Posture 3, where she leaned forward to adjust her skirt, sensing she was "showing too much of herself" (see Figure 39). The shame became a lingering sense of "feeling dirty and cheap," accompanied by the head scratching in Posture 4 (see Figure 40).

Successful interventions into a series of enactment behaviors like these involve their exploration in sequence, identifying the outcome in behavior and affect. Left unattended, Emma would have experienced a low-grade "down" in mood and withdrawn from the group for a while with a vague, undefined sense of guilt over having been "too forward." She was surprised by the depth of emotion which emerged as she reenacted her movements. Several screen memories having to do with scoldings and raising her skirt and sex came to mind immediately. An historical diagnosis of early scenes having to do with sexual guilt which formed a Child ego state is one thing. Concrete awareness of how this ego state operates to inhibit warm feelings and curtail specific transactions with men in the present is another. Successfully addressing both through a seemingly mundane exchange, into which Emma entered with warmth and emerged scratching her head and feeling "dirty," provides a royal opportunity to experiment with different responses of her choosing, without the payoff of bad feelings dictated by her script.

Incidentally, Emma's head scratching is of a different order than "preening" behaviors, described by Scheflen and others, which signal courtship.[9] In fact, it accompanies the opposite response, contraindicating arousal. The persistent recurrence of this phenomenon among a number of clients leads to the following clinical axiom: Women who scratch their heads while discussing sexual matters feel sex is "dirty."

Enactment: Identified Movements expressing a suppressed feeling state.

Dynamics: Denial to Adult awareness.

Structural analysis: Evidence of the Child's anticipation of payoffs to game and script.

Figure 37. Emma: enactment, posture 1

Prescription: Explore and invite the client not to take the payoff.

DENIAL

A sixth type of duplicity is expressed through postures and movements which conceal or close off something in the person, as if to deny its presence. The distinguishing characteristic is the absence of bodily divisions in such efforts. Denial postures are formed through bilateral and cooperative move-ments across bodily quadrants, as though all of a person's kinesics are invested in a concerted effort to repress or close down. I tend to image the conflict as "in-side/outside" in contrast to the other forms of duplicity which tend toward right/left or top/bottom expressions.

Figure 38. Emma: enactment, posture 2

Figure 39. Emma: enactment, posture 3

Laura

Laura entered treatment because she was "frigid." She and her husband had sought sexual counseling from a series of therapists because of her unresponsiveness. Her husband tried to prove himself by working at three jobs and had just resolved in group to set aside time for enjoyment with Laura. This was with considerable insight into his early life in which he gave up being a child to become "a little man" in the face of gross neglect by a busy mother and a wayward father.

"Oh, we can have fun until it comes to sex," observed Laura from across the room, icily discounting the whole process. Her Basic Posture at the moment was a familiar one (see Figure 41). She sat back to the left in her chair, folding her arms tightly across her stomach and rigidly crossing her legs. The manner in which all of her body was co-opted to close herself off from any contact is characteristic of denial postures. So is the failure of verbal interventions which inquire into the origin of her "hostility" or observe the effect of her remark as

Figure 40. Emma: enactment, posture 4

Figure 41. Laura: denial, posture 1

undermining change and protecting the "neurotic bond" of their marriage. The underlying issue with denial postures is seldom a matter of unresolved anger. Usually it is fear surrounding embarrassment, exposure, rejection, or physical harm for which resentment is but a protective measure to avoid the dangers of intimate contact.

The treatment of choice with denial postures is to explore them through exaggeration to their end point and then, where possible, experiment with expressions of their polar opposite.

> Therapist: Laura, will you let yourself experience your posture, exaggerating it more and more, until you are doing it in your body as much as you possibly can?

Laura cooperated by making her arms and legs more and more tense. Then she doubled over in her chair and began complaining of tightness across her chest and a familiar burning feeling in her stomach (see Figure 42).

> Therapist: Will you give the feeling some words . . . whatever comes?
> Laura: Only one word . . . (pause, tears) . . . Alone.

After Laura rested for a few minutes, the therapist invited her to explore the polar opposite of what she had been doing. This was accomplished by asking her to return to the exaggerated end point of her former posture and gradually let herself produce the opposite effect in her body. Normally, this is done with hesitation and considerable uneasiness. The result was a general opening up of her body, first her upper torso, then even more slowly her lower half (see Figure 43).

> Laura: I feel strange . . . very strange . . . two words—open . . . relaxed.
> (Pause) I think we could have more fun together (spontaneously, to her husband).

Third-degree Impasses

Most denial postures have the characteristics of what the Gouldings call a third-degree impasse.[10] Here the impasse is depicted between the natural Child and the adapted Child (see Figure 44). The adaptation is so strong that any opposition to it from the natural Child is totally excluded. The adapted Child has so integrated the archaic message that the person actually experiences himself or herself as passive or bad or stupid or, as in Laura's case, frigid. The lack of any remaining opposition from other ego states is evident in the kinesics of denial posturing. The entire body is co-opted without any contrasting behaviors by a self-protective closing-off posture which prohibits physical or emotional contact.

Third-degree impasses are not amenable to redecision therapy, since the adapted Child accepts the early message and its effects as reality. Only when the client is able to recover and recathect the natural Child ego state in the face of the adaptation is the impasse broken. The Gouldings suggest interventions inviting chair dialogues between the natural Child and the adapted Child ("Have a conversation between 'frigid' Laura and 'warm' Laura").[11] I have found these to be of only limited success without attention to the kinesics of each ego state. The problem lies in the difficulties clients with third-degree im-

Figure 42. Laura: denial, posture 2

Figure 43. Experimental posture: polar opposite

passes have in discovering and investing energy in their natural Child ego state.

Interventions which explore the bodily behaviors of the adapted Child ego state, exaggerating them to their end point, set the stage for experimentation with their polar opposite. The act of assuming the polar opposite posture concretely invites investment of energy and movement in the natural Child. Laura's spontaneous expression of warmth toward her husband at the conclusion of this procedure is characteristic of successful efforts to establish the natural Child

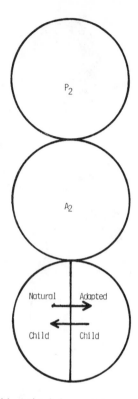

Figure 44. A third-degree impasse

at the point of impasse. Chair dialogues then become possible with the added benefit of contrasting kinesics for each chair, which solidify efforts to behave in each ego state authentically. Radical changes are not unusual when a client, like Laura, establishes the possibility of a free, alternative pattern of responding at the precise point that a third-degree impasse has blocked efforts to change.

Lucille

Denial posturing can take many forms. Masking is one common expression. Lucille expended a great deal of movement to hide portions of her face behind her hands (see Figure 45). This is frequently observed among clients with blemishes, real or imagined ("My nose is too big" or "My chin sticks out"). With Lucille, it was part of a general masking of her body, which she consistently hid beneath baggy clothing. Her shoulders were thrust forward, restricting her breathing and concealing her rather liberal mammary endowment. An exaggeration of this posture brought an immediate declaration from Lucille's Child: "I'm hiding because I'm ugly."

Figure 45. Lucille: denial

Lucille had clearly grown up the "ugly duckling" of her family. She was the source of constant ridicule from father and three brothers. Her mother filled her with messages about the modest estate of the family, which Lucille interpreted as instructions never to act "beyond her level" in matters of dress or personal appearance, even the general decor of her household.

Nowhere is the power of experimenting with opposite or denied behaviors so evident as with such third-degree impasses. When encouraged to discover her polar opposite, Lucille thrust her shoulders back and sat erect, permitting her breath to come deep and full. Her face filled with color and her eyes flashed with excitement. "I feel regal," she said in obvious delight, making immediate resolutions to adorn herself and her home with beautiful things of her choosing. I am increasingly aware through such procedures how much personal beauty is an internal state of being, and so are others who witness the changes. Ugly ducklings transform themselves into swans before our eyes.

Denial: Postures and movements that hide or close off parts of the person, marked by the absence of division across quadrants of the body.

Dynamics: Third-degree impasse.

Structural analysis: Exclusion of the natural Child.

Prescription: Explore to its end point, then experiment with its polar opposite.

SYSTEMIC RESPONSES

The last type of bodily duplicity is the systemic response we sometimes encounter with unresponsive clients. As the term suggests, it is evident through observing bodily behavior that the response we receive does not come back immediately from the ego state we address, but from a system of internal processing involving several ego states. Systemic responses are characterized by significant time lapses between the verbal stimulus and the verbal response. During the interval, we may observe a series of movements suggesting the client has withdrawn momentarily to engage in some type of internal dialogue. The intervening period is often marked by one or more Trunk Shifts indicating changes in ego state.

Doris

Doris, who was hypercritical of herself, provides a clinical example. She had just received a great deal of praise from various members of the group for her involvement in the past half hour. Instead of accepting this, she knit her brow and looked troubled.

> John: Doris, you have passed up all the positive strokes and gone back to the negative ones again.
> Doris: (Silence—13 seconds' worth) (Description: five seconds of eye contact with John, posture erect and squared away, legs crossed, hands in lap. Four seconds of looking upward, posture shifted to upper right quadrant, right hand cupping chin, left hand drawn to left shoulder. Downward frown for three seconds, posture shifted to upper left quadrant, left hand cupping chin, head tilted down, eyes toward floor. One second, before the response, posture shifted back to upper right quadrant, head cocked right and angled to side away from John, open right hand to cheek, eye contact fleeting.) I guess I just can't do anything else (sigh).

With an unresponsive client, the preferred intervention is to explore the internal dialogue during the momentary withdrawal. Some therapists may ask Doris to change her "can't" to a "won't," a verbal technique which encourages her to own responsibility for her silence. But this does not deal with the intrapsychic conflict which leads her to discount her own abilities and John's expectations. An assumption that we confront simple defiance or stubbornness is unwarranted. Failure to do a structural analysis of Doris' internal dialogue abandons our primary aim in treatment, which is to establish the meaning behind her unresponsive behavior.

An exploration of the basic postures and movements during a systemic response is the intervention of choice. This may be undertaken through techniques of mirroring or sculpting, as described in the last chapter. The latter technique, which shaped each posture and repeated each movement slowly with Doris, produced the commentary that follows. The result left her free to experiment with a different style of response, which had already begun in the process (see Figures 46-49).

> Doris: (During five-second period of eye contact) My Adult . . . thinking you are exactly correct. (During the four-second upward look) I feel like a little girl, asking "What do I have to do now?" (During the three-second downward frown) This is crazy . . . I hear my mother saying, "Don't expect too much out of her, John." (During the response, "I guess I just can't do anything else.") I'm my little girl again, resigned. . . . Better to stick with mother than knuckle under to daddy.

Figure 46. Doris: systemic response, posture 1

Internal Dialogues

The internal dialogues which emerge to inhibit or curtail transactions with others often remain vague in the mind of the client and inaccessible to the psychotherapist. Their exploration is always advantageous. Normally, specific bodily behaviors provide the only accurate point of entry into such intrapsychic processes. Often the kinesics are quite subtle and taken for granted by everyone, including the client. Careful exploration of the entire process can release the client from a pattern of long-standing pain and estrangement from others.

Ann frequently required periods of 12-18 seconds between a verbal stimulus and her response. Usually, she would repeat a question or statement upon its reception, if not audibly, under her breath. The shifting of her body was so slight it would normally go unnoticed as it marked a sequence of: 1) looking up right; 2) looking down right; 3) returning to the upward look for a second peri-

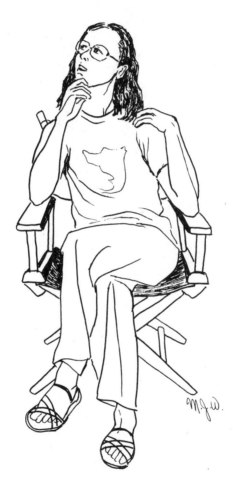

Figure 47. Doris: systemic response, posture 2

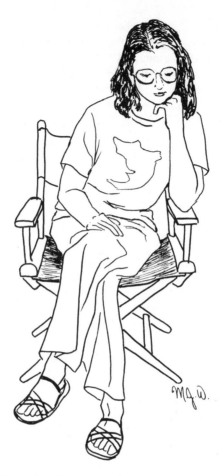

Figure 48. Doris: systemic response, posture 3

od; and 4) reestablishing eye contact to respond. When the therapist attended the process by simply describing each movement and asking her to repeat it, she found herself able to express her internal frame of reference to others for the first time. Initially she repeated everything to herself to make sure she heard correctly (Parent). Then she began by asking herself, "What is the answer?" (looking upward, Child). The downward look accompanied the process of telling herself what to respond (Parent). Sometimes the upward/downward process was repeated several times, until the final upward look, which was accompanied by the following description:

> Ann: I sort of type it out up there, so I can check it over to see if everything is correct. I know this sounds strange, it's not exactly like a typewriter, but I see the words and check them out to make sure they are all there. Weird, but I do that.

Figure 49. Doris: systemic response, posture 4

Group Member: Is your "typing out" in your head like your writing notes and rehearsing everything you are going to say in here before you come?

Ann: Exactly. I see words . . . not every word, but I like paragraphs and key words, so I know where I am going when I start out.

Therapist: Did you "type out" your last response?

Ann: No. (Excited) Hey, I mean I just said what I thought!

The reward for psychotherapists who explore the internal dialogue behind a systemic response often exceeds the immediate advantage of breaking its inhibiting grip. Frequently, clients have had a strange sense of isolation and now feel understood for the first time. Instead of the usual impatience which greets their internal struggle, someone else has entered in with genuine perception of what goes on. A sense of intimacy and trust can develop.

Incidentally, explorations such as I have been describing often conform to patterns of eye movement described by Bandler and Grinder.[12] Eyes drifting up to the left are often accompanied by visual memories, up to the right by the construction of visual images. Lateral movements of the eyes often accompany thoughts of auditory representation, remembered (left) or constructed (right). Eyes down to the right often signal strong kinesthetic representations of feeling; down to the left, eidetic auditory representation. There are enough exceptions to this schema to give the therapist pause in assuming what is going on. For example, Ann was constructing her visual "typing" when gazing up to the right, but she was telling herself Parental sayings when looking down right. For this reason, I favor neutral invitations to people to describe their thoughts, rather than asking a person looking down to the right what he or she is feeling. Otherwise, the therapist through suggestion may access the wrong representational system for the concrete ego states involved in a systemic response.

Systemic responses: Repetitive bodily behaviors occurring between a verbal stimulus and the verbal response.

Dynamics: Preoccupation and withdrawal.

Structural analysis: Internal dialogue between Parent and Child ego states interrupts transactions.

Prescription: Explore each successive Identified Movement for its expression of an intrapsychic conflict.

I once heard someone compare our communication problems as human beings to living in a hotel-room universe, each of us in our own separate room, tapping out messages to one another on the walls. We see only our own room. We assume throughout our tappings that other people's rooms look somewhat like our own. Such assumptions are found to be the source of monstrous distortions. Through paying attention to the bodily behaviors of other people, especially when they express duplicity and conflict, I believe we have a visual means of catching a glimpse of what that other person's room is like. We understand its arrangement, however, only when we permit the other person to invite us in and show us around.

REFERENCE NOTES

1. Goulding, M. M., & Goulding, R. L. *Changing Lives Through Redecision Therapy*. New York: Brunner/Mazel, 1979, pp. 44-49. See Goulding, R. L. Thinking and feeling in psychotherapy: Three impasses. *Voices, 10:*11-13, 1974.
2. Steiner, C. A script checklist. *Transactional Analysis Bulletin, 6:*39, 1967.
3. Berne, E. Trading stamps. *Transactional Analysis Bulletin, 3:* 127, 1964.
4. Berne, E. *What Do You Say After You Say Hello?* New York: Grove Press, 1971, pp. 137-149.
5. Berne, E. *Principles of Group Treatment.* New York: Oxford University Press, 1966, pp. 308-310.
6. English, F. The substitution factor: Rackets and real feelings (Part I). *Transactional Analysis Journal, 1:*27-32, 1971. Also, English, F. Rackets and real feelings (Part II). *Transactional Analysis Journal, 2:*23-25, 1972.
7. Goulding, M. M., & R. L. *Changing Lives Through Redecision Therapy*, pp. 44-49. Goulding, R. L. Thinking and feeling in psychotherapy: Three impasses, pp. 11-13.
8. Berne, E. *Games People Play.* New York: Grove Press, 1964, p. 49.
9. Scheflen, A. E. *How Behavior Means.* New York: Gordon and Breach, 1973, pp. 69-76.
10. Goulding, M. M., & R. L. *Changing Lives Through Redecision Therapy*, pp. 44-49. Goulding, R. L. Thinking and feeling in psychotherapy: Three impasses, pp. 11-13.
11. Ibid.
12. Bandler, R., & Grinder, J. *Frogs into Princes.* Moab, Utah: Real People Press, 1979, p. 25.

6

Signal behaviors

We turn now to consider the range of bodily movements made within the transactional field. Signal behaviors are composed of characteristic postures, movements, and gestures which elicit common responses in our exchanges with others. In contrast to the types of bodily duplicity discussed in the last chapter, signals are more easily sensed and "read" by others who possess quasi-awareness of them. Their repetition is contingent upon the reactions they evoke. Their presence can serve as a sign that something familiar is about to happen. The moves of every psychological game are punctuated by kinesic markers which convey the ulterior alliance carefully disguised from awareness at the level of social exchange.

Our repertoire of signal behaviors is the product of common cultural patterns around us, together with our own individual style of responding acquired throughout our development as persons. I recall watching a young man take a turn the wrong direction into a one-way street. The error brought him face to face with another vehicle which swerved, barely avoiding a head-on collision. Pulling over to the side, the driver leaped from his car and threw up the hood, vigorously examining the engine as if to see if it were still in working condition. Needless to say, the unfortunate turn threatened his survival. Moreover, it threatened his basic sense of security founded upon a belief in his capacity to select proper streets into which to turn and move safely about the world. The rush to check out what was under the hood of his automobile signaled to others his awareness that something had gone wrong.

In one respect, this was a communicative act learned from our culture. Many

138

of us throw up the hood of our automobile when something goes wrong without the slightest capacity to deal with what is underneath. An Ethiopian camel driver would probably not have made the same response before the crowd of onlookers.

At another level, this was a highly individualized reaction in its context, made in symbolic denial of the more threatening confrontation of what went on under the lid of his head. Another person might have sat behind the wheel immobilized and shaking until someone else came. Still another might have uttered recriminations against the other driver or launched into a tirade against city officials who created such a dangerous street system. Each response is derived from common cultural patterns and the individual's own unique way of handling personal crises.

Whether on the street or in the treatment room, any change in the reliable world of transactional order with other persons poses a threat. Interventions interrupt a life process of long standing. Forthright, but gentle, invitations to attend a bodily posture, gesture, or movement need to be cast in an attitude of respect for another's integrity. This makes self-discovery, even of the unpleasant, a worthwhile experience for OK people. We err if we forget that such discoveries usually come as a surprise to the individual involved. The young driver has no conscious awareness of why he so vigorously examines the engine under the hood at that moment. When the threat to survival subsides, he may permit such troublesome self-examination full sway.

REGULATORY SIGNALING

Regulatory signals monitor every social process of interchange between persons.[1] We wander through an alien territory (someone else's yard, another institution, or a strange neighborhood) with lowered head and slumped shoulders so that the chest does not protrude, bringing our hands close to our bodies, or stuffing them in coat pockets. We pass strangers on neutral ground with "civil inattention" at distances of 12-15 feet, looking down and away. We turn faces toward each other and raise our eyebrows, signaling recognition, when we meet a friend. We orient our bodies spatially to indicate whether the conversation will be intimate or formal. Our postures are set to include or to exclude others, or to signal our intentions to participate or be spectators in a larger group. We signal who is to speak by head orientation and bodily shifts to attend. We indicate we are listening with nods, smiles, and raised eyebrows. We knit our brows to indicate we do not understand. We turn at angles or move forward in our chair to signal disengagement and our intention to leave.

Clear lines of commonality exist within every cultural group to provide a ceaseless flow of bodily comment upon verbal exchange. These appear to be banked largely in Parent and Child ego states which employ them elegantly to structure transactions in customary and prescribed ways. A good paradigm for the Adult ego state is the character, Mr. Spock, on the television series *Star Trek*. This Vulcan stands erect and expressionless, engaging in conversation with computer-like rationality, signaling nothing at the level of bodily movement or feeling, since the range of human emotions is completely foreign to his culture. Consequently, he requires lengthy explanations about personal relationships which everyone else takes for granted. Mr. Spock must learn from scratch their common heritage of regulatory signaling.

Speech Markers

One set of bodily movements is made within the context of conversation as kinesic markers to units of speech. Certain trends here are well established.[2] Eyes, head, and hands move in a way synchronized with speech. They drop to indicate the end of a statement. Head position is usually maintained for the duration of a point. The whole body has been observed to shift position to demarcate the beginning or end of larger speech units. There are some common trends in patterns of gesturing which supplement specific units of speech. The sweep of a body part appears with plural nouns and pronouns; movements backward mark past tense verbs, and movements forward accompany the future tense. The rate of representational hand movements appears to be related to fluency and their inhibition affects speech.[3] These movements increase with efforts to describe diffuse visual imagery.

Orientation

Underneath kinesic markers to speech, a whole protocol exists in locating our bodies with postures and distances which orient us to one another and provide a framework for discourse. It is well established that people sit closer to a peer and farther away from an individual with higher or lower status.[4] We sit closer in cooperative situations than in competitive ones, and we sit farthest apart when working independently.[5] Proximity in orientation determines kinesic patterns. There is more head-nodding and self-manipulation when listening to a confederate four feet away than when the partner sits 10 feet away.[6]

Scheflen describes patterns of orientation common to our own culture.[7] North Americans of European descent initiate their intimate relationships at a distance of slightly less than four feet, just beyond tactile range. Formal relationships require a distance of something more than six feet. More intimate conversations are framed by a full bodily orientation vis-à-vis each other, face to face, while acquaintances stand at angles to one another up to 90 degrees. A full orientation toward each other, standing or sitting, tends to exclude others at gatherings. Angular orientation signals the willingness to include them. Persons with durable affiliations orient themselves closer to permit intermittent tactile contact. Ongoing coalitions are signaled by congruent or parallel postures and synchronized movements between partners. Psychotherapists who have worked with couples in their groups know these patterns well, although I have found lengthy attention to them soon reaches a point of diminishing returns. Usually, couples enter group and sit together, maintaining their affiliation for a few sessions until they belong. Often a serious intent to deal with one another is signaled by one member's moving around the circle to an orientation more face to face. For this reason, some group therapists forbid couples to sit together.

Eye Contact

The average middle-class American rarely talks "eyeball to eyeball." Macular vision is fixed at a spot between cheek and shoulder, just out of range for full gazing, eye to eye.[8] The length of glances increases with distance. The blink rate increases with anxiety.[9] Women tend to look at each other more than men do, and mixed groups are marked by reduced eye contact among both sexes. Eye contact decreases significantly with embarrassing questions or negative feedback.[10] A fixed-averted gaze has been regarded as symptomatic of autistic behavior and schizophrenia.[11]

The eyes are marvelously expressive of the kind of relationships we create. Scheflen filmed a mother and son with gaze averted when talking about being home alone and gaze held when discussing being out together.[12] Bakan's studies of conjugate-lateral eye movement (CLEM tendencies) correlate these movements with personality; left movers, for example, being found more subjective, more suggestible in hypnosis, and more emotional.[13] Hess discovered that heterosexual males dilate their pupils to photographs of females, while homosexual males dilate to males.[14] Women dilate to men in a similar fashion. Heterosexual men dilate their pupils more to women whose pupils dilate to them. Perhaps courtship begins when Jack and Jill respond to the dilation in each other's pupils.

For the clinician, an exploration of the client's gaze behavior often yields important information about script. Most clients tend to visually "check out" specific members of their treatment group with regularity and consistency. An examination of their gaze pattern usually reveals their "group imago," a term Berne used to describe the way an individual differentiates other members of the group into roles reminiscent of "significant others."[15] For example, the therapist noticed Oral's gaze shifted repeatedly from Ada to John and back to the therapist, as he discussed a severe conflict at work which threatened his job. Oral was requested to exchange chairs with each person, expressing what he felt that person was thinking. From John's chair Oral declared, "I told you not to take on Roy (the manager), he's too big for you." From Ada's chair Oral said, "I know you must feel terrible, you've worked so hard," and from the therapist's chair, "You never could do anything right." Returning to his own chair, Oral could readily identify each voice as coming from a significant figure in his past—older brother, mother, and father, respectively. Current recipients of regular glances usually prove to be significant candidates in a person's Child ego state for potential activity in script and chosen game behaviors. "Looks," like other signal behaviors, provide significant clues to what is going to happen, either now or eventually.

Affective Response

An elaborate system of bodily behaviors provides a steady stream of signals about our affective response to one another. Among the better known is Scheflen's description of courtship displays.[16] Specific physiological responses emerge within the organism to signal a state of readiness and excitement. The body evidences a high muscle tonus. Sagging disappears; jowling and bagginess around the eyes decrease; slumping gives way to an erect torso; and the eyes brighten. Skin color varies from flush to pallor, and possibly there are changes in water retention and odor. Preening behaviors are usually observable. Women stroke their hair, glance at their makeup in the mirror, or rearrange their clothing. Men comb or stroke their hair, readjust a tie, button a coat, or pull up socks. Changes in postural orientation follow, with partners turning their heads and bodies so as to face each other tête-à-tête, leaning toward one another and placing their chairs or extremities in ways that exclude others.

Efforts have been made to locate different sectors of the body on which the range of affect is signaled. Ekman suggests the head and face give information regarding what emotion is expressed, while the rest of the body registers the intensity of that affect.[17] Birdwhistell thought the upper body and speech denote what is regarded as clean and good, whereas the lower body is associated with affect and what is to be controlled.[18] Shagass made electromyographic readings of increased forearm tension which corresponded to hostility themes among patients in psychotherapy and of increased leg tension with sexual themes among female patients.[19] Ekman emphasized the different sending capacities of different parts of the body. He hypothesized that the face will "lie" the most, the hands next, the feet the least.[20] The reason is that they differ anatomically in terms of mobility and socially in terms of how attended and exposed they are.

Considerable work has been done to isolate characteristic signals of given responses.[21] Positive attitudes have been observed in proximity—forward leaning, indirect body orientation, and increased eye contact. Negative attitudes have been reflected by "arms akimbo" (on hips), reduced eye contact, and a broad, reclining position. High status can be signaled by direct shoulder orientation, greater distance, and moderate eye contact. Low status is reflected in bodily relaxation, a sideways lean, and minimal eye contact. Scheflen and others have attempted to catalog bodily signals for dominance (thumbs hooked in belt, finger pointing, "steepling" fingertips, palms to the back of the neck, etc.) and submission (head down, head cocking or nodding, hand rubbing, slumping).[22]

Learning to read affectual signals from others remains more an art than a science at this point. In fact, judges of nonverbal behavior who showed a strong interest in painting and drama were found to be much more accurate than analytic faculty members who did rather poorly at the task.[23] The intuitive skills of the Child ego state prove much more valuable than logical efforts to correlate a specific gesture with a specific meaning. Excessive concentration on any one aspect of the process distorts the effect of the whole. Any interpretation of specific movements can be made accurately only when the observer assesses the social context together with the entire psychophysiological state of the person. Jones, for example, clearly showed that persons who had drunk a lot of water and were forced to wait increased substantially their number of genital and pedal movements.[24]

SYNTONIC AND DYSTONIC SIGNALING

We can distinguish between two broad categories of signal behaviors, those that are *syntonic* to a chosen ego state and those that are *dystonic* to it. Syntonic signals are in tune with an executive ego state and congruous with its purposes. They enhance the aim of chosen discourse, rather than subvert or disrupt it. For example, John shifts forward in his chair, extends his right hand toward George, smiles, and says, "I really want you to know I like you when you come on strong like that."

Dystonic signal behaviors are discordant to the executive ego state or out of tune with it. I use the term *dystonic* to indicate an essential difference in tone from the manifest purpose of ongoing transactions, so as to communicate something incongruous with it. For example, Harry states that he really desires emotional involvement with other members of the group. At the same time, he stiffens his body, crosses his legs, and folds his arms over his stomach. Dystonic signal behaviors serve as a cue to the emergence of unbound energy from another ego state bidding for executive control.

Syntonic Signals

The absence of syntonic signaling evidences just as many problems as the presence of disruptive dystonic signals. Norman, for example, declared he was "awfully distraught" over his wife's decision to leave him the previous week. He talked in steady Adult tones, relating the facts dispassionately, offering no discernible bodily expression of his distress. His detached demeanor created uneasiness among everyone in the group. Instead of effectively communicating, Norman's executive Adult was met by mounting irritation from others: "You don't look upset"; "You sound like you're talking about your car"; "I don't get any feeling from you." The three most common problems indicated by the absence of *syntonic* signals are exclusions, discounting, and grief.

1) Norman may be functioning in an excluding Adult ego state which prohibits investment of energy in any other. Compulsive thinking and detachment always involve contamination of the Adult by an adapted Child whose early experience forbids emotional expression. A similar contamination of the Adult is evident among persons described as paranoid personalities whose logical and objective descriptions of conspiracies against them follow consistently once the original premise is granted. The kinesics are strikingly similar.

2) Norman may also be engaged in a characteristic pattern of discounting at times of severe threat, either at the level of the existence of the problem or at the level of its significance. The absence of appropriate signal behaviors to ascribe emotional meaning to a crisis is among the more reliable indicators of discounting at these levels. If unconfronted, the anxiety of those around will rise, giving occasion to crossed transactions and "helping" games. Problem-solving

will not be resumed until syntonic behaviors appropriate to the situation have been manifested.

3) In some instances, an individual like Norman is found to be in an early stage of grief, described as denial.[25] This is decidedly different from habitual discounts of the existence or significance of a problem. In the face of a massive loss, the organism defends itself against overwhelming pain through shock and disbelief. Successful movement through the grief process is contingent upon Norman's permitting himself to express feelings surrounding his loss in manageable portions with encouragement and support.

Effective interventions when syntonic signaling is absent involve forthright invitations on the part of the therapist and others to express appropriate affect. Often expressions of our own reaction are helpful: "That's almost unbelievable," or "I can hardly accept that." A few well chosen words of this kind, with appropriate nurturing syntonic to them, are most effective with this kind of problem, since they convey both respect for the defense and an invitation to move beneath it to realistic expressions of suppressed feelings.

Dystonic Signals

Dystonic signal behaviors constitute what Berne called an ulterior transaction, duplex type.[26] They communicate another message at the psychological level from an ego state different from the one engaged at the social level. When Libby addressed Greg, it was with conscious intent to supply observations about how his actions were affecting others. He had requested this information and she sought to provide it objectively and clearly. And she did, experiencing herself as functioning in her Adult ego state. She was surprised when several others "read" disapproval into what she was saying. Her voice on tape did not sound disapproving. Only her Identified Movements which were mirrored by another group member appeared dystonic to her Adult intentions. Libby gestured predominantly with her right hand, moving it up and down rapidly in cadence with her speech, pausing at the end to rest a pointed finger on her thigh. Repeating the gesture herself, Libby uttered, "I'm not sure he's listening. And even if he is, I'm not sure he'll do anything about it (punching her knee vigorously several times with her finger)."

The gesture marked the emergence of unbound energy in Libby's disapproving Parent. She had not yet shifted free cathexis to that ego state, experiencing herself, as she did so often at home, as responsible for making someone else "do right." Her central complaint was that she felt she had to be constantly in charge and keep everyone else under control. Dystonic signaling is the first cue to ulterior transactions in which another ego state emerges to determine the outcome of what is going on. The intervention of choice is to attend such signals, giving Libby added social control in actively choosing which ego state she favors.

Some Concerns about Structure and Function

The task of conceptualizing these movement displays poses some problems. We have little difficulty in depicting *dystonic* signals through traditional diagrams of ulterior transactions. For example, Libby's unbound energy emerging from her Parent ego state beneath her executive Adult can be shown as an ulterior transaction between her Parent and Greg's Child (see Figure 50). The issue becomes more complex when we start to draw a diagram of *syntonic* signals in a similar situation. Let us suppose that Libby gives the information (Adult) with some friendly humor (Child), accompanied by vibes that this is good and helpful (nurturing Parent). The executive ego state would be determined by customary means of behavioral diagnosis, according to the predominant trend in voice, posture, gesture, demeanor, etc. Then we have the

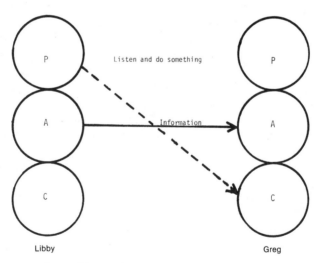

Figure 50. An ulterior transaction, duplex type

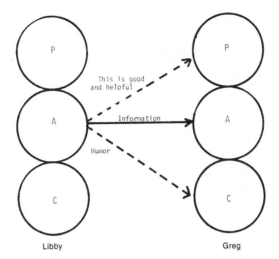

Figure 51. An ulterior transaction, angular type

option of drawing the syntonic behaviors as ulterior transactions of an angular type to other ego states in Greg (see Figure 51). Karpman termed this transaction a "bullseye," since it appealed to all three parts of his personality.[27] Or, we have the option of drawing these syntonic expressions from aspects of Libby's own personality functioning congruously with her Adult (see Figure 52).

Our choice between considering ulterior syntonic behaviors as angular transactions from one ego state or simultaneous displays from several ego states involves us in distinctions between the structure and function of ego states in general. Berne originally described ego states as phenomenological realities.[28] By this, he meant that they were observed as functional displays of three psychic organs, the *exteropsyche,* the *neopsyche,* and the *archeopsyche.* The *exteropsyche* was judgmental and incorporated from parents, the *neopsyche* engaged in data processing in accord with previous information, and the *archeopsyche* was composed of the relics of childhood which have survived as complete ego states, often based upon prelogical thinking. These psychic organs were different from their observable functional displays which he colloquially called Parent, Adult, and Child ego states. Berne then proceeded to use all these terms interchangeably to designate both psychic organs and observable expressions emanating from them. He did not believe that the methodological

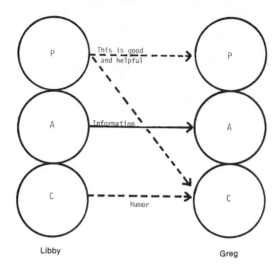

Figure 52. Syntonic signals

problems involved "in moving from organs to phenomena to substantives" were relevant to practical applications.[29]

Berne's last conclusion may have been premature. Bill Holloway, for example, has conducted a lengthy discussion of the confusion created by mixing structure and function.[30] The psychic organ model lends itself to a conception of behavior as originating in a given ego state around which we can draw a boundary, like a circle. The mental picture is of a self-contained unit, which may be further divided into parts. Our concerns in depicting behavior are with locating what belongs inside of what part. The functional display model is more flexible, lending itself to a description of ego states as governed by a constantly shifting process of psychic energy capable of becoming bound and unbound throughout component parts at any moment. I tend to picture a large keyboard upon which are mounted three different colors of lights, with varying shades in each color, intermingled, so that one is capable of creating a limitless range of colors by pressing different combinations. The latter model is far superior for comprehending the movement displays observed throughout this research.

These issues between thinking structurally and thinking functionally surface around questions of whether the Adult ego state has feelings qua Adult. In his earlier writings, Berne addressed this problem by conceiving of the Adult as incorporating *ethos,* or a grown-up sense of ethical responsibility from the Parent, and *pathos,* or charm and openness reminiscent of the Child.[31] He never developed the idea further, only observing that the mechanism of integration was different from the contamination process and remained to be elucidated. James and Jongeward described the "integrated Adult" which they felt they had observed in persons reaching their human potential.[32] Such persons possess the honest concern and commitment toward others of a good parent, the intelligence to solve problems characteristic of the Adult, and the ability to create, express awe, and show affection characteristic of happy and healthy children.

I prefer to think of such integrations functionally, not structurally. It is an integration "around" and not "into." Otherwise the Adult ego state is cast in the preferred position for the self-actualized person, as if to suggest the goal of health is to be Adult. A concept of structural integration seems to preclude a larger process of integration across various ego states in the total personality, drawing boundaries between them which our clinical observations do not support. I am disposed to view these integrations functionally as "between" psychic organs which remain intact, an integration across boundaries in the form of increasing syntonic behaviors, congruent with one another in our chosen purposes. *Syntonic* behaviors, then, from ulterior ego states fulfill the following criteria of congruence with the executive ego state:

1) The ulterior message does not conflict with the overt one.

2) Positions are consistently maintained across ego state boundaries so that ulterior transactions do not contradict an ostensible position (I'm OK—You're OK) at the social level.

3) No ego state is excluded from unbound expression in the transactional process. Exclusion may be indicated when thinking ceases or criticism is impossible or compromise is forbidden.

4) Whatever shifts in cathexis among ego states transpire, the essential social contract between the persons continues uninterrupted and enhanced.

ULTERIOR SIGNALING

A major concern in psychotherapy is with dystonic signals which mark the emergence of another ego state at the ulterior level to claim executive power. Dystonic movements indicate the presence of unbound energy from another ego state competing with the ostensible purpose at hand. As such, they serve as cues that "it" is going to happen again, whatever "it" is. Friends and intimates develop a nagging uneasiness that something is awry. Those who seek a place among the vibrations of the signaler's world consistently "get the message," although they rarely know what has cued them.

Characteristics

Emily described in detail a conflict she was having with her teenage daughter. Soon her information was punctuated by a twirling, outward gesture with her right hand, palm up. She began to glance upwards as her voice slowly rose. Then she stopped abruptly, dropping gestures and eye contact. Two other women who were mothers immediately identified with her and expressed similar problems ("Ain't it awful"), while other members of the group began to supply suggestions and solutions. Soon all of the energy came from them.

Dystonic signal behaviors have five characteristics:

1) Their discordant tone is denied to Adult awareness. If asked, Emily would report she is earnestly seeking a solution, quite unaware that her adapted Child has emerged to subvert the process.

2) Unbound energy from a second ego state increases without any internal conflict. Emily's adapted Child makes its bid for executive power unopposed. The subtle transition from realistic problem-solving to redefining the situation as hopeless is a smooth one. All conflict is quietly bestowed externally upon others, at least for the moment.

3) A response of mild anxiety and uneasiness is engendered in others which sometimes rises to states of excitation. Well-intentioned suggestions at the Adult level and efforts to support or comfort Emily, Parent to Child, fail to alter her response to her dilemma.

4) Dystonic signals herald a change in ego state that will be forthcoming at some stage of the process. This was observable as a Trunk Shift into the upper right quadrant for Emily with a commensurate shifting of executive control to her adapted Child. The final step in the process was to transfer free cathexis to her Child, at which point ulterior transactions ceased and Emily experienced herself as "unable to cope."

5) Finally, dystonic signals serve to preserve unresolved conflicts by curtailing problem-solving and eliciting familiar responses from others in accord with archaic Child feelings. The transactional result is either a racket or a psychological game. The precise relationship between the two remains obscure. We have

described the manipulative quality of rackets in which an individual elicits strokes from others for a familiar feeling dictated by the script, in Emily's case sympathy strokes for hopelessness. The same payoff in hopeless feelings can be procured through rejecting solutions proposed by others until they become angry in the psychological game "Can you help me, yes, but . . .," with the added excitement of disconcerting Parents who are "Only trying to help." Fanita English has suggested that the racket feeling is more basic than the game and that an individual progresses to moves in the game only when the racket fails to elicit its customary response.[33] I am inclined to believe it works the other way, and many behaviors identified as rackets are early moves in an ongoing game process, particularly when the game is extended over larger spans of time in the person's life. Whatever the case, dystonic signaling to others involves them in a familiar pattern of response where the outcome is determined at the ulterior level.

Interventions of choice attend and explore the ulterior messages sent through dystonic signals. Once they are admitted to Adult awareness, everyone involved possesses a renewed opportunity to experiment with doing something else. Three basic levels of dystonic signaling are encountered in treatment: 1) *cueing*, which offers kinesic invitations for others to respond in a chosen way; 2) *positioning*, which establishes the transactional stance between persons; and 3) *pacing*, which constitutes a series of cues exchanged with others as if to conduct their behavior in concert with one's own.

Cueing

Any number of postures and movements in the face, head, and appendages can serve as cues for others to respond in a characteristic way. Roselyn sat rigidly erect and furrowed her brow while relating how well she had done in working out her differences with her husband. Her troubled look and tense posture signaled otherwise. She acted surprised and irritated when several members of the group challenged her well-being with pointed questions indicating doubt. We know now from such signals that Roselyn will shortly exclaim, "Why doesn't anyone ever believe me when I tell them something?" ("Why does this always happen to me?")

Barbara leaned forward in thought to respond to a question, firing a quick glance and open movement of her hand toward her husband. Invariably, her husband would interrupt and explain for her within five seconds, although he had established no Adult awareness as to why. Barbara, interestingly enough, objected vigorously when he did so and always after the fact. ("If it weren't for you, I could express myself.")

Eugene complained that people did not listen to him. His conversation was punctuated with circular movements of his hands which occasionally went to his head for light scratching. When asked to exaggerate those dystonic signals, the circular movements brought feelings of "having to dish it out" for others lest they be displeased. The scratching produced feelings of "confusion over what everyone wants from me." At the time the therapist interrupted the conversation to explore Eugene's kinesics, several members of the group reported they had begun to "tune him out," although they were uncertain exactly why.

Interventions which attend cueing behavior are only effective when the client's Adult can be cathected. Since all dystonic signals are out of Adult awareness, their interruption is often interpreted as crude criticism. Observations are best timed either at the point of their first display, while the Adult is still in the executive, or after the game has progressed to payoff, or the racket has run its course, and everyone is temporarily disengaged from the process. At this point, an agreement to figure out together what went on is often possible. Cues can be reconstructed through description, mirroring, or sculpting in a procedure with possibilities for pleasurable insight.

Positioning

Positioning involves a mutual cueing process of signals which establish the ulterior transactional stance from which persons will interact. Bob and Carol sat down in the treatment room and after ritual greetings were exchanged 1) made glances toward each other, 2) extended hands toward each other, 3) shifted back in their chairs to wait, and 4) again exchanged glances. The series of cues represented their jockeying for reactive superiority. Finally, Bob broke the Alphonse-Gaston routine by "going first." It later proved that when he did so, in their version of "Courtroom," he not only laid himself open to critical rebuttal for omitted facts, but forfeited his right "to have the last word." Such maneuvering is a common pattern among persons who rush to occupy the same transactional position (in this case, "I'm OK—You're not OK"). Genuine advantages may be gained by the person who holds out longest, demanding considerable sacrifice from the one who "gives in first." Bob and Carol could structure days in "the cold treatment" at home after a disagreement through such positioning maneuvers.

For persons with complementary positions, the process moves more smoothly. Ted ("I'm not OK—You're OK") sat next to Alice ("I'm not OK—You're not OK") with a radical shift of his torso away from her (see Figure 53). Alice leaned forward with a protruding finger upon her knee, eager "to bring something up." When she began to speak about his drinking the past weekend, which ended in an affair, Ted shifted farther into the left quadrant, turning his body a good 45 degrees and ducking his head under the cover of his left hand (see Figure 54). This was followed by a sweeping gesture of his right when she paused, accompanied by his declaration, "I said I was sorry, and it won't happen again." Their positioning polarized the group between those who sided with the contrite Ted (rescuers) and those who sided with the offended Alice

Figure 53. Ted and Alice: complementary positioning, posture 1

Figure 54. Ted and Alice: complementary positioning, posture 2

(persecutors), who had already forgiven his drinking episode 70 times 7 and turned all four cheeks. The result was a continuation of their alcoholic game "Drunk and Proud" within the group.[34] For readers unfamiliar with the game, "It" places his wife in the compromising position of being a merciless, unforgiving persecutor or a patsy who is powerless to protect herself through repeated episodes of bad behavior followed by profuse apologies at the right moment. Effective interventions address the original positioning process between the two (irate mother and bad boy, now contrite), for once the transactional stance is set in motion, the untoward outcome is well nigh irresistible, even for supposedly disinterested bystanders in a therapy group.

Ordinarily, positioning behaviors are communicated through a more subtle range of facial and psychomotor activity unique to the persons involved. An assortment of smiles, scowls, glances, open and closed postures, finger drumming or chin pulling, flicks of hands or feet, etc. form a cueing system characteristic of each individual. Mitch began discussions of his difficulties with his wife matter-of-factly, sounding Adult. At the same time, he began to pick lint, specks, and whatever from socks and pants legs in deliberate fashion. Soon he would be quietly finding fault with his wife who, in turn, would accuse him of "nit-picking," the petty criticism which infuriated her. Mitch's picking behavior became a reliable signal for the onset of his game of "Kick Me." The probable outcome could be effectively read in his wife's listening posture, leaning forward, sitting on her hands restlessly, followed by the emergence of a series of tiny flicks of her right foot. Feet prove marvelously sensitive centers of movement for discerning a forthcoming switch to angry exchanges between persons. Whenever Dan and Evelyn began calm and reasonable discussions, while their feet quietly but decidedly kicked toward one another, we could accurately predict another ending in "Uproar."

Pacing

Pacing designates a series of cues exchanged between persons as if to conduct the other's behavior in concert with one's own. Even with the closest observation, it is difficult, if not impossible, to determine at a given moment who leads and who follows. In well-established relationships, an antiphonal chorus of signals appears, as if the task of conducting the next movement is mutually shared.

Jeannie insisted her husband Frank come for treatment because he dominated her and treated her like a little girl. Sure enough, he did, carefully telling her what to do and say in response to her halting efforts to participate. When confronted, Frank promptly resolved to stop. The occasion provided the therapist a rare opportunity to isolate Frank's signal behaviors, which continued his directions as effectively as his words.

When Jeannie began to talk about how hurt she was that her husband controlled her, made all the decisions, and didn't give her credit for anything, Frank sat across the room in studied and progressive inattention, folding his arms and crossing his legs (see Figure 55). Soon Jeannie stopped her com-

Figure 55. Frank: pacing, posture 1

plaints as if in answer to a series of slight head shakes, "No." At the precise moment Frank shifted forward in his chair and folded his hands, Jeannie exclaimed, "I know what it is. It all goes back to my first husband" (see Figure 56). A thorough recitation of his abuses followed, which Frank attended with intermittent eye contact. Then, while Frank assumed his third posture by shifting back into the upper left quadrant and producing a sweeping movement of his arms outward, Jeannie launched into a flood of tears (see Figure 57). She remained unresponsive and helpless until her husband again leaned forward and, sitting on his hands, spoke for the first time something to the effect that she had "been through enough for now" (see Figure 58).

Some similar sequence of mutual cueing marks the major moves of every psychological game. Partners pace themselves to each other's offerings in ways so well established that each senses the proper moment for the next move. This is most evident with individuals who have etched the process into their transactional patterns through years of living together, like Jeannie and Frank. It is less evident and often more cumbersome when acquaintances are involved, which

Figure 56. Frank: pacing, posture 2

Figure 57. Frank: pacing, posture 3

often accounts for the long and drawn-out processes of psychological games played in treatment groups among persons who lack such familiarity with pacing signals.

Interventions which explore pacing patterns are rarely successful until after the game has run its full course to payoff. Later, when each partner has disengaged and withdrawn for a brief period, invitations may be issued to figure out what happened between them. For example, Frank and Jeannie were able to reconstruct an ulterior message with each successive posture as Frank resumed it and repeated its movements. These appear under the appropriate posture in Figures 55-58.

Posture 1: "Don't blame me for all this."
Posture 2: "You know your suffering all goes back to your first husband."

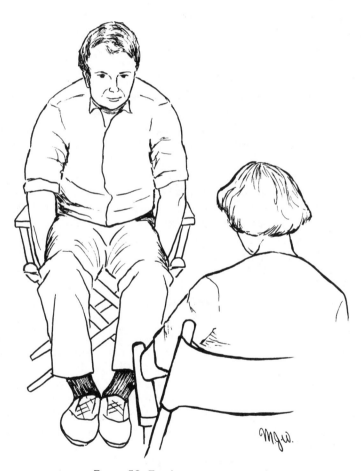

Figure 58. Frank: pacing, posture 4

Posture 3: "See what I am up against with her? What's the use?"
Posture 4: "Leave her alone, you are just upsetting her more and she's too fragile to handle all this."

I also encourage persons conducting such an analysis of the moves to their game to give that game their own name, rather than searching for a textbook label. Frank's choice was much more descriptive than anything we could have produced from the literature: "See, she can't . . . ."

Parallelism is a common kinesic indicator of the pacing process. Scheflen recorded instances of mirror image parallelism among couples in which extremities were placed in opposite relations, so that one posture "mirrors" the other.[35] Even when partners sit across the room, postural changes and gesturing appeared synchronized in some process of mutual cueing. An interesting variation of this which I have observed on occasion is the emergence of parallel posturing among various group members who become affiliated through a common role in another member's game. Edna, for example, launched a critical attack upon the way others in the group avoided certain issues important to her. Around the circle, the therapist observed as four members of the group shifted and crossed their legs, placing hands to mouth and chin as if to hold back their speech.

Everyone who has done family therapy has witnessed the elegant system of signal behaviors which govern interaction among members. Figure 59 reconstructs from photographs the Raygood family, 15 minutes into a session, discussing 12-year-old LeRoy's truancy from school. The positioning process was interesting. LeRoy rushed to the far end of the couch and began the hour fidgeting. His sister, Ruth (age 16), stationed herself at the other end, as close to father as possible, but with her back slightly turned. Father sat down stiffly in the middle and looked uncomfortable. Mother completed the seating arrangement in a "J" fashion by pulling her chair around for a principle view of all members. Everyone's silence forcefully cued her role as spokesperson. After relating incidents of the past week, mother began to blame father for not being home and helping, threatening to leave if he did not show more interest and consideration of her needs. Father sat cool and rigid, being "reasonable" about his wife's demands and his son's misconduct. At the precise moment the photograph was taken, LeRoy had just giggled and looked away in an effort to distract mother by saying something irrelevant about the apple trees outside. Ruth then burst into tears and began threatening to "be bad," if her father didn't do something to keep mother from leaving.

At this moment, everyone in the Raygood family was making a characteristic response to a family crisis. Each person's movements emanate from a charac-

Figure 59. The Raygood Family: positioning

teristic ego state with which that person has learned to face threats to well-being. Mother ordinarily blames someone else for her misfortune. Father sits rigidly, looking down and away, intellectualizing when his employer is dissatisfied with his work. LeRoy giggles and distracts at school when he doesn't understand what is going on. Ruth cries with her boy friend and threatens to do something to herself, if he isn't nice to her. What the family therapist initially sees in each individual's response within the family system constitutes a protocol which is extended to the breadth of that individual's transactions outside the home in the world around. This makes persistent dystonic signal behaviors a proper focus for lasting cure in any approach to psychotherapy.

SIGNAL INTERVENTIONS

On occasion, a knowledge of the signaling process enables the psychotherapist to make interventions at that level of communication itself. Signal interventions consciously alter cues or positioning without verbal comment. When effective, such measures change an ulterior transactional stance between persons by removing the complementary dystonic signaling and replacing it with signals syntonic to the desired executive ego states. Signal interventions are particularly valuable in presenting an antithesis to a psychological game or racket.

Cueing

Signal interventions at the level of cueing involve the therapist in a process of: 1) establishing awareness of dystonic signals coming from the client; 2) identifying the therapist's own corresponding response to these cues in the emergence of unbound energy from an ulterior ego state within oneself; and 3) restoring undivided executive power to the ego state of our choice producing signals syntonic to that new position.

Rita was becoming agitated during her second visit to me. Her expressed desire was to rid herself of guilt surrounding her mother's death. The circumstances were that three years ago Rita returned home for a visit and had a bad argument, in which she told her mother she hoped she would die. And mother did die suddenly the next night. Rita spoke with great effort, stopping frequently to choke back tears. When I encouraged her to express her feelings, she stopped altogether and exclaimed, "I can't." The process repeated itself twice in about five minutes, until I became aware of the dystonic cues we exchanged. While Rita made increasing gestures with her hands which were jerky and "frantic" in quality, I leaned forward as if to "pull" the experience from her (see Figure 60).

As it later proved, any effort from men to push Rita in a given direction was met with fierce and fearful resistance. This was not without good cause, given her history of abuse by significant males. All that was apparent at the moment was that the ulterior signals between my nurturing Parent and her mistrustful adapted Child proved dystonic to her discussion of her mother's death, yielding increasing agitation. With this awareness, I chose to shift my posture back into the chair, resting my hands upon its arms. Within 10 seconds, Rita had readjusted her posture back into her chair and begun to talk in solid tones about her guilt with appropriate affect (see Figure 61).

Several things are important to the therapist in choosing to alter cueing behavior in this fashion. A knowledge of one's own ego states is necessary, together with what signal behaviors are syntonic to them. My own nurturing Parent does, on occasion, tend to pull things from clients—particularly distressed women—and my predominant movement is from the left when I do so. Disengagement for me is often effective when I can cathect my natural Child who is more curious than understanding, more imaginative than caring, and not near-

Figure 60. Rita: posture 1

ly so serious about helping someone else. At the moment I shifted back in my chair to do this, I chose to engage in a series of intuitive fantasies about the kind of childhood Rita must have had. Selecting a pattern of thought that goes with the type of syntonic signals we wish to send is a vital part of using ourselves to make signal interventions. Without an authentic change in ego state, such interventions are wooden and lack genuineness.

Figure 61. Rita: posture 2

The selection of an ego state antithetical to the ulterior, complementary one is the other important consideration. The antithesis to any psychological game is more effectively undertaken from an ego state in no way complicated with the roles the game requires others to play. In Rita's case, the abusive and exploitive roles played by men, particularly her dominating father, seemed to call for a curious natural Child as an antithesis, completely outside the bounds of any controlling Parental involvement. The Adult alone is seldom a sufficient ego state to provide the antithesis because of its involvement in previous ulterior transactions. I think of Edmund whose anxiety attacks persisted to points of agitation in group until one day I calmly sat back, grinned broadly and said, "I'll be OK." This had to be repeated several times to an astonished Edmund, who finally burst out laughing at his failure to alarm everyone else with his escalations. His anxiety attacks promptly ceased when his wife provided the same antithesis. They were resumed only during lengthy telephone conversations with his overly concerned mother. These he also discarded eventually as an unproductive way to spend his time. Such interventions are similar to those reputedly advocated by Harry Stack Sullivan when he recommended that the psychotherapist think of what everyone else in one's society would say and say the opposite.

Positioning

Signal interventions at another level can accomplish profound transactional changes simply by altering the positioning pattern between persons without comment. This is particularly true in family therapy. A simple rearrangement of an existing bodily orientation at the right moment can change the ulterior alliances of a family system. Mother and father always seated themselves on opposite sides of the room with their 13-year-old son, Bert, between them. It soon became evident that this was the family structure when it addressed Bert's consistent failures to follow his diet as a diabetic, a source of great concern to everyone. By eating the forbidden, getting sick, missing school, and sneak-eating again despite constant parental monitoring, Bert had successfully divided and conquered his parents.

The roles in this diabetic game were persistent, as was the outcome. Father adopted a tough, critical stance toward his son, precipitating a nurturing and protective role for mother who constantly mediated between them. This made mother an "easy touch" for favors from Bert which heightened father's resentment of her "wishy-washyness." Bert was defined as "a diabetic patient" necessitating continual care and control. This involved trips away with mother for the latest in treatment and instruction for diabetic management, together with all sorts of privileges, including the avoidance of any number of feared social situations in his life. ("Can't go swimming because of the needle marks"; "But nobody else will notice.")

Near the end of the session, the therapist asked father to move over and sit beside mother on the couch. After an awkward silence, Bert exclaimed, "This doesn't seem right." He went on to express amazement at how "weird" things were this way, obviously pleased at some level with the change. Father and mother were also in a position to relate differently. They began conversation about how little they were together recently, which led to resolutions to do more things with each other, regardless of how sick Bert was. The positioning intervention served to reduce the boundary between parents and strengthen the boundary between parents and child, marking the beginning of cooperation to present a more united front to Bert than the current one, divided into perse-cutor and rescuer roles. Salvador Minuchin has described such changes in boundaries as a formative measure in altering the family system.[36] In this fam-ily, it marked the first step toward strengthening the marriage itself and shifting responsibility for dietary control firmly over to Bert, an effective antithesis to the diabetic game.

Pacing

On occasion a pacing intervention can prove valuable, particularly with per-sons who are anxious or agitated. To intervene by pacing, the therapist under-takes a series of cues at the nonverbal level of bodily behavior in an effort to direct the client's behavior toward a more desirable ego state. Through their studies of Milton Erickson and others, Bandler and Grinder have described this procedure.[37] The therapist assumes a parallel posture to the client which accu-rately reflects its tone and movement. The effort is to reproduce in oneself as nearly as possible the bodily experience observed in the other. Breathing at the same rate is an excellent measure of pacing oneself into the rhythm of another's kinesics. Then, through slowly and gradually altering one's own breath rate, movement, and posture, the client is directed toward corresponding and paral-lel changes. Agitation subsides before the measured leadership of the thera-pist's own movement behavior. The desired result effects a change in the client to an ego state more amenable to problem-solving. Pacing is a more difficult procedure in group therapy than in individual treatment, but can be under-taken beneath the level of verbal transactions with a person who is escalating bad feelings in that setting as well.

THE TALE OF TWO SINGLES

The intuitive Child in all of us possesses elegant abilities to send, receive, and respond to signal behaviors. Their constant presence in all that we do defines the way we go about being in the world, accomplishing our personal destiny. The entire process is seldom admitted to the daylight of Adult awareness. This was tellingly demonstrated by two single persons in two different groups, which met hours apart in the same room. Neither knew the other. Both were lonely, in search of a companion of the opposite sex, and bewildered as to "where in the world you can meet someone." One was male, the other female. Each possessed the proper dilation of the pupils in their eyes, just no one to dilate to.

I had often wished, as I imagine many therapists do, that I possessed a cosmic whistle with which to stop the world one night in order to get all the nice, unattached men I knew into the same room with all the nice, unattached women I knew. It happened in microcosm one night, without whistle or anything. We learned the following week that these two singles each made the scene at Harlow's the previous Saturday night, as "luck" would have it, disastrously.

Jack sauntered in around 9:00 P.M. alone and stood side by side with a buddy he met at the bar for an hour, watching couples dance. He started to break in once, but no one else seemed to be doing that, so he settled onto a bar stool from which he bought a gregarious blond a drink around 10:30, only to have her leave abruptly with another man a half hour later. He retired, utterly defeated, at 11:15, sadder but no wiser.

Jill made her entrance with a girl friend sometime around 9:30 P.M. The two settled themselves in a square booth behind the bar and at the opposite end from the dance floor. There they sat for an hour and a half, watching no one come up. They did manage to strike up a conversation with two elderly couples in the next booth. They left hurriedly soon thereafter, Jill with an uneasy feeling that others might gain the impression they were a lesbian pair.

In each group, we were fortunate to have a cocktail waitress, one of whom had actually worked at Harlow's. Both were experts on singles bar protocol. They quickly supplied both Jack and Jill with accurate readings of their bodily behavior. The square booths on the perimeter were the habitat of spectators, older couples, and isolates who ordered mixed drinks and conducted lengthy conversations with one another, which went uninterrupted because their position vis-à-vis one another excluded others. They came together, never met anyone else in the square space they chose, and left alone or paired, as they came.

The locale for congregating and introductions was in the round-tabled area where various groups could quickly pull up chairs together with easy access to the dance floor. Beer sold in this area and there was a rapid turnover from one table to another. The bar stools were for hard-drinking men and women positioning themselves for immediate pickup, which was usually executed quickly to avoid excessive social comment. Jack, whose contract was "to stop getting shot down by women," could manage to meet just the wrong type there. And

Jill, whose contract was "to stop withdrawing from men," found just the appropriate place to prove there were no eligible males extant.

Jack and Jill represent the style with which all of us move about our world signaling to others the way we are. We play our own individual numbers in the customary keys of nonverbal communication which we have learned to employ consistently to further our respective destinies. Effective changes in psychotherapy involve sorting out those signal behaviors which serve us well from those belonging to archaic patterns which do not. A change in chosen direction is immediately sensed by others through new signals syntonic to that purpose.

REFERENCE NOTES

1. An excellent summary of regulatory signaling is found in Scheflen, A. E. *Body Language and Social Order.* Englewood Cliffs, N.J.: Prentice-Hall, 1972.
2. Scheflen, A. E. *How Behavior Means.* New York: Gordon and Breach, 1973, pp. 33-43.
3. Hoffman, S. P. An experimental study of representational hand movements. Ph.D. Dissertation, New York University, 1968.
4. Lott, D. F., & Sommer, R. Seating arrangements and status. *Journal of Personality and Social Psychology, 7:*90-95, 1967.
5. Norum, G. A., Russo, N. J., & Sommer, R. Seating patterns and group task. *Psychology in the Schools, 4:*276-280, 1967.
6. Kleck, R. E. Interaction distance and non-verbal agreeing responses. *British Journal of Social and Clinical Psychology, 9:*180-182, 1970.
7. Scheflen, A. E. *How Behavior Means,* pp. 53-63.
8. Ibid., p. 65.
9. Harris, C. S., Thackray, R. T., & Schoenberger, R. W. Blink rate as a function of induced muscular tension and manifest anxiety. *Perceptual and Motor Skills, 22:*155-160, 1966.
10. Exline, R. V. Explorations in the process of personal perception: Visual interaction in relation to competition, sex, and need for affiliation. *Journal of Personality, 31:*1-20, 1963. Exline, R. V., & Winters, L. C. Affective relations and mutual glances in dyads. In *Affect, Cognition, and Personality.* Ed. by Tomkins, S. S., & Izard, C. E. New York: Springer Publishing Co., 1965, pp. 319-350.
11. Hutt, C., & Ounsted, C. The biological significance of gaze-aversion, with particular reference to the syndrome of infantile autism. *Behavioral Science, 11:*346-356, 1966.
12. Scheflen, A. E. Communication and regulation in psychotherapy. *Psychiatry, 26:*126-136, 1963.
13. Bakan, P. The eyes have it. *Psychology Today, 4:*64-67, 1971.
14. Hess, E. H. Pupillometric assessment. In *Research in Psychotherapy,* Vol. III. Ed. by J. M. Schlien. Washington: American Psychological Association, 1968, pp. 573-583.
15. Berne, E. *Principles of Group Treatment.* New York: Oxford University Press, 1966, pp. 153-156.
16. Scheflen, *How Behavior Means,* pp. 69-76.
17. Ekman, P. Differential communication of affect by head and body cues. *Journal of Personality and Social Psychology, 2:*726-735, 1965.
18. Birdwhistell, R. L. Nonverbal communication in the courtroom: What message is the jury getting? In *Persuasion: The Key to Damages.* Ann Arbor, Mich.: The Institute of Continuing Legal Education, 1969, pp. 189-204.
19. Shagass, C., & Malmo, R. B. Psychodynamic themes and socialized muscular tension. *Psy-*

chosomatic Medicine, 16:295-313, 1954.

20. Ekman, P., & Friesen, W. V. Nonverbal leakage and clues to deception. *Psychiatry, 32*:88-105, 1969.

21. See Mehrabian, A. Significance of posture and position in the communication of attitude and status relationships. *Psychological Bulletin, 71*:359-372, 1969.

22. Scheflen, A. E. *Body Language and Social Order*, pp. 23-26. Nierenberg, G. I., & Calero, A. H. *How to Read a Person Like a Book*. New York: Cornerstone Library, 1973, pp. 138-147.

23. Estes, S. G. Judging personality from expressive behavior. *Journal of Abnormal and Social Psychology, 33*:217-236, 1938.

24. Jones, M. R. Studies in "nervous" movements: II. The effect of inhibition of micturition on the frequency and patterning of movements. *Journal of General Psychology, 29*:303-312, 1943.

25. See Kübler-Ross, E. *On Death and Dying*. New York: The Macmillan Co., 1969, pp. 38-49.

26. Berne, E. *Games People Play*. New York: Grove Press, 1964, pp. 33, 34.

27. Karpman, S. Options. *Transactional Analysis Journal, 1*:83, 1971.

28. Berne, E. *Transactional Analysis in Psychotherapy*. New York: Grove Press, 1961, pp. 3, 29-37.

29. Ibid., p. 3.

30. Holloway, W. H. Transactional analysis: An integrative view. In *Transactional Analysis After Eric Berne*. New York: Harper & Row, 1977, pp. 169-221.

31. Berne, E. *Transactional Analysis in Psychotherapy*, pp. 194, 195.

32. James, M., & Jongeward, D. *Born to Win*. Reading, Mass.: Addison Wesley Publishing Company, 1971, pp. 269-271.

33. English, F. Racketeering. *Transactional Analysis Journal, 6*:78-81, 1976.

34. See Steiner, C. The alcoholic game. *Transactional Analysis Bulletin, 7*:6-16, 1968.

35. Scheflen, A. E. The significance of posture in communication systems. *Psychiatry, 27*:316-331, 1964.

36. Minuchin, S. *Families and Family Therapy*. Cambridge, MA: Harvard University Press, 1974.

37. Bandler, R., & Grinder, J. *Patterns of the Hypnotic Techniques of Milton H. Erickson, M.D.*, Vol. I. Cupertino, Calif.: Meta Publications, 1975, pp. 137-148.

7

Script signs

"For each patient," observed Berne, "there is a characteristic posture, gesture, mannerism, tic, or symptom which signifies he is living 'in his script,' or has 'gone into' his script."[1] So long as it occurs, the patient is not cured, no matter how much progress has been made. The script sign is usually first perceived intuitively by the therapist's Child ego state, Berne added. When taken over by the Adult, we recognize it as so characteristic of the patient as to wonder why it was never noticed before.

At the same time, Berne spoke about a larger process of which the script sign is but a single marker. In his own inimitable fashion, he wrote about the "reward" for the group therapist who "watches *every movement of every patient at every moment during the session.*"[2] One may observe a patient going through his script in condensed form in the space of a few seconds. These few seconds may tell the story of the patient's life, which the therapist might otherwise need laborious months to dig out and clarify. Berne believed this probably happens with every patient at every group meeting in some form, more or less heavily disguised or coded. A good beginning is to look for what is so obvious about the person that we are apt to ignore it.

Script signs are specific bodily expressions of those ego states surrounding an individual's central life conflict. When we address them, we are focusing our attention on the formative process of how that person developed a life plan to be this way and not another. In this chapter, I undertake to create a workable classification of movement behaviors around the script matrix.

THE SCRIPT MATRIX

One reason psychotherapy may take so long is that we are constantly missing the forest for the trees. We concentrate upon a particular incident or spoken phrase or feeling without getting the larger picture. The larger picture is always a whole life process. Most of us believe this process is comprehensible, has a beginning and an end, and is governed by some chain of cause and effect. What we witness, at any rate, is an intricate system of interrelated events that is ongoing. This person, unhappily married to that person, with these failures at work and those failures with children and friends, is talking about this thing with us. The force of the whole governs the expression of each part. What is of central concern is always beyond our grasp in the particular matter at hand.

Script analysis always carries us into the larger process that shaped this person's place in the world. It forces us to deal with the particular system of relationships operating in the family of origin where initial learning about how a person is to be takes place. It involves us in what family therapists call a "multigenerational transmission" of family themes to a person's present situation in life.[3] It requires that we learn how a sense of personal destiny plays itself out against the background of the social structures of the time. And it thrusts us into examining each individual's own, unique way of being in this world with a developing set of beliefs, attitudes, thoughts, and feelings. When this way of being is deeply troubled, every psychotherapist must find a workable way to address it.

The *script matrix* constitutes one effort to simplify this larger life process for understanding and redecision. Numerous diagrams have been proposed since Claude Steiner advanced the original one to depict the structure in which the life script takes shape.[4] Of necessity, such diagrams carry with them the oversimplification of shorthand efforts to reduce to words the complex processes of interaction between the child and significant others. My own version in Figure 62 contains the three elements common to all of them: *injunctions, program,* and *counterinjunctions.* When we come to address movement behavior as script signs, these elements form the most usable frame of reference around which to arrange our perceptions.

Injunctions

Berne described injunctions as negative or prohibitive commands coming from a parent, more specifically from the Child ego state of the parent.[5] Their binding and irrational quality follows from unresolved conflicts in the parents

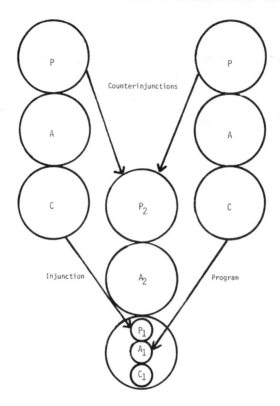

Figure 62. The script matrix

themselves. Bob and Mary Goulding prefer to talk about injunctions as messages which the Child accepts from the parents, rejecting Berne's notion that
they come as commands inserted into the Child like an "electrode."[6] In fact,
they believe children, on occasion, may fantasize or invent their own injunctions, as the child who loses a beloved father and decides never to be close to
anyone again. At any rate, the injunction is seen as functioning to forbid some
important, natural aspect of an individual's strivings.

As we encounter them clinically, injunctions appear to have been delivered
through a process which is largely nonverbal in which (1) an issue is made of
some behavior, and (2) its satisfactory resolution or mastery is forbidden. A
small child is encouraged to be loving, close, and warm, and then is rejected or
abandoned when engaging in repeated efforts to do so. Berne described this

process through what he called *script controls,* which normally consist of a *provocation,* in which the Child is invited to do something, and a *stopper,* which precludes its accomplishment or satisfactory completion.[7] These primitive parental messages are represented in structural analysis as an archaic Parent (P_1) governing behavior of the Child ego state quite independent of contemporary Parental values (P_2) or rational thought (A_2). An early decision to accept the force of an injunction is made by the Child (A_1) without benefit of the logic and perceptions acquired in later development and with strong feelings (C_1) which usually follow upon some sensed threat to survival. The resulting pattern of behavior becomes generalized throughout the course of life, taking on the character of a *script payoff* which prescribes how a lifetime is to be spent and ended.

Bob and Mary Goulding have compiled a list of injunctions frequently encountered in their work which, although not exhaustive, provide the clinician with a workable list of different types.[8] So long as the therapist remembers they are verbal shorthand for a whole series of events and transactions, largely nonverbal, that surround parental messages, they can serve to guide our search with clients for injunctive materials. I will correlate certain script signs with the Goulding list, although in treatment I always employ the client's own terms which emerge in the process.

1) *"Don't"* is an injunction given by fearful parents who will not allow the child to do normal things, producing a belief that nothing one does is right or safe.

2) *"Don't be"* is the most lethal message delivered to an unwanted child, nonverbally by the way the child is touched and in subtle suggestions that the child is a detriment to mother or father or significant others.

3) *"Don't be close"* follows upon parental discouragement of the child's desires for physical touch and positive stroking or the interruption of these through loss.

4) *"Don't be important"* as an injunction represents the child's conclusion that what he or she says and does won't count or that conspicuous achievement may incur danger or threat.

5) *"Don't be a child"* injunctions are frequent among older children who must grow up fast and take care of the younger ones or become "little men" or "little women" for their parents.

6) *"Don't grow"* injunctions are often delivered to younger children who are not supposed to mature and leave their parents and who for

some reason develop the notion that becoming an adult will threaten a parent sexually or dissolve the parents' marriage.

7) *"Don't succeed"* is a message given by a parent who cannot tolerate being outdone by a child or who subjects the child to constant criticism in a perfectionistic vein.

8) *"Don't be you"* is the most frequent message given to the child who is the "wrong" sex (e.g., third girl) or a child who sees all the favors belonging to siblings of the other sex.

9) *"Don't be sane"* or *"Don't be well"* messages are conveyed by parents who model and reward crazy behavior, failing to correct it, or by parents who constantly attend children who become sick while neglecting them at other times.

10) *"Don't belong"* injunctions are given by parenting figures who constantly act as though they should be somewhere else or create a climate of isolation and suspicion of others.

One set of *script signs* appears to accompany the response of the Child to the injunction itself. These are either 1) characteristic Basic Postures which literally embody the Child's response to an archaic message, or 2) specific physiological components that somehow represent a kinesic marker to its continuing presence. The former are readily observable in the treatment room. The latter present a more mixed picture to the clinician. Sometimes a physiological component like pronounced anxiety or chronic headaches is so prominent that a treatment contract may be established around its cure. More often, it is so constant and familiar a companion, like high blood pressure, chronic muscular tension, or cold extremities, that clients ignore, conceal, or fail to mention it. Seldom, if ever, is the emotional significance of the physiological component established in Adult awareness. This quality of embeddedness-in-tissue marks all script signs which accompany the injunction.

The Program

The *program* is a specific pattern of behaviors adopted by the Child in order to do what the injunction dictates. The norm is for the parent of the opposite sex to tell the Child what to do (deliver the injunction) and the parent of the same sex to show the Child how (provide the program). In actual practice there are many variations. In the program, a sequence of behaviors surrounding an injunction (e.g., *"Don't be"*) becomes stylized and set (getting more and more depressed), and its outcome successively approaches the ending called for by the *script payoff* (suicide). Berne insisted this pattern of behavior was acquired in the form of Adult instruction as information on carrying out injunctions in real life.[9] I choose to diagram it on the script matrix from the Child of the parent, since the archaic thinking (A_1) which governs the script protocol always appears to be remote from the abstract and logical reasoning we encounter in contemporary Adult thought (A_2). The program constitutes more than a set of ways to act in compliance with script controls. It also contains a notion of character and destiny, taking the form of "a story to tell" that may be embellished for a lifetime.

Script signs of the program are observed in repetitive behavioral sequences involving a series of postural shifts, characteristic patterns of Identified Movements, and specific gestural displays which reveal the essential activity and rhythm of an individual's life course. Often a recurrent set of postures or a series of gestures proves representative of one's larger life process when explored intuitively. A well disguised intentionality becomes evident, governed by a sense of progression to a familiar outcome. In contrast to the physiological component or the scripted posture that embodies an individual's response to the injunction, the injunction must be inferred from the resulting sequence of activity in script signs accompanying the program.

The Counterscript

The term *counterscript* designates the body of parental training accumulated in the client's Parent ego state (P_2). Its relationship to the basic scripting in the Child is twofold. First, the counterscript contains moral precepts on how to live, which prescribe worthwhile things to do (like working hard) while waiting for the essential drama of the script (drinking, failing, suicide). Counterscript often governs strivings of the adapted Child which appear counter to the script protocol and serve to raise hope again to be dashed (e.g., being sober for three months).

The second function of specific counterinjunctions in the client's Parent ego state is to command behaviors (e.g., "Always do your best") which are forbidden by the script injunction ("Don't succeed"), serving to drive the individual into repeated failures. Taibi Kahler and Hedges Capers have identified five types of "drivers" which, like the Gouldings' typology for injunctions, can serve to guide the therapist to relevant counterscript messages: "Be Perfect," "Please Me," "Hurry Up," "Try Hard," and "Be Strong."[10] Again, I prefer to identify drivers in the client's own words. Counterinjunctions are much more available to verbal recall than injunctions, since they are normally acquired through verbal instruction and much later, developmentally.

Signs of the counterscript are more subtle and escape easy detection. Since counterscript is lodged in the client's Parent ego state, its influence is usually accompanied by displays from the client's adapted Child which makes strong efforts ("will power") to obey its directives. Specific bodily behavior from the Parent becomes distinguishable among the sequences of postural shifts and Identified Movements patterning themselves according to the script program. Such counterscript displays are part of script signs in this category. They are important for the psychotherapist to watch for during periods of "improvement" and "progress" or what some have called "counterscript cure," in which the client's adapted Child is "trying harder" to be a good patient or a good group member. Their presence through occasional flurries of specific gestures or mannerisms signal the continuing grip of the client's unresolved script issues waiting in the wings, while presently denied expression.

It is against the background of this larger process that the clinician looks for specific script signs. What we call *the* script sign is commonly the bodily behavior we see first or come to regard as predominant according to our perceptions. If we stop there, we will unquestionably miss the forest for this one tree. Surrounding any reliable kinesic marker of the script is a whole process of movement that conveys precisely what we are after in script analysis. Keeping our peripheral vision upon the client's script enables us to comprehend each item as a part of that larger system governing destiny.

THE PHYSIOLOGICAL COMPONENT

Any sudden onset of symptoms, according to Berne, is usually also a script sign.[11] Headaches, anxiety attacks, sudden outbreaks of asthma, allergies, ulcerative colitis, or perforated gastric ulcers all come under suspicion as physiological components of the script. The term "physiological component" refers to any prominent symptom representing the individual's own unique response to the script injunction. Its appearance is evidence of the ongoing presence and effects of that injunction throughout the course of life.

Think Sphincter

When searching for the physiological component, Berne offered the script analyst the slogan, "Think sphincter."[12] He regarded the sphincters as the organs of final display or script payoff. Developmental issues surrounding the formation of ego states have received considerable attention among transactional analysts.[13] From the standpoint of observable bodily behaviors within the treatment room, which is the focus of this present study, Berne's slogan has some merit. We will presently discuss hand-to-mouth gesturing, which elegantly preserves psychodynamics surrounding an individual's mastery of needs of nurture, the incorporation of care, and issues surrounding what Erikson described as "basic trust versus mistrust."[14]

With other developmental periods, the picture is not quite so clear. I have been unable to determine a reliable set of bodily behaviors arranging themselves for classification around activities of the anal sphincter. On several occasions, problems related to the regulation of bowel movements directly reveal issues surrounding autonomy, defiance, and compliance. The common problem transactionally is over doing things and who is in control. I think of Warren, a 29-year-old psychologist, who struggled with periods of diarrhea so uncontrollable that he was reluctant to go to parties, fearful he could not make it to the bathroom in time and would soil his trousers. His wife responded with mounting anger, detachment, and demands for change. Warren's history revealed a long-standing struggle with a dominant mother whom he could never please. His diarrhea did not cease until he received permission to do two things. The first was to defy his wife openly by refusing some of her demands, coupled with making some of his own. The second was permission to go ahead and soil his breeches at the next party and quietly remedy the situation any way he chose. He never needed to exercise the latter, although permission to do it his way was vital.

Karen evidenced the same tendencies toward overcompliance and rebellion. She was the third-generation female in her family to have colitis. Grandmother, mother, and she shared in common marriages to demanding but emotionally detached men who proved inadequate to meet their needs for intimacy. A similar permission to do things her own way alleviated the symptom. Subsequently, Karen became one of the few clients in this 10-year study who broke her contract to terminate group treatment over a three-week period. A note which followed expressed her decision vividly. It read, "When I was little, my mother told me to wipe three times and I would be clean. Never again!"

Developmental issues surrounding the genitals are of such similar breadth that I have declined to address the task of classifying bodily movements in terms of them. Among our earliest subjects, we were able to correlate flurries of gestural enactments which corresponded to sexual behaviors. Subject X1, whom we discussed in Chapter 3, made argumentative movements with his arm extending rigidly, then suddenly falling limp and "helpless" to his side, which corresponded to his impotence in the bedroom. Berne noted that premature ejaculation arises from, is part of, and contributes to a script that is usually a

"failure" script in many areas besides sex.[15] Scripted postures of the "protective" type, which I will discuss later, represent not only tendencies to shut off
members of the opposite sex in fear of violation, but also transactional tendencies in styling an individual's relationship to these same persons in social situations and at work. Some may be traced directly to an early developmental period. Others represent the larger process of development across several stages
in accord with the client's early decision. Whatever the case, it is the early decision itself that is crucial to unearth. Once a more satisfactory resolution of the
circumstances surrounding it has been found, the physiological component re-
linquishes its troublesome hold.

The method of organizing script signs under the categories in which they appear requires some explanation. Since the main focus of my study has been on
specific movement behaviors, script signs are classified wherever possible
under particular postural or gestural displays. For example, "thinking sphincter," I could well discuss oral displays under Physiological Components. However, since specific hand/mouth movements are the main observable source, I
will include oral script signs under Gestural Sequences. A thorough discussion
of physiological components of the life script is impossible within the scope of
this study. I restrict myself to selected physiological states that appear frequently in the course of treatment, such as anxiety or obesity, and specific physical
symptoms or signs that accompany the script, such as chronic muscular tension
or pronounced coloration of the skin. To qualify as physiological components,
these states reveal the individual's basic response to the script injunction and
are not associated with any observable pattern of repetitive gesturing. The list is
suggestive rather than exhaustive.

Anxiety

Any sudden display of anxiety symptoms at a judicious point of emotional
exchange is normally a script sign. Such physiological components of the script
manifest themselves in profuse perspiring, rapid breathing, dizziness, palpita-
tions, or chest pains. Thinking and problem-solving cease. Bert suddenly became dizzy and reported pains in his chest when discussing a meeting with his
estranged wife to close the sale of their home. He had felt "sick" the same way
that day. Instead of walking outside as he normally did, Bert was invited to
place his head between his legs until the dizziness subsided, then picture himself
in the scene with his wife. He bitterly opposed the divorce and suppressed the
impulse to scream "Don't leave me!" Procedures developed by the Gouldings
are helpful with persons like Bert who can be encouraged to recall similar scenes
when he felt the same way.[16] Bert produced a screen memory of having rheu-

matic fever, when he was five, at a time of family crisis because father was leaving. Mother's message was, "Stay sick and I'll take care of you ('Don't be well')."

Anxiety symptoms appear at times when the fundamental premise of the script is threatened. The events surrounding their onset may be quite positive, bewildering friends and intimates as well as the client until the script is understood. Ralph, a businessman who had struggled all his life to succeed, underwent two hospitalizations and three comprehensive physical examinations for chest pains and difficulty in getting his breath. Upon referral for psychological evaluation, he insisted nothing was bothering him. For the first time in his life he had gotten out from under all the pressure. His attacks mysteriously began on the day he signed the final document that extricated his company from four years of threatened bankruptcy and put it "out of danger." Such success, it turned out later, threatened a life pattern of struggle and failure. "Don't succeed," "Don't be well," and, on occasion, "Don't be (exist)" are the most common injunctions encountered in anxiety reactions.

Overweight

Obesity is usually a script sign. Weight problems can be classified into three broad script types. Type 1 is seen in individuals who are 10-25 pounds overweight, constantly on and off diets, and hassled by others about appearance. Family and friends are carefully trained to be critical of their eating habits so that scenes with a significant Parental figure can be repeated. Type 1's weight problems will rarely increase beyond their moderate level, and others with different scripting would disregard them. The aim is to rebel against internal and external Parental control, blemish oneself, and avoid intimacy. The more common injunctions are "Don't be close" and "Don't grow up."

Type 2 scripting is observed among persons who are 25-50 pounds overweight and have been for a substantial period of time. Type 2 eaters have settled for a body image of "being fat." Sometimes this dates from early childhood, sometimes from puberty, and sometimes from the birth of a child. Often there was a period of weight loss in late adolescence or young adulthood surrounding courtship and marriage. The common factor is a surrender of good and pleasurable feelings about themselves as sexual beings. Whereas Type 1 eaters play the role of rebellious Child with others, Type 2 eaters usually have an overdeveloped Parent ego state and structure most of their time in caretaking; hence, they are stroke-deprived, constantly giving more than they receive. The overeating provides a measure of self-stroking to fill up this deficit. They seldom speak easily about their weight or their secret wants to others.

And their weight problem may progress to the point of tissue damage and serious physical problems. The most common injunctions are "Don't be sexual" and "Don't be you (a man or a woman)."

Persons whose obesity is in excess of 50 pounds overweight are likely to have Type 3 scripting. Normal life routine is seriously curtailed in an eating pattern that will produce severe physical problems. Type 3 eaters have a tragic script which calls for them to "eat themselves to death." This is evident in their eating habits which are often self-punitive to the point of painful overconsumption, followed by periods of physical discomfort and lonely self-recrimination. Persons with Type 3 scripts usually define themselves as "different from others" and often dissociate themselves from their bodies to think of the "self" as existing somewhere buried beneath fatty tissue. This may account for some of the difficulty we have in pursuing bodily movements with them. Gestural displays and movement behaviors are greatly curtailed, and these persons are uncommonly resistant to attending them. Although they occasionally become preoccupied with issues that persons in Type 1 and 2 scripting have, the underlying issue with Type 3 eaters surrounds a basic injunction, "Don't be (exist)." This must be dealt with first, or nothing else is accomplished.

Anyone who has worked with persons who are overweight is well acquainted with the difficulties. Type 2 eaters may engage in programs of successful weight loss, but these are never permanent until their fears of unbridled sexual expression surface and are resolved. Type 3 eaters have the added problem of dealing with the same issues after redeciding their right to exist in the world and often the task of addressing a normal life proves overwhelming, necessitating something short of complete weight loss as a defense. The same script issues are present among non-eaters (anorexia nervosa), although the problems common to each seem quickly combined. In the four cases studied during this period of research, relationships with significant others were consistently structured according to the Type 1 protocol with Parental figures coaxing, insisting, and exhausting themselves in efforts to feed the rebellious Child. However, the issues of Type 2 overeaters surrounding the denial of sexuality were present beneath the surface, and the problem can quickly progress to the self-destructive dimensions of a Type 3 script necessitating hospitalizations and intravenous feedings.

Nasal and Respiratory Displays

Sniffles and runny noses which suddenly appear are always worthy of attention. Snifflers tend to be verbally facile, deny warm feelings, and have doubts about their adequacy. Bill would get the sniffles whenever he argued with his wife. By his report, he felt like a "snotty-nosed kid" being fussed at by his mother. Elaine got the sniffles when worrying whether she could come to love her boy friend. When we called attention to her runny nose, she reported a sudden onset of the same symptom the other night as she started to make love. What Bill described as a tendency to "live by his wits" and outsmart others is a trait that appears in snifflers. The more common injunctions are "Don't grow up" and "Don't be you" with attendant problems in self-assertion.

Respiratory disturbances in the treatment room, such as hyperventilation, are often physiological components to the script. Usually they represent the response of a fearful Child to an intolerable emotional situation from which there was no escape. Often the anxiety is so pronounced that efforts to talk about the experience only heighten somatic distress and panic. Jill had worked with several psychotherapists on a vivid memory of being locked in the closet while her parents had a violent argument in the kitchen. Each time, she hyperventilated and sought to regain stability by blowing and puffing so vigorously that psychotherapy became impossible. The incident remained in a snarl of unresolvable panic, which she experienced regularly when challenged by her angry husband.

In such instances where the kinesthetic channel is so overloaded, interventions which elicit communication in the visual mode are indicated. Jill was asked to project a movie of the scene upon the wall, describing it so that every member of the group could "see" it. This she was able to do, switching it off when the hyperventilation returned at several points to decommission thought. Such visual procedures lend themselves to restoring the intuitive Child (A_1) who can "see clearly" ways to resolve a situation heretofore too overwhelming with affect. Jill ran the movie to an ending of her own choosing in which the little girl found her way out of the dark closet, faced her parents in the kitchen, and saw that their argument was neither lethal nor a signal of desertion. Bandler and Grinder have recently refined this technique, described as a visual-kinesthetic dissociation.[17] Frequently the injunctions are *hamartic* or tragic: "Don't be (exist)," "Don't be well," or "Don't be sane."

Eye Signs

Our eyes are the strongest center for nonverbal communication. They change constantly within conversation to signal the range of human affect. Eye "contact" is the chief nontactile means of staying "in touch." When the expression in a person's eyes does not change, evidencing the same "look" for sustained periods of time, it is probably a physiological component of the script. Seeing and not seeing become important issues. Some persistent disruption of contact in primary relationships is preserved in the gaze, as opposed to bright, constantly changing eyes which accompany health and signal cure. Again we confront the problem of overlap in classification. I will discuss winking and blinking behavior here, although these could just as easily be included under gestural displays. Here I present six common types of eye expression observed in treatment that persist for sustained periods incongruent to a person's overall pattern of movement behavior.

1) *Moist eyes.* Moist eyes are one familiar marker casting expressions of unresolved sadness over a person's general appearance. They may remain in quiet background to ongoing transactions or flood in tears disproportionate to the loss (if any), or both. George was representative of the constant, non-tearful type. He launched into lengthy, rational discussions of his difficulties with his wife which others characterized as "speeches." Only the sad-moist "look" in his eyes revealed his inner yearning for emotional contact. His wife's mounting impatience with his "speeches" and his "hurt look" brought the two of them to treatment. Joy cried with all of her emotions—happy, sad, angry, or fearful. Her tearful displays constituted periodic rebellion against counterinjunctions to act in accord with her name, always "happy and cheerful." Her tears ceased when she dealt with her plucky, cheerful response to the death of her father when she was five. George's injunction was "Don't feel"; Joy's was "Don't grow up."

2) *Clouded eyes.* Dark, clouded eyes accompanied by a knit and furrowed brow are a common physiological component of depression. Bob was chronically depressed for three years while he underwent business reversals, a divorce, and estrangement from his friends. His injunction, "Don't be a child," yielded years of dutiful striving and neglect of personal wants. Four months into group treatment, his redecision to express that ego state was followed by floods of angry, sad, and joyful feelings, the appearance of which were marked by a clear departure of darkness from around his eyes. The cloudy eyes of depression seldom shed tears to satiation, nor come to life long enough for flashes of anger to pierce their gloomy pall. The clinician should be alert to injunctions against existence ("Don't be").

3) *Piercing eyes.* Piercing eyes, wide or narrow, present clinicians with script signs they rarely miss but seldom explore. Usually a mixture of fear and anger blends into one stark "look" that occurs at times of threat. Jane in Figure 63 is shown switching from her normal to her piercing expression. When the therapist called attention to it, she could switch back and forth at will and did so for photographs. When her eyes were piercing, she reported feeling as though a tube extended down behind them into her lower abdomen. She was again a

Figure 63. Jane: piercing eyes

small girl, locked in a closet, unable to see. She feared her mother striking her about the face and thought about leaving home to find her separated father. "Don't be," "Don't be you," and "Don't belong" are the more common injunctions encountered with this eye sign.

LeRoy produced a similar stark and piercing stare for much longer periods, often for an entire group session. The abiding character of this physiological component of his script earned him the childhood nickname, "Hawkeye." Hawkeye evidenced two characteristics common to piercing eye signs: He had great verbal facility and often failed to see clearly hurtful aspects of his relationships to the opposite sex. For example, he failed to see a growing estrangement with his wife which was marked, he later learned, by an affair that could scarcely go unnoticed. He also failed to see seductive patterns which led to a number of sexual liaisons among men and women in his therapy groups. At age five, Hawkeye experienced the trauma of his mother exposing her genitals to him and then scolding him viciously for looking. The stark, piercing expression in his eyes held within it the waves of fear and anger which he quietly harbored as disgust.

Successful interventions with script signs of this type involve measures of reclaiming the original affect and then returning to the visual channel to "see" the situation clearly to some resolution. Hawkeye was encouraged to see the scene again, fully imaging it mentally until he could express the strong fears of inadequacy he felt before his mother, together with his rage at both her invitation and her rebuke. Once these measures are undertaken to the client's satisfaction, the crucial intervention is to encourage the person to "keep looking at the scene until you see everything you need to see." Successful resolution comes when persons like Hawkeye and Jane see the severe damage done to their development was by parents who were themselves inadequate and acting in their own Child ego state at such times. Such measures are vital to the treatment of suspicious persons evidencing similar eye signs whom we sometimes call "paranoid."

4) *Blinking eyes.* Recurrent blinking is a similar script sign and is usually accompanied by confusion and failure to see things clearly. Rita often blinked uncontrollably when she began talking about herself. On two occasions she got lost coming to group, although she had successfully driven there for several weeks. She did not "see" her turn, nor did she "see" her reluctance to come on those evenings. She also failed to see any rebellion in her marriage to a person of another race, even though her father who was a fundamentalist preacher opposed it bitterly. Often there is some underlying trauma which accompanies blinking, coupled with a fear of injury or untoward consequences. Margo blinked rapidly when someone became angry and, at other times, produced a series of squints or half-blinks while looking aside and contemplating something painful from her past. She carried with her a fear of being struck near the eye across the left side of her face, with a vague sense that this had once happened to her as an infant in her crib. She was also terrified at the thought that someone would punch her in the eyes, reflecting the memory of the small boy next door who punched out the eyes of her three kittens while she watched helplessly. The frequent occurrence of such phenomena leads me to posit still another injunction alongside the familiar ones we have discussed—the injunction, "Don't see." Effective redecisions are followed by strong self-assertion and the willingness to look at situations in one's life and see them clearly.

One of the more interesting encounters between persons with eye signs developed when Hawkeye, whom we described earlier, took as a client a woman who had just completed a year of unsuccessful behavioral therapy for her blinking symptoms. Hawkeye's client experienced periods when she could not reopen her eyes for three to four seconds after they closed to blink. Our clinical seminar scheduled the case as "Hawkeye meets the Blinker." The successful outcome was encouraging to those who are willing to explore physiological components, not just as isolated symptoms, but as representative of larger script processes. Hawkeye cured the Blinker in three individual sessions by insisting she describe her relationship to her domineering and abusive husband. She saw him clearly for the first time, initiated divorce proceedings, and ceased her blinking symptoms within the span of one week.

5) *Winking.* Involuntary winking is a different phenomenon. Two types of winks are observed in treatment. One is the overt kind, a clear expression of jest, camaraderie, or affection that is sent and "read" as kinesic shorthand for "We've got something on here between us." The other is a covert type of wink which is incongruous to the context and, more often than not, ignored by its recipients. Carol's wink (discussed in Chapter 2) was of this type. Usually, the winker is unaware of winking when the winkee calls attention to it. In the eight cases of covert winking I have identified during the course of this study, massive deceptions of oneself or others were either in the making or in progress.

Upton is representative. He earnestly protested his innocence when his wife accused him of failing to break off an extramarital relationship. His self-justifications were so convincing that several group members joined him in marital pleas for her to trust him. Others, by reason of vibrations they could not identify, were uneasy. When two new paramours surfaced several weeks later, their skepticism was vindicated. Only then did the therapist note and respond to the subtle winks which occasionally punctuated Upton's earnest negotiating. They proved to be an acquisition from early scenes with father, who silently signaled him with an equally "not-so-knowing" set of winks to exploit women and not take them seriously. Upton and others like him have taught me to be especially attentive to contracts they establish which leave all sorts of legal loopholes. Upton did, in fact, fulfill his agreement to "get rid of the girl" which carefully preserved his absence of any commitment to avoid other relationships.

6) *Unfocused eyes.* Fuzzy, unfocused eyes constitute still another script sign. Unlike blinkers, the blank stare of fuzzers is normally accompanied by curtailment of verbal expression, evasiveness, and nonchalance. The more common injunction is "Don't succeed," with "Don't be you" a close second. Walt is shown fuzzing his eyes in Figure 64. This he could do at will, once the process was identified, although he previously had no conscious awareness of when

Figure 64. Walt: unfocused eyes

and how. Walt was sure he fuzzed his eyes when he was a teenager during conversations with his domineering father. He caught himself doing it in contemporary conversations, particularly when his father, who was his employer in the
family business, was requiring him to work long hours for a low salary with no
assurance of advancement. The most characteristic thing about Walt was his inability to focus on anything and complete it. He held a graduate degree in art,
but stopped painting when his efforts failed to support his family. To please his
mother, who resented his father's sternness, Walt developed a playful Child
ego state in which he drank too much, never succeeded, and got by with characteristic charm. His fuzzy, unfocused eyes served as an apt expression of what

he termed as his way of "bugging out." Clarity and focus came when he began to see his scripting and make his own decisions.

Muscular Displays

Any chronic tension or discomfort in the musculature may serve as a physiological component of the script. Often the location is symbolic, as "a pain in the neck" or "the weight of the world on one's shoulders." During treatment, clients often touch or stroke an area of tension or adopt postures which convey the discomfort. Harry, who nodded yes constantly when told things to do, shifted his torso forward, placed his elbows upon his knees, and repeatedly rubbed his stiff neck muscles which pained him sufficiently to require regular doses of Valium. He experienced considerable relief by exploring his "polar opposite" of sitting erect and vigorously shaking his head no.

Bea presented a more dramatic embodiment of developmental problems. Characteristically she tended to draw her head down and thrust her shoulders up, giving the appearance of what the group members called "turtling." Bea entered treatment after two years of neurological examinations for severe pain in her upper back and neck. For three months she remained utterly mute concerning anything unsettled in her emotional life, except for expressing some mild irritation with her solicitous husband who failed to treat her as an equal. Then she requested a private hour and told the therapist of being raped when she was 12 by a neighboring farm boy who threatened her life. The reality of the threat was borne out 10 months later when he strangled another girl in a nearby mental institution. She had literally carried this around ever since, never telling family, friends, husband, or doctors. As she talked about it, she began waves of violent, convulsive shaking that moved up and down her trunk. She subsequently told the group and then her husband, with similar periods of shaking. The result was cure for her chronic pain, together with a redecision that she was neither "bad" nor "ruined" and was entitled to "hold her head high."

Tics, twitches, and the like are a special, localized muscular display which accompany the curtailment of unacceptable feelings. On occasion, Pat produced noticeable twitching around the corner of her mouth. She was mildly phobic, avoiding parties and fearful of going to the grocery store alone. If she went to the latter, she was afraid she would faint. Pat twitched uncontrollably, just thinking about it. Procedures of visualization and action, which the Gouldings have outlined, are the most effective here.[18] Pat was encouraged to sit back, breathe deeply, and progressively relax, then to visualize herself entering the grocery store and fainting. When she did, she was awakened by a dark, handsome butcher toward whom she was sexually attracted. Visual completion of the feared outcome and emotional ownership of the forbidden feeling was the first step. The next was a brief psychodrama enacted by the group in which Pat went to the grocery store and noticed particularly attractive men. The final step was an actual solo trip on the way home from group to buy pork chops for dinner, while a supportive group member waited outside in the parking lot. The common trend among muscular displays that are script signs is to reveal injunctions against anger and sexual expression, the former being more frequent among men, the latter among women.

Skin Displays

Sudden changes in color or temperature of the skin can be a physiological component of the script. A similar suppression of unacceptable feelings is usually involved. One example is the hard-white-tense appearance some persons take on around the face and neck when addressing significant conflicts. Babs displayed this look when she talked about her abuse as a child. The colloquial expression is rather accurate, describing persons turning "white" with either fear or rage. Babs, it proved, turned white with both, usually with a mixture of the two.

Some clinical principles are worthy of note here. Chronically suppressed feelings are rarely one single emotional trend. The usual picture is to see at least two strong emotions so intertwined that the individual cannot accurately report what is being felt. With Babs it was a picture of fear and anger so confused that neither could receive full focus and expression. Interventions of choice separate the two and permit the client to deal with one thing at a time. Resolutions of fear are best undertaken on the visual channel through "facing" the fearful object or situation. Babs literally could not remember exactly what happened in her memory of being "attacked and raped" by her brother. When encouraged to assume a state of deep relaxation and see the scene all over again, she visualized the entire series of events which took place in a family bedroom, deciding for the first time that she had not really been violated. Instead, she saw herself as capable of self-protection.

Suppressed rage is best dealt with on the kinesthetic level with measures permitting concrete bodily expression. When mixed with fear, as in Babs' case, the fear needs to be dealt with first. Once issues surrounding survival and self-protection have received sufficient resolution, an individual may address the rage in which the issue is that of protecting others. Babs was encouraged to do a rage reduction procedure in which other members of the group held her down, providing protective limits, while she discharged all her angry feelings toward each member of her family. This took Babs 40 minutes with intermittent periods of rest from exhaustion. At the conclusion, her hard-white pallor was gone and an even reddening to normal coloration was distributed over visible parts of her body. It remained for the rest of the day and, with repeated practice in emotional expression, gradually became a part of her appearance, together with normal amounts of warmth in her chronically cold hands and feet.

Similar changes in bodily color often appear when the client has completed a meaningful redecision. Bob, a physician, made a deathbed pact with his mother when he was eight to take care of the family. In chair work with his mother's "ghost," he decided he had fulfilled his obligation and could end his self-denial and overprotectiveness of others. Immediately, he lost the rigid, whitish appearance around his face, his glasses came off, and several people in the group remarked how handsome he suddenly appeared. "Don't be a child" and "Don't feel" are the more common injunctions accompanying hard-white coloration.

Red splotching and flushing are similar physiological components of the script. These phenomena are usually most visible around the neck, shoulders, and lower face. In contrast to those who whiten, the reddeners usually embody some conflict between the expression of angry and pleasurable impulses with a similar result of inhibition. Interventions of choice encourage these individuals to "let their color out." Carl formed noticeable red splotches upon his neck while discussing the completion of his slowly moving doctoral research. He reported similar splotching whenever criticized by parishioners of his church, by his wife, or by colleagues. When encouraged to give all the "red" in him full expression, he shouted, "Goddammit, I want to do it my way!" Immediately his splotches distributed themselves evenly into steady coloration across his countenance and he reported pleasurable sensations at self-assertion. Carl's injunction belongs in the "Don't" category ("Don't do anything unless you do it my way.").

Janet's reddening was a type frequently observed among women. Large red splotches formed on her neck and shoulders, even her upper arms, as she discussed conflicts with her husband. Their most recent argument produced a night in separate beds. When encouraged to "become" her redness and "play" what it had to say, Janet began, "I am red. I am red all over the place. I am warm, hot, exciting, filled with color (giggle)."

Janet's mixture of anger with pleasurable warmth is not uncommon. She is a particularly good illustration because of her strong responses to stress in her skin and bodily temperature. On one occasion, when she feared her husband might leave, she developed red welts like the hives she recalled having at age five. This was a time in her development when her father withdrew his earlier attention and lavished it upon her younger brother. She also evidenced a noticeable difference in bodily temperature between her right hand, which was chronically cold, and her left hand, which was warm. Members of her group could confirm the difference by touch. She characteristically moved her left hand when in Parent and her right hand when expressing Child feelings, which were "cold and shut down." Once she talked about wanting to go to a party and then stilled the gestures in her right hand with her left as she reminded herself that she had been sick and needed rest and sleep. Concrete acts of letting her color out through verbal and bodily expression brought full color to her face and warmth to both sides of her body.

Physiological components involving changes in skin color and temperature often go together. Script issues surround problems of physical and emotional contact with others, often with the suppression of profound affect. A number of injunctions are possible. Usually the person has permission to be (exist). But a great deal of self-expression has been cut off in survival compromises involving themes of "Don't feel," "Don't be well," "Don't be assertive," and "Don't (do anything)."

In rare instances where the Child ego state is completely excluded, even more radical skin changes can occur. On one occasion I witnessed the appearance of stigmata. It was the first time I saw Leta, the young woman in nurses' training whom I discussed in Chapter 4. She came because she was unexplainably failing, even though she had superior grades throughout her studies. Quite rationally, she reported plans to return home and care for her alcoholic father upon graduation. Suddenly two large welts appeared upon her face. I asked if her father had ever struck her. She answered, "Yes," registering surprise at the question. When I asked her where, she pointed just above her right eye and to the upper part of her left check. I took a mirror from the corner and showed her the two red welts where she had pointed, one just above her right eye, the other on her left cheek. Only then did she relate how father had beaten her in an alcoholic rage when she was small and how she would "rather take a beating" than return home.

SCRIPTED POSTURES

Sometimes a posture becomes so characteristic of a person that it serves as a script sign. We have distinguished between *Rest Postures,* in which an individual engages others from a range of ego states and *Cathected Postures,* which invariably signal the emergence of one ego state over and over again. Among the latter we can sometimes identify a Scripted Posture. In pure form, it presents the adjustment originally made to formative figures, displaying a person's bodily responses to an injunction. Whenever it is assumed, we can count on that person's behaving in a certain way, reading familiar lines, and adopting a custmary stance toward life which arrests realistic problem-solving and change. The client tends to cling to a given perimeter of thought and affect as if survival depended upon it. An intuitive exploration of such script signs usually reveals the injunction. The six types listed below are the more common ones encountered in treatment.

Protective

The first type is best characterized as protective. Berne described a protective posture he observed among women as a script sign.[19] It was formed by crossing their knees and winding the upper instep around the lower ankle, often simultaneously crossing their arms over their chests. It seemed to constitute a triple or quadruple protection against violation. Within our scheme it appears as a top/bottom division between upper and lower quadrants, as observed with Evelyn, who even added a pillow to her lap (see Figure 65). In the upper quadrants, she moved freely as she spoke about ending an affair with a married man at work. She entered treatment because she had never succeeded in sustaining a relationship that was emotionally close.

One effective intervention with scripted postures is to encourage the client to exaggerate the posture to its natural end point. As in the case of Evelyn, this permits the individual to experience the full bodily impact of what he or she is doing. When she did so, Evelyn first reported extreme tightness in her legs. There were sensations of "being in control" and "protecting herself" and, finally, a "wave of nausea" as she doubled over, encircling her knees with her arms. Evelyn's father was absent for sustained periods of time when she was very young. Her mother taught her to be strong and competent. Later, she developed intense resentment toward her pretty younger sister, who gained father's attention by "making a fuss" over him when he returned from trips. Evelyn never questioned her professional competence in her rising career. Only when considering intimacy with men did she close up in this way.

Sometimes such divisions between upper and lower quadrants appear to preserve a corresponding landmark in the development of bodily structure. Glenda was a large, hippy woman with a narrow trunk and a girlish look about her face, reminiscent of pubescence. She appeared "alive" and vivacious in the upper half of her body, making vigorous movements with both arms and offer-

Figure 65. Evelyn: protective posture

ing facial expressions which took on a "cute little girl" quality. She rarely made any movements in the lower quadrants, appearing thick, bulky, and "dead" from the waist down. Her history revealed a great deal of attention from father as a preadolescent girl; this was sharply curtailed when she "came of age" following a late menarche. She was able to verbalize feeling between 12 and 14 years old from the waist up and "dammed up" or "sluggish" from her hips down. In this case, a protective posture revealed an early decision to stay a little girl ("Don't grow up") which preserved a preadolescent pattern of movement above, coupled with flabby underdevelopment below. However, the clinician should not assume that protective posturing always has the same meaning. Beth, who underwent a series of intense love affairs with several males, proved a notable exception. When the therapist called attention to her protective posture, she blithely reported this was the posture in which she masturbated.

Among men, an assortment of closed posturing expresses the same protective script sign. Arms are frequently folded across the abdomen, legs crossed, and various kinesic barriers erected between oneself and others. George, a highly successful executive, represents the male counterpart to Evelyn. He entered treatment complaining of indecision in his private life centering around his marriage of 18 years which was marred by four lengthy separations, three divorce proceedings, and numerous affairs. Two women in the group complained about the way George ignored them when they spoke, by turning to address another man, appearing annoyed as if they were intruding.

When he was asked to respond to a woman, George invariably moved to a protective stance, shifting back into the upper right quadrant, crossing his right leg over his left, and either (1) folding his arms cross his stomach, or (2) joining his hands across his groin (see Figure 66). He reported feeling "uneasy" and began to perspire visibly. He was eager to "get back to work" which meant discussing his life at a rational level with a man. When he was five, George's father started an eight-year period of separating from his mother which culminated in divorce. His mother demanded he side with her. When he was unwilling and acted confused, she lavished attention on his younger brother and George began a lifelong pattern of working hard like father, while avoiding emotional involvement with women at all costs.

Upon identifying such postures as script signs, the intervention of choice is to attend the posture rather than continue the conversation at the social level of interchange. The usual response among men is one of confusion (racket), marked by such slogans as "I never understood women, anyway." Beneath the anxiety is a struggle with covert anger which they feel forbidden to express. Women, on the other hand, usually express anger which masks their need for protection against feared violation or control. Until the underlying injunction is identified and resolved, contact with members of the opposite sex, sexual and otherwise, will be evasive, exploitive, or both.

Posture: Protective

Injunction: "Don't be close," sometimes "Don't grow up"

Counterinjunction: "Be strong"

Program: Competent, successful, and distant

Figure 66. George: protective posture

Position: I'm OK—You're not OK

Script payoff: Loneliness

Prescription: Explore underlying feelings toward members of the opposite sex and experiment with options approaching intimacy.

Diminutive

Diminutive postures form the second major type of script signs. In Basic Posture and Identified Movements, there is a noticeable effort to make oneself appear smaller. Diminutive postures are sufficiently asexual to chart out almost identically for males and females. Protection does not appear to be an issue, since the individual seems to have achieved sufficient safety in acting "little." All four quadrants of the body appear to be conscripted for congruous movement and there is no duplicity. The general picture is one of curling up in flexion. The reader can gain a sense of such cozy contraction by curling fingers into the palm of the hand, then extending the fingers outward into space, creating the opposite effect. Gestural movements with hands and arms are made close to and in front of the body, normally with palms up. Basic Postures reveal radical departures of the trunk from its vertical axis forward, backward, or to one side. Characteristically, one or both feet are withdrawn from the floor, tucked under the body, or crossed Indian style. We rarely witness consistent behavior from an ego state other than Child when both feet are removed from the floor. The following are clinical examples of diminutive posturing.

Eddie complained he "couldn't hack it" with women and constantly struggled to "be a man" through getting dates or holding jobs (see Figure 67). He frequently angered members of his group by making conspicuous late entries, distracting noises, and futile attempts at problem-solving which ended in his inability to handle something. He often compared himself to a successful older brother, dropped out of graduate school, lost numerous jobs, and failed to get better through 18 months of reparenting in another setting with a lot of regressive work. In his initial interview with me, Eddie asked if I would hold him. I refused.

Babbs, at 23 years of age, was the "ugly duckling" of three sisters, though actually rather attractive. Her first treatment contract was to leave home. She masterfully elicited advice and suggestions from parental figures, whether in or out of group, and reported feeling secure so long as she was being "guided in the right direction." She began changing precisely at the point she altered her diminutive stance and placed her feet on the floor, which happened at about

Figure 67. Eddie: diminutive posture

the same time she got a job that permitted her to get her own apartment, move out, and "stand on her own two feet."

Louise adopted a similar dimunitive stance, but with a decidedly different history. She was the youngest of four children, and her father died of a coronary when she was four years of age. Her characteristic posture in group was assumed by tucking her feet underneath her and folding her hands, often rubbing them together as if to warm them (see Figure 68). Her shoulders were bowed inward, restricting her breathing. She complained of coldness in her extremities and sat that way to keep her hands and feet warm. Although the stance was diminutive, it had a quality of isolation about it that suggested a small girl taking care of herself without anybody else's help. Exaggeration of the posture caused Louise to double up and report an overwhelming sense of emptiness in her stomach. She recalled being left alone following the death of her father. This led to her childhood decision to stay small, not cause trouble, and never again be so vulnerable to anyone.

When Louise was encouraged to adopt a posture exactly opposite to the one above, she placed both feet flat on the floor and opened her shoulders backward, permitting deep breaths to enter her abdomen. At first, she reported being very uncomfortable. Then, a few moments later, she expressed a sense of calm and peace, like "one of the Pharoahs of Egypt," her hands set firmly on the arms of her chair. Her voice became more deliberate and mature. At the

Figure 68. Louise: diminutive posture

conclusion, she reported extreme coldness in her hands and feet, doubling them beneath her again. Several week later, after expressing affection to another group member and reaching out to take his hands, she was able to maintain bodily heat in both extremities for the first time over an entire group session. This change marked considerable initiative at home to express warmth to her husband and children.

Posture: Diminutive

Injunction: "Don't grow up"

Counterinjunction: "Please me"

Program: Try hard and fail

Position: I'm not OK—You're Ok

Script payoff: Being taken care of

Prescription: Experimentation with muscular extension instead of flexion and contraction.

Ascendant

Ascendant postures form a third group of script signs. They are witnessed among persons who repeatedly assume the dominant position in a Parent-Child symbiosis. The clinician needs to distinguish them from the normal repertoire of postures in a Parent ego state which persons acquire culturally. These are well-known among the studies of dominance and submission in nonverbal communication.[20] The ascendant postures I am describing are more subtle and continue without interruption for sustained periods of time, forming a persistent level of ulterior duplicity while the person is seemingly Adult. The executive Parent may remain disguised while the individual "submits" to psychotherapy. The distinguishing feature in ascendant postures is the exclusion of the Child ego state, or its firm constraint. These two expressions, *exclusion* and *constraint,* constitute the two major types.

Exclusion. Bert, shown in Figure 69 provides an example of the excluding type. He was observed to sit in this posture 90 percent of the time during his first six sessions of marital therapy with his wife, Ann. His history is characteristic of persons with ascendant posturing who exclude their Child ego state. He was the eldest of a number of siblings with a father who deserted the family when he was nine, necessitating the full assumption of a Parental role in the family system. In the marriage, Ann provided the Child functions which included a con-

Figure 69. Bert: ascendant posture, excluding type

tinual flow of fears and emotional "upsets" regarding children and kinfolks, along with the inability to do things for herself. The trade-off in such relationships usually involves an unacknowledged pact in which each protects the other from feared situations. The wife is willing to provide the emotional energy and excitement for the relationship, protecting her husband from facing fears about his own Child feelings which are interpreted as weak or dangerous. The husband, in turn, protects his wife from a feared assumption of grown-up responsibility and its risks in the interpersonal world around. Bert's benefits were portrayed in his seemingly relaxed posture, shifted over and away into the upper left quadrant, gesturing calmly with arc-like movements of his left hand, palm down. He was invulnerably present in therapy to help his wife cope with her difficulties, sometimes interrupting to speak for her, remembering things she forgot, and constantly encouraging her to share her distressing thoughts with the therapist.

The quality of ascendancy in this type of posture is not to be confused with actually dominating or controlling the other person. For Bert, the issue was self-control, staying in charge of his own feelings. This could be safely undertaken by remaining ascendant. Ann was then free to control him through her help-lessness and emotional displays, demanding huge concessions in time, energy, and responsibility. Whenever she escalated feelings which were uncomfortable for Bert, he took over to do her bidding. For example, when Ann became frightened that a fire built by other couples on a weekend camping trip would spread, Bert consented to go get the others to put it out. When Bert choked on his food during the same trip, Ann became "hysterical," and Bert retired to the rest room to care for himself. So long as Ann remained confused, weak, and unable, Bert remained strong, capable, and untroubled. The symbiosis protected him from dealing with his own unresolved needs and wants. Successful resolution of his script involved a succession of sensitive permissions to express his excluded Child ego state and abandon his program of always being "bigger" than he is.

Constraint. Some expression of bodily duplicity restraining the Child ego state marks the second type of ascendant posturing. Here a broader range of injunctions may be present, including those against expressing certain feelings ("Don't feel") or accomplishing things ("Don't succeed"). Reeba, who had experienced severe periods of depression which occasioned medication and a series of electroconvulsive shock treatments in the past, is an excellent example. During times when her depressed Child was not in control, she maintained a strong executive Parent that had little patience for her own feelings or for those of anyone else. She readily dispensed tough advice to other members of her group, insisting that they "snap out of it" and do something constructive immediately. To her credit, she was much more intolerant of any indolence of her own, continually forcing herself to do all sorts of things "for her own good."

Reeba's posture, shown in Figure 70, evidences the characteristic one-sidedness of this type of ascendant constraint. Her trunk was shifted left in the chair while she gestured entirely with her left hand. Her right hand lay dormant and lifeless in her lap. Occasionally, her left hand drifted across to restrain her right

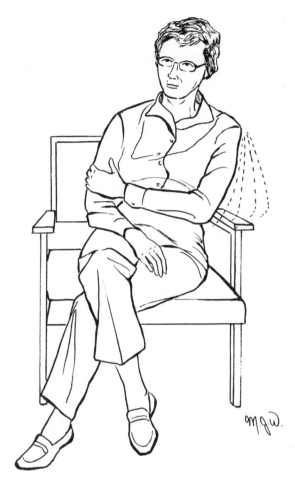

Figure 70. Reeba: ascendant posture, constraining type

arm visibly at points when she spoke of unacceptable feelings of anger toward her husband, her children, or her employer. The overriding force of Reeba's Parent was to tolerate "no child's play whatsoever." She could successfully force herself into periods of rigorous labor or caretaking, until her neglected Child ego state protested in despair with sizeable depressions. Although she had in the past succeeded in working herself out of these to keep going, the inevitable question became "For what—more of this?"

Such constraint is normally expressed through the type of right/left divisions in bodily duplicity which we discussed in Chapter 5. An assortment of cupped fists, restrained hands and forearms, or other modes of holding oneself back are their hallmark. The Child is visibly curbed rather than quietly excluded by an ascendant Parent ego state. In either case, the treatment of choice is to provide delicate and measured invitations to express the neglected Child. Reeba was encouraged to speak from the other side of her body by increasing movement and affect. For success, both her Parent and her Child must become convinced there will be no permanent loss of self-control. Momentary and repeated excursions into the neglected "side" build confidence in the safety of expressing forbidden anger, warmth, fear, or grief. While this is being done, persons with ascendant postures usually go through a stormy period with considerable unease for both themselves and their intimates. Reeba, for example, began openly expressing anger at home, while experiencing disturbing warmth and sexual feelings toward men other than her husband. This was followed by a movement into unexpected grief centering around the loss of her mother when she was three years of age. Some similar unresolved grief of long standing appears beneath most script decisions made by persons with ascendant stances to be strong, refuse to be a child, and stay "in charge."

Posture: Ascendant: excluding and constraining types

Injunction: "Don't be a child"; and sometimes a range of others like "Don't be," "Don't succeed," and "Don't feel"

Counterinjunction: "Be strong," "Be perfect"

Program: Take care of everything and everybody

Position: I'm OK—You're not OK

Script payoff: See how hard I tried

Prescription: Permission to pursue Child needs and wants.

Discordant

Discordant postures constitute the fourth type of postural script signs. They are so termed because they possess an overriding quality of awkwardness or gracelessness. An otherwise mature and attractive person suddenly cathects a Child ego state marked by noticeably poor coordination and a pattern of movement that appears inappropriate to that individual's age level and sexuality. Acknowledged feelings of discomfort or of being "ill-at-ease" accompany such discordant postures. Attention to the quality of movement provides a developmental key to the way the scripted Child views a current life situation.

Albert, a tall, handsome 32-year-old politician, professed fear of a second marriage. He was deeply involved with Rebecca, an attractive professional woman who complained that Albert was too serious, too ambitious, and too inhibited to have fun. Although Albert was known as a liberal and powerful public figure, his intimate relationships were marked by continually frustrated efforts to placate others and to be what they wanted him to be. As Rebecca sought to reshape his interests away from a crowded schedule toward listening to music, going on picnics, and sharing feelings openly, Albert grew increasingly anxious. His anxiety decreased when he stood up for his own interests and reduced his efforts to please, whereupon Rebecca suddenly became more interested in a permanent relationship.

Figure 71 depicts the series of postures Albert assumed when telling his group of a discussion the two had about getting married. Each posture was marked by uneasy shifting in his chair, poorly coordinated movements from both sides of his body, and such visible discomfort that the therapist stopped him to attend what was going on. Repeating the discordant movement, Albert reported feeling like a gawky adolescent. His thoughts focused on a home movie, made when he was 16, which he had viewed during a recent vacation. In the film, he had just received a National Honor Society pin which was placed on his coat lapel. He stood up awkwardly in the group, demonstrating how he appeared, feeling too tall, too thin, and too ill at ease to laugh at his free-spirited sister who turned cartwheels before him. His eyes took on a characteristic darkening in sadness.

"I have always felt like a 'klutz,' " said Albert. "If I got the ball in the basket, it was the most clumsy way you could do it." The scripted posture of a sad 16-year-old boy for whom life was all work and achievement extended his present awareness to a series of early scenes in which mother shaped his interests toward becoming "an outstanding man." Father provided the model as a brilliant but emotionally detached mechanical engineer. Albert's awkwardness in this Child ego state stood in sharp contrast to later achievements of coordination in golf, which he played with manly grace. Discordant postures preserve the awkward lack of coordination of a previous age. Prescriptions for Albert outside group involved experiences in creative dance, yoga, and swimming, along with other chosen measures, to reestablish his graceful natural Child. Success was marked by a brightening of the eyes and increasing gracefulness in emotional situations with women.

The central dynamic in discordant posturing appears to be a parent forcing a child to do something beyond the child's emerging natural inclinations. The re-

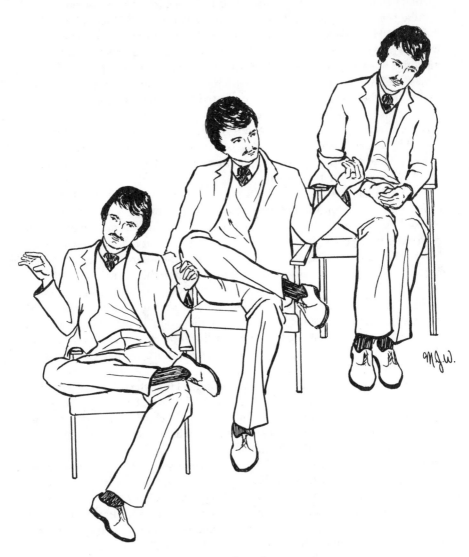

Figure 71. Albert: discordant postures

sult is overdevelopment of one function and the neglect of others. In one way or another, the child is told in effect: "Don't be you, be something else." The child's efforts to placate the demanding parent are made at the sacrifice of coordination and the development of movement patterns appropriate to age and sex. This is particularly true in issues of sexual identity. A female prototype is the third or fourth girl in the family who should have been a boy for father. Often she was a tomboy when she was young. Sometimes the rejection of feminine beauty is linked with some blemish like crooked teeth. She may be too tall or too skinny or too fat. The discordant postures remain to bracket the rejection of sexual grace. The gangly "Good Ole' Boy" who can't "make it" with a woman is the male counterpart.

Ravel provided an interesting expression of such discordance. She took ballet under her mother's constant tutelage from age five to age 19, when she abruptly abandoned her career and got married. Her contract was to "stop pleasing people." She is shown in Figure 72 in a posture she maintained for 15 minutes, her weight shifted forward in the chair. Without awareness, she had made what the therapist learned was a relevé (the ballet term for raising the foot from a flat position to demi pointe or full pointe). If you can assume the same position for five minutes without abandoning it with exhausted calf muscles, you receive the endurance prize. What was of importance to the script analyst was the discordant presence of the graceful relevé beneath an otherwise angular, ungraceful posture marked by choppy, uncoordinated gesturing. Figure 73 represents another sample of the rather masculine quality of stance and movement. Ravel worked as a serviceperson repairing computers. She took great pride in her rational and intellectual abilities which were equally discordant to her childlike efforts to please others. An exploration of her posture revealed the struggle for identity between mother and father. Ballet with its precise gracefulness was for mother, while her rejection of mother as a model of femininity was represented in her adoption of her accountant father's discordant movements.

Posture: Discordant

Injunction: "Don't be you"

Counterinjunction: "Please me"

Program: Prolonged efforts to be what someone else wants with sacrifice of natural grace and/or sexuality

Position: I'm not OK—You're OK

Script payoff: Loveless

Prescription: Permission to claim natural grace and beauty.

Figure 72. Ravel: discordant posture 1

Passive

Another group of scripted postures presents an overriding quality of passivity. Usually the trunk is shifted back and away into one of the top quadrants in a
manner approaching recline. Legs are extended or crossed, and the stance
somehow invites others to take initiative in movement toward the individual,
since the posture lacks protective features or barriers, such as arms folded
across the abdomen. Passive postures are distinguished from ordinary rest pos-

tures in that they appear at points where problem-solving has become arrested or the person experiences some threat which is met by a characteristic pattern of doing nothing. There are two major subtypes: *benign* and *angular*.

Benign. Passive postures of the benign type are formed in apparent restfulness. Identified Movements are slow and seem to lack energy. Frequently a hand in the dominant quadrant props the chin. Don, shown in Figure 74, is a

Figure 73. Ravel: discordant posture 2

Figure 74. Don: passive posture, benign type

good clinical example. Don consented to enter his father's business because he didn't know what he wanted to do instead. Now he only knew he had to get away because he couldn't "hack" the competitive world of sales. But he could not bring himself to tell his father, make the break, and commit himself to some other course. So he did nothing.

A number of characteristic problems present themselves with the benignly passive. Discounting is usually at the level of the individual's ability to solve problems, although occasionally at the level of the solvability or significance of the problem itself. The passive postures reveal the most benign expression of the "I'm not OK—You're not OK" life position. Others are rendered impotent, unreasonable, or helpless in their efforts to pull action from this individual. Consequently, treatment usually gets nowhere. This is a third-degree impasse, since there is no measurable internal conflict surrounding this person's compromise with life. As Don would say, "It's just not my nature to be an aggressive go-getter."

The passivity is successfully broken only through finding a way to assist Don in cathecting his natural Child ego state. Efforts to solve problems at the Adult level will be ineffectual until the scripted posture is abandoned with its passive stance. Successful interventions at the kinesthetic level can be undertaken by encouraging Don to discover the polar opposite of his passive posture ("Experiment with doing the exact opposite of what you are doing now in your body"). Movement and verbal expressions from the opposite side often assist persons like Don to get in touch with their denied and energetic natural Child.

Angular. Passive angular postures are distinguished by the presence of a more pointed, harsh arrangement of limbs around the reclining trunk, furnishing the essential picture of angularity. Ken in Figure 75 is depicted in several positions which were charted and photographed. There was a quality of challenge about his bodily presence. One forceful representation was formed by folding his hands behind his neck with elbows extended outward and occasionally swung forward toward the person he addressed. Ken felt trapped in a bad marriage from which he saw no way of extricating himself, and his problems were compounded by substandard performance in his work, threatening his career.

The main characteristics of passive angular postures are their pointed, protruding quality that seems to challenge others, and the subtle, clever combat that anyone who addresses these persons may anticipate. Crafty, witty rebuttal meets every expectation of change, and confrontations seem to miss. One gets the feeling of dealing with a defiant adolescent whose response is symbolized by the angular leveling of the body toward a horizontal position, in which anything aimed his or her way will glance off and fall harmlessly beyond.

Benign and angular passive postures provide excellent diagnostic criteria for what have been termed passive-aggressive character disorders and can serve to distinguish accurately between passive-dependent and passive-aggressive types.

Posture: Passive: benign and angular types

Injunction: "Don't succeed," "Don't," and "Don't grow up"

Figure 75. Ken: passive posture, angular type

Counterinjunction: "Be perfect"

Program: Do nothing, with passive-aggressive forms of rebellion ("You can't make me")

Position: I'm not OK — You're not OK

Script payoff: Failure

Prescription: Measures to cathect and energize the neglected natural Child ego state.

Quiescent

I term the last type of scripted posture *quiescent* because of its inactive, still, motionless quality. Whatever gestures accompany it are made slowly and deliberately. Although the individual may give the appearance of being relaxed and casual, there is usually an awareness of considerable muscular tension. The absence of apparent agitation generally conceals internal feelings of despair and sensations of being ready to "explode." This posture is essentially the same for both men and women. Its other characteristic is the absence of physical contact, either with oneself in patterns of self-stroking (joining hands, grasping arm or leg) or stroking others with warmth of presence or touch.

Raymond, who is shown in Figure 76, was regularly charted in this quiescent posture. He sat still and rigid in this manner throughout months of treatment, responding reasonably in quiet tones, rarely showing any glint of affect, either positive or negative. Raymond's presenting problem was a series of painful rejections by women which he recounted logically and dispassionately. His detached presence soon evoked anger from several women in his group which he accepted matter-of-factly. Raymond's father was away a great deal as an Air Force pilot while Raymond was between three and five years of age. Once, father brought his pilot's helmet home, placed it upon his son's head, and mercilessly blew air through the hose into his ears while Raymond sat quietly, unable to object to the pain. Father also bought him a treasured camera for a gift, only to return it several days later because it cost too much. Mother was equally rejecting, busy, detached, and nonloving. The motionlessness of Raymond's quiescent posture represented his decision to sit still and wait until it was safe to feel and desire things for himself.

Quiescent postures, unlike discordant ones, preserve the essential gracefulness and coordination appropriate to sex and age. These postures are held stiffly with an erect torso in contrast to passive postures. Their essential stillness and retarded movement are common to both men and women. One experimental

Figure 76. Raymond: quiescent posture

subject in the phase of video research was charted sitting for sustained periods of time in the same inactive manner. Her reasonable verbal tones baffled the audio team who could not determine whether she was in her Adult ego state or her adapted Child. Her history revealed repeated psychotic episodes precipitated by her early responses to a physically abusive father and a distant, rejecting mother.

Allison, shown in Figure 77, provided a less stark example of a female without any history of psychosis. She was troubled by a disturbing lack of memory regarding large periods of her childhood. When she was four, she went to live with her grandparents while the family regrouped due to mother's severe illness and an economic crisis. Her quiescence dominated her behavior in group, where she sat for long periods of time saying nothing. When verbal, she was reasonable, clear, and direct. But she repeatedly voiced the sense that she should not be there taking up time and space that someone else could use. A turning point in her treatment came when she folded her hands and placed her extended forefingers over her mouth while listening to her therapist speak. She was encouraged to brandish this gesture, then to leave her chair and use it to make physical contact with her therapist, putting any words to the situation she felt like saying. Allison finally poked her fingers into her therapist's ribs and repeated several times, "You can't make me, you can't make me, you can't make me!"

Persons with quiescent postures maintain their still, motionless stance for good reason. It was originally adopted at some point when survival was threatened or autonomy forbidden. Affect could not be expressed out of fear. Action could not be taken because it was prohibited or impossible. Allison's stillness in the face of rage at being abandoned by her parents was a reasonable coping device for a small girl, fearful that whatever had precipitated her removal from the family would be dangerously aggravated by any overt objection. Her quiescence embodied her protest, as did the gesture (termed "The gun," as we shall see presently) imposed upon her lips to restrain vocal expressions. Successful resolution of quiescent scripting always involves some encouragement by the therapist and the group to express and act upon feelings long forbidden.

Posture: Quiescent

Injunction: "Don't feel," "Don't belong," "Don't be important"

Counterinjunction: "Try hard and stay still"

Program: Struggle to survive and to avoid disapproval of any kind

Position: I'm not OK—You're not OK

Figure 77. Allison: quiescent posture

Script payoff: Rejection

Prescription: Encourage forbidden movement to pointed expression.

Scripted postures are assumed at points where the original adaptation that formed the script is threatened. The contemporary scene becomes reminiscent of the formative one. Usually, the links between the archaic and the contemporary have long since become obscured. All that remains is a stance—protective, diminutive, ascendant, discordant, passive, or quiescent—that embodies that individual's basic response to the injunction. The scripted posture is characteristically assumed and held until the threat subsides.

On those occasions when an individual does move out of the scripted posture, the first movement is usually highly significant. It can often be seen to represent earlier, unsuccessful efforts to do what the injunction forbids. And it can serve to point the way beyond the impasse that the script creates. Raymond's first movement from his quiescent posture provides an excellent example. He was relating a conversation with his girl friend who professed love for him. She had been offered a job in another city and was deciding whether to accept. Raymond dispassionately discussed the relative merits of respective positions, ignoring her obvious, but unspoken, plea for a permanent relationship.

The normal procedure for working in group with relationships outside the room involves getting a chair for Raymond's girl friend and requesting him to have the unspoken conversation, playing both parts. When it came time for him to speak, Raymond abandoned his quiescent posture for the first time, leaned forward, placed his right elbow on his thigh, his fist to his chin ("The Thinker"), and declared he did not trust her feelings for him. Then he sat back in his former position and remarked to the group, "She doesn't make me feel anything."

Raymond was invited to repeat the process several times, thrusting his torso forward toward his girl friend to experience his feelings, then leaning back and tuning them out, feeling "nothing." He reported he felt "involved" when he shifted forward, "aggressive," "exerting himself," and "angry." Then he reported feeling "empty and hollow inside," expressing the fear he would "break apart." After making a quick, clinging gesture with his hands, he sat back in his quiescent posture, reporting he was just waiting and hoping he could feel.

This procedure laid bare for Raymond the dynamics of formative scenes with his mother. Placing her in the chair, he could experience vivid sensations of "breaking apart" in anger, which came in response to the "empty, hollow" feelings inside, representing his hunger for affirming affection. His first movement from his quiescent position pointed the way beyond his impasse with women. He could lean forward and get involved, express feelings without "breaking apart," reach out with his hands and let go without the fearful weight of early rejection he had experienced as a child.

We turn now to consider sequential movements as script signs. Instead of the static and continuing adaptation to an injunction which we see in physiological components and scripted postures, we observe repetitive movement behaviors in the same pattern. These sequences of posture and gesture preserve in present behavior the essential movement of formative interpersonal scenes and serve to reveal the program a person has adopted in response to the injunction.

REFERENCE NOTES

1. Berne, E. *What Do You Say After You Say Hello?* New York: Grove Press, 1971, p. 315.
2. Ibid., p. 346.
3. See Bowen, M. *Family Therapy in Clinical Practice.* New York: Jason Aronson, 1978.
4. See Steiner, C. Script and counterscript. *Transactional Analysis Bulletin, 5:*133-135, 1966. Steiner, C. *Scripts People Live.* New York: Grove Press, 1974, pp. 85-92. Berne, E. *What Do You Say After You Say Hello?* pp. 100-109. Woollams, S. Formation of the script. *Transactional Analysis Journal, 3:*36, 1973.
5. Berne, E. *What Do You Say After You Say Hello?* p. 113.
6. Goulding, M. M., & Goulding, R. L. *Changing Lives Through Redecision Therapy.* New York: Brunner/Mazel, 1979, p. 39.
7. Berne, E. *What Do You Say After You Say Hello?* p. 107, 113-116.
8. Goulding, M. M., & Goulding, R. L. *Changing Lives Through Redecision Therapy,* pp. 35-38.
9. Berne, E. *What Do You Say After You Say Hello?* p. 108.
10. Kahler, T., & Capers, H. The miniscript. *Transactional Analysis Journal, 4:*26-42, 1974.
11. Berne, E. *What Do You Say After You Say Hello?* p. 318.
12. Berne, E. Preliminary orientation. *Transactional Analysis Bulletin, 5:*172, 1966.
13. See Schiff, J., & Schiff, A. Reparenting Schizophrenics. *Transactional Analysis Bulletin, 9:* 47-71, 1969. Falzett, B., & Maxwell, J. *OK Childing and Parenting.* El Paso: TA Institute of El Paso, 1974. Woollams, S., & Brown, M. *Transactional Analysis: A Modern and Comprehensive Text of TA Theory and Practice.* Dexter, MI: Huron Valley Press, 1978, pp. 93-105. Levin, P. *Becoming the Way We Are.* Berkeley, CA: Pam Levin, 1974. Schiff, J. L. *Cathexis Reader.* New York: Harper & Row, 1975, pp. 32-48.
14. Erikson, E. H. *Identity and the Life Cycle.* New York: International Universities Press, 1959, pp. 55-65.
15. Berne, E. *What Do You Say After You Say Hello?* p. 319.
16. Goulding, M. M., & Goulding, R. L. *Changing Lives Through Redecision Therapy,* pp. 185-214.
17. Bandler, R., & Grinder, J. *Frogs into Princes.* Moab, UT: Real People Press, 1979, pp. 79-136.
18. Goulding, M. M., & Goulding, R. L. *Changing Lives Through Redecision Therapy,* pp. 185-214.
19. Berne, E. *What Do You Say After You Say Hello?* pp. 316, 317.
20. See Scheflen, A. E. *Body Language and Social Order.* Englewood Cliffs, N.J.: Prentice Hall, 1972, pp. 23-26.

8

Sequential movement and script

Every injunction cuts off part of our being. Options natural to our development as human beings cease to present themselves. We observe this bodily in tendencies toward repetitious movements among persons who are in script. The same sequence of posture and gesture appears over and over again. It is as though the individual still seeks what was originally denied, now without the possibility of obtaining it. He or she goes about fulfilling emotional needs as well as possible in the face of an injunction which forbids their satiation.

Sequential movements become script signs when they reveal the program called for by the script. Repetitive movement behavior surrounding the script can be classified into two major types: 1) *postural shifts* which follow one another in characteristic patterns, and 2) *gestural displays* which more symbolically reveal the person's sense of destiny. In this chapter I will discuss these two types of script signs and consider appropriate interventions when they are observed.

POSTURAL SHIFTS

Persons who repeatedly display sequences of postural shifts can be divided into three major groups. The first group evidences bodily duplicity between the right and left quadrants and engages in repeated patterns of *side-to-side* shifting. Group two displays sequences of shifting *forward and backward* in their

217

chairs, alternately thrusting their torso toward others and then away from them. Members of this group may or may not evidence marked duplicity between right and left. A third group reveals a distinct pattern of assuming a posture shifted to one side for a period of time, then making a decisive shift over into the opposite quadrant and stopping, a pattern I came to term *side-arrest*.

We distinguish this type of script sign from the scripted postures discussed in Chapter 7 by its characteristic repetition during short spans of time, while the individual is talking to others or interacting with them. This is in contrast to those with scripted postures who sit and talk for sustained periods in the same Basic Posture. In a relatively few number of cases, I have observed repeated postural shifting in a restless, uncoordinated fashion with movements so radical as to create discomfort for others around. In each instance, the individual was making a marginal social adjustment, felt isolated and misunderstood by others, and behaved in ways often described under the diagnostic term, schizoid personality. I will discuss only the three major types.

Side-to-side Shifting

Trunk Shifts side-to-side appear in persons who tend to have an "always" dimension to their script. Our first video subject, Alpha, whom I described in Chapter 3, shifted back and forth from left to right. She was "always" trying to make herself do something successfully and failing. Edna, whom I will present here as a representative of this group, was "always" caught "in between" two men and having to get away. The ongoing and unending quality of repeated shifting from one side to the other seems to express the character of the life course.

Edna's vacillations. Edna was separated from her second husband for the eighth time in a stormy 14-year marriage. She began her work in group by announcing "I have decided to go back with my husband." Her first posture (see Figure 78) shows her trunk shifted into the upper right quadrant, her right elbow resting on her left hand, her right hand the dominant one for gesturing. She then proceeded to recite all the circumstances surrounding the last time she left: her husband's verbal abuse, his late hours, his unreasonable demands. At the end of this speech unit, she shifted her trunk over into the left quadrant, made several rapid movements with her left hand, and excitedly reported how she finally "had to leave" (see Figure 79). Then she shifted farther over into the right quadrant and folded her hands together (see Figure 80). Here she launched into a pensive description of "the worst thing that could happen," which proved to be a repetition of the misunderstandings that had prevailed, coupled with

Figure 78. Edna: posture 1

Figure 79. Edna: posture 2

periods of sullen withdrawal to separate bedrooms. She concluded her monologue with a sharp Trunk Shift back into the left quadrant, placing her left elbow
upon her right hand, and announced with a note of triumph, "I can always
leave again" (see Figure 81).

A number of details are important here concerning script signs revealed in
postural shifts.

Figure 80. Edna: posture 3

Figure 81. Edna: posture 4

1) An examination of the specific series of postures reveals progression in an internal Parent-Child dialogue to a definite ending. The dominant right gestures in Posture 1 accompany Parental messages about how Edna "ought" to make a go of her marriage and hold things together, despite conflict. The flurry of gestures in Posture 2 from her left accompanies memories of having to leave, in times past, her Child response to such precepts. In Posture 3 the Parent re-

turns and is enlisted by the Child to remember all the bad treatment by her husband and to be realistically on guard for repeated affronts. Symbolically, the Parental right hand enfolds the Child's left hand. In Posture 4, the left hand again moves in concert with fantasies of escape, now not only extricated from the weight of the Parental left, but also subjecting it under elbow to the conclusion she can always leave again. The definitive ending in leaving is the script payoff.

2) To the clinician familiar with Edna's life course, this sequence of postures contains its essential movements. The side-to-side shifting marks the vacillations which constitute the "story of her life," one of clinging to men and then having to get away. In childhood, she was overly close to her father as the youngest daughter. Mother shunned her and unwittingly pushed her closer to him in family arguments, where she always took Daddy's side. In adolescence, father bitterly opposed her dating and she finally left by running away to get married. In young adulthood, her first marriage became so stormy that she finally left for her second husband. Currently, she would have to leave her husband for sojourns home to care for her ailing father, then have to get away by returning to "make a go" of her marriage. The rhythm of forcing herself into new periods of effort, collecting frustration, and having to get away was vividly expressed in the sequence of her postures shifting from side-to-side. This is a familiar movement pattern for persons with scripts that have "always" themes of frustrating repetition.

3) Stringent interactive standards in some therapy groups may preclude witnessing such patterns of life description and movement as a whole. Edna's monologue lasted approximately four and a half minutes. Had we insisted upon immediate "group interaction" or that she confine her conversation to "what is going on in the room," material of some other kind would have emerged. For this reason, I seek to create a climate in the group where all members are free to claim time to use in their own way. This is based upon the pragmatic assumption that what an individual does in group will constitute a significant rendition in that setting of what he or she does everywhere with significant life problems. The task of making "good group members" is an insignificant byproduct, since when this happens, the individual is usually ready to terminate anyway.

4) When a sequence of scripted postures appears, the client will interact with his or her chosen game. Based upon previous transactional analysis with Edna's vacillating Child, we could reasonably predict what would have happened had the group engaged in interchange about her announced decision. Edna would have either: (a) elicited support for her decision to move back with her husband and, after considerable attention, switched to being unable to do it wholeheartedly or happily; or (b) evoked critical attack of her plan, only to insist at the end

that she must go through with it anyway. Both were subtle, social forms of her version of the game "Frigid Woman," which always ended with a payoff of not being able to do or feel what she wanted, whether it be to come up with a satisfactory solution to her problem, to make a go of her marriage, or to have an orgasm.

5) When the scripted Child emerges beneath ostensible Adult discussion of a current crisis, we are wiser to attend the script signs at the ulterior level than to direct our attention to the present dilemma. Invariably, the Adult ego state is preempted by "script blindness" and reason is discolored by primitive perceptions of the Child. Until the contemporary drama is placed within the context of the life plan, objective thinking will be superseded. More important, until the Child ego state is convinced it no longer needs to repeat past protocol, no alternative is really viable.

The miniscript. A series of postural shifts of this type often fits the miniscript sequences described by Tabai Kahler and Hedges Capers.[1] The miniscript portrays the tendency we have been describing to go through a mini-version of the life script within the span of a few minutes. Edna's miniscript is shown in Figure 82. It begins with the "Driver" in her Parent ego state ("Try hard") telling her she "ought to go back and try again to make a go of her marriage." The flurry of activity from her left which follows may well represent the "Stopper," the product of her injunction, "Don't be close," which propels her to remember having to get away before. The "Final Miniscript Payoff" is the fantasied act of leaving, which terminates the process. The "Vengeful Child" who emerges in retaliation against the continuing grip of the "Driver" can well be represented in the process of tallying grievances to justify leaving and in games of "Frigid Woman" with those who want her to feel good about what she forces herself to do.

Although the miniscript may provide the clinician with a useful tool to identify the repertoire of ego states surrounding the client's script, its viability in treatment is questionable. Kahler suggests we address the Driver, since it is this counterinjunction that propels the client into scripty behavior. If it can be changed or eliminated, the sequence of behaviors dictated by the script need not be activated. I have not found such measures effective until the Child ego state in which the script is vested is de-confused and convinced it is safe to disobey the injunction. Edna provides an excellent example. She operated with only two alternatives with men: to try hard to be close to them or to leave. The removal of the Driver would only activate the option of leaving. Every therapist should be alert to this possibility of precipitating the script payoff through superficial efforts to change a Parental message, without concurrence and consent of the Child.

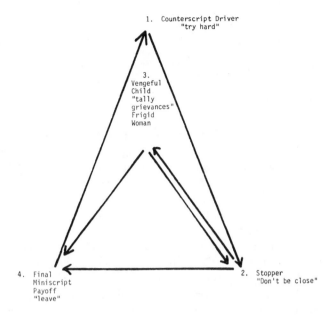

Figure 82. Edna's miniscript

The common factor among side-to-side shifters is their lateral pattern of movement on a plane perpendicular to others. Rarely does one of them move toward others to establish lasting and effective contact. Treatment issues center here. Until the Child is convinced it is safe to establish pleasurable contact with others, no measurable change can occur. This also involves the freedom to initiate and terminate intimacy with persons of one's own choosing and at times of one's own choosing. We know we are becoming successful when movements back away from others appear at times when self-protection is appropriate, as well as movements forward toward others to establish significant emotional contact.

Trunk Shifts: Side-to-side

Injunction: "Don't be close," sometimes "Don't succeed"

Counterinjunction: "Try hard," "Be strong"

Program: Always try and fail, stay strong and disappointed

Position: I'm OK—You're not OK

Script payoff: Leaving

Prescription: Appropriate movement toward and away from others.

Shifting Forward and Backward

Repetitive Trunk Shifts forward and backward characterize the second type of sequential posturing. What is immediately evident is the "over and over again" quality these people reveal in their life course. They lose jobs, repeat arguments, or get kicked over and over again, moving from episode to episode with decreasing confidence in themselves. This, however, never seems to dampen their efforts. In contrast to side shifters, they are capable of intense involvement with others, and their periods of rocking back in despair are short-lived interludes before the return of new striving all over again.

Rosemary is pictured in Figure 83 in the forward phase. This posture could serve at different times for either her Parent ego state, trying very hard to help someone else, or her Child ego state, making lengthy explanations, trying to "get something out," or attempting to please the other person in one way or another. Technically, the Parent phase of this posture was the archaic Parent (P_1) in her Child engaged in efforts to rescue others from various woes and disabilities. Both were expressions of her long-standing adaptation as a little girl to placate others in search of acceptance and affection. Figure 84 represents her characteristic Trunk Shift back and away, "giving up" either effort in frustration and despair, evidencing feelings of helplessness. In both postures, Rosemary's trunk was shifted over into the right quadrant, and her gestures were made predominantly with her right hand.

Forward/backward shifters present a mixed picture in terms of bodily duplicity. Gary, for example, evidenced no similar one-sidedness in his Identified Movements as he shifted forward or away. His trunk was aligned much more closely to the vertical axis, and he gestured bilaterally in equal Expenditures with both hands. Gary tended to become anxious when he remained in the forward position too long, fearing he would "fall flat on his face." Parental messages about "being too forward" or "imposing himself on others" governed his responses and shut off efforts toward self-assertion. Shifts backward in the chair were marked by the return of internal security, although at the price of resignation. This is a common characteristic of this group. Even though the argument has been lost, help has been refused, or someone has rejected their efforts, comfort returns with retreat. Often, the posture in the backward shift evidences some bilateral resolution of anxiety through attachment gestures that join

Figure 83. Rosemary: posture 1

hands as if to represent fears of departing from some long-standing dependency.

The other characteristic common to forward/backward shifters is the difficulty they have acknowledging anger. The Parent ego state is usually chosen to express hostile feelings which are frequently disguised as nurture or "helpful criticism." Transactionally, the response these forward/backward shifters elicit can be observed in the corresponding postures forward and backward which others adopt in concert, like two tall bushes in the wind being blown first one way, then the other. This indicates some productive directions for treatment. Front/back shifters are moving out of their script when they can shift forward to meet others who are shifted forward to meet them, or can be "laid back" along-

Figure 84. Rosemary: posture 2

side of others who are "laid back" with them. Such a departure from familiar posturing usually represents a surrender of rescuer, subtle persecutor, and victim roles, which forward/backward shifters can play equally well with significant others in diverse situations.

Trunk Shifts: Forward/backward

Injunction: "Don't be important," "Don't succeed," and "Don't"

Counterinjunction: "Please Me," sometimes "Hurry up"

Program: If at first you don't succeed, then try, try again

Script payoff: Sisyphus and the Rock

Prescription: Permission to be forward and laid back with others.

Side Arrest

The third major script sign found in postural sequences is best described by the term "side arrest." This group of persons will talk to others for a period of time with predominant movement from one quadrant (right or left), and then make a decisive Trunk Shift over to the other side (quadrant) and stop. Their movements convey a dimension of "never" in their life course. Never will they get love, care, fulfillment, happiness, or whatever it is they treasure. It is as though these individuals are living with a curse, constantly holding out for something they never got and never will; just when it appears they may, it is tragically denied.

Steve began talking with his group about his marriage, assuming the posture shown in Figure 85. For years he had sought affection and wholehearted sexual participation from his wife. She explained her reticence in terms of the inner turmoil, which she had taken to another psychotherapist for several years. Now she had reported a series of disturbing dreams which she related to Steve with liberal interpretations surrounding her fear of men, violence, anger, and intimacy of any kind. Having presented these facts with gestures predominantly from his right side, Steve precipitously shifted over into the left quadrant with a radical tilt of his torso, placed his left hand despondently to his face, looked down, and uttered what he had said to his wife, "You mean to tell me after trying for five years, I never had a chance?" (see Figure 86).

Those who shift to side-arrest invariably stop at this point to remain for a considerable period of time in the characteristic feeling that accompanies their script payoff. For Steve, it was bitter anger, which he would aim at anyone expressing hope or the simplest expectation of problem-solving. For Evie, a comparable Trunk Shift left with a similar look downward, her left hand extended to hide her eyes from others, signaled she would be withdrawn, noncommunicative, and depressed, in spite of any well-meaning approaches others would make.

People with this postural sequence tend to organize their emotional life around a basic human need that is never satisfied. Their scripts are like that of Tantalus, doomed for eternity to hunger in full sight of food never to be eaten. Still another example is Joan, shown in Figure 87, recounting the events of an unsatisfactory affair with a married man, making small gestures of a futile qual-

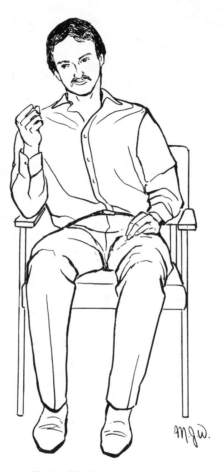

Figure 85. Steve: posture 1

ity with her right hand extended on the back of the couch. Occasionally, as she talked about being hurt, her left hand moved from her lap to stroke her hair, as if to extend small amounts of comfort. This was followed by a radical Trunk Shift over into the upper right quadrant, forming the "L" posture which, as we shall presently see, is so characteristic of those who deny needs for nurture (see Figure 88). Her conversation shifted to never finding a permanent, caring relationship, starting with the experience of never being really cared for by her father. Upon exploring this posture, she became aware of pain in her stomach which she covered with her left arm, recalling between ages six and nine when, in order to gain attention, she refused to eat and was often physically ill.

The basic treatment problem with those who shift to side-arrests centers around this task of satiation. So long as their rhythms of bodily movement are attuned to the less-than-satisfying measures of nurture and attention that they receive by giving up and stopping their pursuits for the real thing, the "never" dimension of their program prevails. They usually have cold hands. Depar-

Figure 86. Steve: posture 2

Figure 87. Joan: posture 1

tures from the script are marked by forward movements to reach out toward others, assuming responsibility to satisfy their own needs. Often this can happen only after more appropriate choices of companions are made, outside the selective processes of the life script.

Trunk Shifts: Side-arrest

Injunctions: "Don't be close," "Don't grow up"

Counterinjunctions: "Be strong," "Please me," "Try hard"

Program: Never getting love, care, or fulfillment

Position: I'm not OK—You're OK, sometimes
I'm not OK—You're not OK

Script payoff: Starved

Prescription: Reach out and touch someone.

GESTURAL DISPLAYS

As we have examined script signs associated with posturing, we have increasingly noted certain gestural displays accompanying them as a significant source of information. For example, Joan's hair-stroking and arrangement of

Figure 88. Joan: posture 2

her arms in the "L" position (see page 245) are important cues to the quality of feeling accompanying each posture. We turn now to consider gestural displays themselves as script signs. They are the most symbolic of bodily movements we have considered from the standpoint of script. When they become the script sign, the gestural display is made from a Basic Posture which, in and of itself, indicates little about the script. It is the specific set of Identified Movements the person makes that reveals the program.

We need to bear in mind that any classification of movement behavior into subtypes runs some risk of fragmenting our perceptions of the process as a whole. It is not my intent to separate gestures from their postures or our structural analysis of bodily duplicity from our search for meaningful script signs. We will deal here with many materials we could have discussed in Chapters 5 and 6. Some enactment gestures presented under the heading of bodily duplicity also serve as script signs. In addition, a number of specific signal behaviors reveal significant dimensions of an individual's life script. The difference is that we are now looking at these phenomena through clinical glasses attuned to script analysis. They are organized under two major categories: 1) simple *hand enactments,* which come to represent symbolically an individual's larger life process; and 2) *hand-body enactments,* which often reveal important steps in an individual's psychosocial development.

Hand Enactments

Occasionally, persons in therapy will evidence a repetitive gesture with hands and arms at points where major script issues come into play. Myra provides a good example. She is shown in Figure 89 responding to Elmer, who was popping his knuckles as he listened to her talk about difficulties with her dominating husband. Elmer openly acknowledged he was "turning her off." Her bilateral gesture, the right hand moving in toward her bosom, her left hand thrust outward toward Elmer, accompanied Myra's response, "But I thought we had been close. I have given a lot of myself to you."

Myra's central complaint about her husband was that he lacked the capacity for emotional closeness. He was always a "big Parent" like her physician father, who was protective but distant and never expressed feelings. Elmer's impatience triggered a script scene for her in which she made her characteristic response to significant males. The whole tenor of her long struggle to pull the other closer, while defending herself against domineering control, received vivid expression in her simple hand enactment. This dimension which her script cast upon the scene was not available for exploration in the verbal interchange alone.

Hand enactments frequently involve a number of gestures in sequence. Rhonda began to talk by steepling her fingertips (see Figure 90) and calmly discussing her chronic dissatisfaction at home. Something was missing in a life of housework, child care, and business, which seemed never ending. Upon reenactment, Rhonda was able to identify feelings of self-control and sensations of keeping everything together which were associated with this gesture. Next, she placed her hands together, knuckle to knuckle, with fingers dangling downward. This gesture accompanied an account of her desires for more time with her husband—time spent talking, dancing, in mutual activities like cooking, going to the theater, or talking about the meaning of a play afterward. Abruptly, she stopped and discarded her wishes, pronouncing them unimportant, selfish, and not cognizant of the basic differences between the two of them. The

Figure 89. Myra: hand enactment

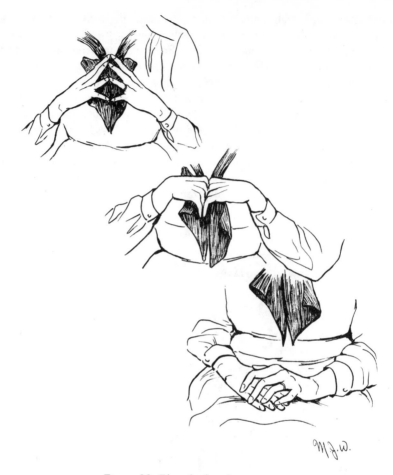

Figure 90. Rhonda: hand enactments

impasse, expressed by her hands which pushed against each other, was re-solved by carefully folding them together in her lap, which coincided with her beginning to talk about how good her husband was to her, how hard he worked, and how long he had tolerated her unhappiness. It represented her primary at-tachment, based upon a deep need for security.

Rhonda's gestural sequence punctuated her verbal account of a script pro-gram calling for her to hold things together, wish for better but surrender her desires before irreconcilable differences, and cling to her primary attachment, counting her blessings. The clinician could undertake to analyze the action through talk therapy, paying attention to exactly what was said. Such efforts are usually fraught with frustration. For one thing, Rhonda has talked this way for so long that she takes what she says for granted, as the way life really has to be. Efforts to challenge her assumptions will be met with confusion, disbelief, and argumentation over detail. More important, the graphic movement of the gestures preserves the larger life process of which her current complaint is but a single manifestation. Careful reenactment of each gesture in sequence permitted Rhonda to experience fresh sensations with each Identified Movement and to place the entire process within the larger context of the script program.

Specific gestures expressing attachment, restraint, or enactment such as those discussed under bodily duplicity often occur as key components in a series of movements constituting a gestural display of the script. In addition, there are a number of other gestures involving hands and arms that appear with such frequency as to merit discussion. Although specific meanings vary from individual to individual, there is sufficient common meaning attached to them that the clinician can be alerted to their significance.

The gun. The gun is an excellent example of the symbolic character of many gestures. It is formed by folding the hands together, extending both forefingers to a point, and lifting the thumbs (see Figure 91). Sometimes it appears in the lap, other times between the legs as the individual leans forward with elbows on thighs; at other times it is tipped upward with pointed fingers across the lips. I have termed this gesture "the gun" because this is the most common way it has been identified by clients.

George formed the gun between his legs when beginning lengthy conversations with the group in which he was characteristically pointed and contentious. Evelyn formed the gun over her lips while listening to criticism and forming her soft, but firm, rebuttal. Robert formed the gun while denying he was the least bit upset by the way others challenged his logic about quitting his job. When this gesture is extended toward others, many persons are surprised by the uncanny accuracy of its aim toward a particularly troublesome individual and often exclaim, "Bang! Bang!" or "Ratta-tat-tat." I have also heard the same gesture described as a "boat" (sailing off, prow to the wind), a "stick" (whap-whap in the face), and a "penis."

My tendency is to downplay symbolic interpretations of the gesture as a penis. For one thing, I find this gesture to occur as frequently among women as men. In some cases, however, such symbolism merits consideration. Herbert was an interesting example. This 48-year-old professor was referred by his family physician because of recurrent depression following the death of his

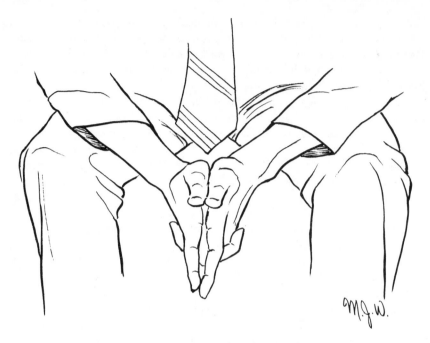

Figure 91. The gun

mother, with whom he had lived for most of his adult life. He suffered from hypogonadism, which early caused him to abandon any hope of marriage because of the extraordinarily small size of his penis. Herbert's initial contract in group was "to stop procrastinating," because he kept putting off measures to deal with a pattern of excessive drinking (approaching alcoholism), the nonpayment of bills (including taxes over the past three years since mother's death), and general lethargy in maintaining his household, his diet, and his personal appearance.

Herbert's characteristic posture when working in group was accompanied by intermittent displays of the gun, usually between his legs, as he leaned forward to conduct elaborate flurries of intellectual sparring with the other members. He often contended over the precise meaning of words in the same way he toured the country giving speeches to professional societies concerning the proper use of the English language. His constant, critical argumentativeness set him apart as "different." During his 10 months in group, Herbert: 1) curtailed his drinking to a chosen amount on social occasions; 2) dealt with his sexual embarrassment to the point where he actually undertook pleasurable sexual intercourse for the first time with his childhood sweetheart, since widowed, and promptly married her; and 3) set his house in order financially and physically for his new bride, who proved a considerable asset in the process. But Herbert still "procrastinated," made contentious speeches about the precise use of language, and punctuated conversations with his "gun." He finally terminated group treatment, stating that he was "too different" and did not "fit in with the others." I consider him my most successful failure.

Gesture: The gun

Style: Contentious

Dynamics: Suppressed anger, Child ego state

Message: "Someone's going to get it."

Steepling. The steepling of fingertips is another common hand enactment (see Figure 92). This particular gesture has been discussed by others as a nonverbal signal of dominance. In repeated instances that I have observed, the issue is more frequently described by the person as one of self-control. Make the gesture yourself, experiencing the sense of precision and propriety it can convey. Most persons report sensations of holding everything together and keeping it in its place. Although the person's style of relatedness may well seek to control the responses others make, the primary efforts of the individual are toward self-control, as if to "hold things together, lest they get out of hand."

Some typical clinical examples follow. Albert steepled his fingertips while discussing a business crisis with his partner. His quiet, vindictive manner, which led him to deny reasonable solutions to their conflict, caused a wave of alarm among group members. This he met with calm and efficient logic to buttress his position. Alice made the same steepling gesture when members of her group questioned her father's noble and silent retreats from her mother's pickiness and dominance. While others challenged her father's conciliatory spirit as withdrawal from the threat of conflict rather than altruistic sacrifice for peace, Alice steadfastly defended the purity of his motives. An interesting variation of the steeple was made by Edgar who insisted, with halting speech and characteristic confusion, that he was "worthless," leaning back in his chair and steepling his fingertips across his forehead from temples to eyebrows. When asked by his therapist to experience the gesture, Edgar pressed his fingers with increasing firmness across his head, saying, "It's like I'm holding everything in, as if I'm keeping everything from blowing apart."

Figure 92. Steepling

Gesture: The steeple

Style: Precision and control, especially self-control

Dynamics: Compulsiveness and denial

Message: "Things will *not* get out of hand."

Arms akimbo. Arms akimbo (hands on hips) have been broadly recognized as a signal of dominance.[2] When expressed standing, with both hands on hips, as, for example, when a parent stands over a small child and demands every bit of a mess be cleaned up, the dominance is nakedly visible. In psychotherapy, seated in chairs, an individual can rarely be observed placing both arms in the akimbo position. More commonly, we observe one arm placed at the hip while movement is undertaken with the other (see Figure 93). This usually signals the

Figure 93. Arm akimbo

presence of a more subtle attempt to dominate, accompanied by various shades of defiance and stubbornness in the Child ego state. As such, the arm akimbo often represents part of a simple division in which the client expresses an agitated form of passivity, stubbornly clinging to a point of view, despite all the good intentions of others seeking to extricate him or her from it. Claude is an excellent example. He rebelliously messed up all kinds of assignments from his supervisor with severe self-accusations and confessions of failure. His *mea culpa* attitude so effectively disarmed anyone of the right to expect something better from him that he could dominate vast portions of a group session with his struggles, which rarely brought progress, let alone change. The left arm akimbo was an impeccable signal of his passive defiance.

Gesture: Arms akimbo

Style: Dominance, either passive or aggressive

Dynamics: Critical Parent or rebellious Child

Message: "You can't make me; I'll make you."

The bowl. Scheflen[3] cited the frequency with which psychotherapists form a bowl gesture with both hands while sharing a fantasy about a patient (see Figure 94). Basic Posture is normally shifted forward as if to offer the other person something useful or valuable. In my experience, the bowl signals a whole range of helpful or caring intentions which are syntonic to offering information, insight, opinions, and the like. Twirling gestures with either hand or both hands simultaneously, as if to "dish out" something for another, commonly accompany it. When it appears within a gestural display of the script, it is usually abandoned in futility or resignation. The progression of the gestural sequence is toward some ending in rejection dictated by the program. The bowl also appears frequently among early responses in variations of the psychological game, "I'm only trying to help you."

Gesture: The bowl

Style: Helpful and giving

Dynamics: Ulterior nurturing Parent

Message: "Try it; you'll like it."

The hand outstretched. The most common of all hand gestures is a one-sided, twirling motion, palm up, often made with pronounced repetition and effort. Invariably, clients who exaggerate it report feelings of helplessness and

Figure 94. The bowl

frustration, together with a sense of "trying hard and getting nowhere." The ego state is adapted Child, and the bid for relationship is in search of recognition and strokes for having struggled so hard. The gesture signals something decidedly dystonic to problem-solving and resolution. If we divide the world into "helpers" and "helpees," this individual falls in the latter category, wandering around looking for a "handout."

Gesture: The hand outstretched

Style: Helpless and struggling

Dynamics: Adapted Child in search of recognition

Message: "Gimme somethin'."

Hands behind neck. Another common gestural signal is formed by folding one's hands behind the neck and frequently accompanies a postural shift back into a radical recline in the chair (see Figure 95). Unlike most of the gestural displays we have been considering, which do not follow sexual roles, this one is predominantly male. The common meaning attached to it is one of challenge. The style is adolescent and rebellious, expressed through a stance that is so an-

Figure 95. Hands behind neck

gular that any confrontation appears to glance off the person and pass on unabsorbed. Christopher assumed this stance repeatedly when challenging the group to catch him in his recurrent capers with authority figures, who were always critical of his efforts. Bob produced the same gesture when he got others to "mother" him with suggestions which he invariably would not follow.

Gesture: Hands behind neck

Style: Challenging and angular

Dynamics: Rebellious Child

Message: "Nobody tells me what to do."

The "L". One final gesture worthy of note is the "L" formed by placing one arm across the abdomen and resting the other elbow upon the back of the hand, extending this arm in the air with hand elevated, to the cheek, or to the mouth (see Figure 96). This is predominantly a female gesture and has been noted among women who characteristically present a strong front and deny their needs for nurture. Sometimes a cigarette is flourished in the ascendant hand. Occasionally, the fingers move to the edge of the mouth. Ruth made the "L" while insisting she wasn't hungry, when she chose to miss the evening meal at an out-of-town workshop rather than to ask someone for transportation to a restaurant. Linda assumed the same gesture when she described the way she was becoming "independent" from her husband who seemed to ignore her. When the "L" is made as part of a gestural display revealing the script program, it is usually assumed and held at the end of a series of Identified Movements. The general stance of the gesture is to cover an individual's "soft underbelly" and squelch one's visceral needs for love, attention, and care.

Gesture: The "L"

Style: Independent and strong front

Dynamics: Denial of needs for nurture

Message: "I can take care of myself."

Hand-Body Enactments

In contrast to simple hand gestures, hand-body enactments normally involve repeated contact with a selected part of the body. The quality of this chosen contact is often symbolic of developmental issues as well as indicative of re-

Figure 96. The "L"

peated trends in current behavior. Brenda began her work in group by stating that she was disturbed over turning off sexually to Ben, her fiancé. As she spoke, she sat cupping her chin in the palm of her right hand, extending the fingers to her mouth, gently stroking her lips. Before she said anything else, she removed her right hand from her chin, made a fist, and struck the arm of the chair three times lightly. Then she placed her right hand flat upon her lap, palm down, covering her genital area.

An exploration of this gestural sequence revealed the program of her script which governed her present perceptions. She began with fantasies about her desires for loving care (hand cupping chin, fingers stroking lips). These were followed by angry doubts as to whether Ben actually did care for her or only wanted to use her sexually (first striking the arm of the chair). The gestural display ended with "cold sensations" and a desire to withdraw from him (covering her genitals). Developmentally, this hand-body enactment symbolized the way she learned to manage her sexual identity in her family of origin. Both father and brothers regarded women as sex objects and people of little importance otherwise. Mother's pattern for the program was one of feeling used, collecting resentment, and withdrawing affection, eventually leading to the termination of the marriage. Brenda was unaware that this program, which was revealed in her gestural display, governed her perception of her current relationship with Ben, who, in most respects, did not fit the male figures of her past at all in attitude or action.

Specific patterns. Within the course of the gestural displays we are considering, there are specific patterns of hand-body contact which recur with frequency. As with all such movement behaviors, their meaning varies from individual to individual. However, we can note certain trends to which the clinician can be alert.

1) Fingers to the nose usually signal disbelief.[4] A flurry of such gestures often appears around the circle when someone persuasively "tries to sell something others aren't buying." Within the sequential displays we are considering, this gesture normally signals that something has gone awry in the categories of credibility or truth. The origin of this movement could be a throwback to such childhood expressions as "that stinks" or "something's rotten here."

2) Fingers above the lip, below the nose, can signal that a convention is about to be broken.[5] Others make this gesture when a member is breaking rules established by the group. I have noticed this gesture among numbers of persons who are contemplating breaking their own personal conventions with some behavior. Another possible conjecture as to its origin has to do with restraining a sneeze in public, a convention widely held in our culture.

3) Hands to the groin is not an exclusively male gesture, although it is much more common in men. It occurs at some point of threat. Men invariably report a sense of protecting themselves when attending it and often make the latest colloquial remarks about "keeping their gonads." As women increasingly wear jeans and slacks, I believe they are free to make more hand-to-groin movements instead of the traditional protective posturing which we have described. Clinicians who have not watched bodily behaviors will be amazed at the frequency with which persons move to protect private parts from exposure and danger within gestural displays.

4) Hands to hair is usually a significant gesture, but it has so many varied meanings for different persons that it is difficult to isolate common themes. Preening is one. Hair-smoothing and adjustment have been noted as expressions of courtship and sexual interest.[6] We have noted scratching to accompany confusion and feelings of "being dirty." Various styles of self-stroking, such as hair-twirling, -pulling, or -braiding can be observed to accompany adapted Child ego states of long standing. Jan pulled her hair out to a point during discussions of her lonely childhood. When questioned about the gesture, she reported memories of her mother pulling out broken ends of her hair, one of the rare moments when she received any stroking of a physical nature.

Hand-to-mouth. Hand-mouth behavior is one of the most consistent script signs of issues surrounding nurture. Precisely at moments when one desires to be cared for, protected, or supported, fingers drift to the mouth. Developmentally, the issue is normally around basic trust as opposed to mistrust. Others around cannot be trusted to supply the needed love, care, understanding, or whatever, so the individual regresses to self-stroking of an oral character. The three major types of hand-mouth activity are sucking, biting, and shushing.

1) Sucking behaviors can be observed when a person touches one or more fingers to the lips, gently inserting the tips into the mouth, or occasionally thrusting a thumb into the edge or center of the mouth. Most persons report a momentary soothing effect reminiscent of fantasies of the breast. The average grown person will not permit more than a few seconds of such pleasure uninterrupted, but may leave fingers touching a cheek or stroking the lips for longer periods. Suckers are different from biters in that the finger makes contact with the tongue and inner lips, not the teeth. In accord with the colloquial term, "suckers" tend to be gullible and incorporate ideas and suggestions from others. They also tend to remain in a helpless, victim position, failing to take initiative to meet their needs.

2) Biting of fingers and nails is a similar display of hand-mouth activity with the same desires for nurture and caring. The added dimension is mounting agitation and frustration. Cheek-biting, tongue-chewing, and teeth-grinding evidence the same emotional picture. It is commonly one of a small boy frustrated by excessive demands who finally gives up. Lawrence used to bite his nails. Now he runs his teeth underneath them, occasionally breaking one off, grinds his teeth, and clenches his jaws when trying hard. Beneath the strong expectations both parents placed upon him was his mother's warm response when he struggled and didn't make it. With biters, the primary needs for nurture are pur-

chased at the price of self-defeat and failure. They commonly reject help while suckers will take it in. After lengthy efforts to please, biters often become agitated and rebel, finding some way to bite back.

3) With the acquisition of speech comes another type of hand-mouth activity, colloquially known as "shushing." Fingers, hands, and sometimes fists are brought over the mouth, stopping conversation. To the careful observer, it is as if someone said, "Shush your mouth." Each of the three types of hand-mouth gestures represents a different response to those whose continuing care is needed. Biters clench their teeth and tend to stop short. Suckers are gullible and will swallow a lot to keep others around. Shushers are tight-lipped and usually operate with the auditory representational system as the favored one. What is said and heard is of paramount importance but they are forbidden to "speak out." Ralph was typical, quietly covering his mouth with his hand and sitting expressionless when challenged to assert himself. He also characteristically cleared his throat when about to talk. He remembered with embarrassment his unsuccessful father doing the same before praying publicly in church. Shushers seldom talk things out. Therapeutic interventions which get them into the kinesthetic communicational mode are often effective, enabling them to express themselves through doing something.

Noncommunicative clients. Sometimes with noncommunicative clients who have a great deal of difficulty verbalizing their life experience a gestural display can serve to introduce us to the basic adaptation of the script. Amie was such a person. She sat quietly in group for several months and talked haltingly in individual sessions designed to provide a supportive structure until she became comfortable working in the group setting. One particular gestural sequence was repeated a number of times during the long silences when Amie was thinking about what to say next.

1) Resting her elbow on the arm of the chair, Amie placed the fingers of her left hand lightly to her cheek, sticking the third and fourth just inside her open mouth.

2) Soon the finger or fingers were bitten or quietly gnawed for several seconds before they were drawn back to the left corner of her mouth.

3) Then the left hand was placed in front of her mouth and formed into a fist which was either held there or drawn back toward the lips in deliberate tapping.

4) Finally, the fist was opened, and the fingers dangled limply before

her face at which point eye contact was restored expectantly. She
either spoke or signaled her therapist to speak.

The entire process took from 10-12 seconds. After viewing it several times to
assure himself of the sequence, the therapist requested Amie to reenact it step
by step, showing her each gesture by repeating it himself. The following content was elicited from her as she explored the display, gesture by gesture, reporting her thoughts and feelings.

1) The fingers were caring initially, touching cheek, lips, and mouth,
   reminiscent of childhood scenes when Amie wanted to suck her
   thumb. She was acutely aware of her mother's harshness and the absence of such caring activity.

2) The finger-biting hurt and brought to mind incidents Amie had not
   discussed before in which she had inflicted injury upon herself. Recently she felt compelled to jab her knee with a knitting needle. As a
   teenager, she cut herself on the wrist several times with a knife and
   burned herself on the stove. Somehow she linked the finger-biting
   with her aversion to physical touch. Pleasurable contact turned into
   hurt. Then she recalled an early scene in which she had tearfully ap-
   proached her mother for comfort and was spanked instead, being
   told, "I'll give you something to cry about."

3) The fist in front of her mouth quietly embodied her urge to strike
   back. Instead of becoming an instrument to express anger, however,
   it served only to mute verbal responses of any kind. The tapping
   movements on her lips only made her more "tight-lipped." She
   never talked back or struck back.

4) Opening the fist and limply dangling the fingers before her face constituted her characteristic response to conflict—withdraw quietly, go
   into hiding, and say nothing.

The best explanation I can make for such phenomena is that the Child ego
state in Amie preserves in this particular gestural display an often repeated sequence of events in her formative years. The process begins with the desire for
nurture, care, and love. Efforts to satiate this need end painfully, and eventually Amie integrated this pain into the scheme in which she bites herself until it
hurts, in the same manner small children integrate Parental responses into their
own behavior and smack themselves upon the hand when caught reaching for

the cookie jar. The remaining Identified Movements preserve Amie's characteristic response of muted anger followed by giving up and withdrawing in silence. The value of exploring such hand-body gestures to the task of script analysis is obvious, whether or not the client is noncummunicative.

The way these repetitive sequences of postural and gestural displays become integrated into an individual's behavior during development remains to be discussed in the final chapter. But first, we need to return to signal behaviors to consider a special class of repetitive transactions with others that become so characteristic of a person that they, too, can serve as script signs.

REFERENCE NOTES

1. Kahler, T., and Capers, H. The miniscript. *Transactional Analysis Journal,* 4:26-42, 1974.
2. Scheflen, A. E. *Body Language and Social Order.* Englewood Cliffs, NJ: Prentice Hall, 1972, p. 24.
3. Scheflen, A. E. *How Behavior Means.* New York: Gordon Breach, 1973, pp. 129-143.
4. See Nierenberg, G. I., and Carelo, H. H. *How to Read a Person Like a Book.* New York: Cornerstone Library, 1973, pp. 64-67.
5. See Scheflen, A. E. *Body Language and Social Order,* p. 108.
6. See Scheflen, A. E. *How Behavior Means,* pp. 69-71.

9

Spontaneous commentaries

When people "go into" their scripts, we can expect them to relate to others in ways that are characteristic of the program the script calls them to live out. We turn now to consider a special class of signal behaviors, which I term *spontaneous commentaries,* as script signs. Spontaneous commentaries are involuntary, uncalculated expressions from ulterior ego states which signal the type of relationship a person is seeking. They usually emerge among initial transactions or at key points where the executive ego state professes another purpose, so as to be dystonic to the desired outcome. As such, they provide an immediate comment upon the psychological level of a developing pattern of ulterior transactions, serving as a reasonable predictor of what will, in fact, happen.

Whereas some spontaneous commentaries serve as common signals without any great significance to the individual, others are so characteristic of major trends in the person's life that their exploration immediately involves the client in formative scenes that determined the life script. In this chapter, I will discuss selected *paralinguistic phenomena* such as nonlanguage sounds, yawns, and coughs, together with their verbal first cousins composed of characteristic expressions and habitual phrases which, instead of furthering what is being said, subvert it at the ulterior level. Specific movements associated with rings and things, along with dress and paraphernalia brought into the treatment room, also will be examined for their commentary upon the life script.

252

PARALINGUISTIC EXPRESSIONS

A number of paralinguistic expressions accompanying speech serve as spontaneous commentaries upon the kind of relationship a person is creating. More often than not, such sighs, grunts, noises, and yawns go ignored within the process of psychotherapy. When they appear repetitiously within a person's conversation, particularly at points where major life conflicts are addressed in characteristically unsuccessful ways, they are usually script signs. The intervention of choice is to encourage persons to attend them, explore their transactional meaning, and experiment with other, more congruent ways of expressing themselves.

Sighs

Sighs which accompany descriptions of personal conflict merit attention. They usually convey an emotional stance of long standing. Arnold came to a week-long workshop to determine his professional future. His enthusiasm for his work as pastor of a large church had waned. He had difficulty sustaining programs he believed in, particularly as his concern for social issues went unshared by increasing numbers of his parishioners. His verbal expressions were alert and precise as he described his disillusionment. An occasional sigh of two-to-three seconds' duration formed the only emotional comment on his thoughts. When the therapist called attention to it, Arnold described himself as "a tired old man of 52." He immediately recounted the vigorous activities into which he had thrown himself following his wife's death in an automobile accident eight years earlier. He had never stopped to cry, even though plagued by doubts that he could "keep going" after it happened. Exploration of Arnold's sigh cast the course of treatment toward expressing the grief which he had never permitted himself, assuming he must "hold up well" as an example for others.

Sighs have different meanings within the life course of each individual. A common feature is prolonged periods of trying hard, in which the sigh is usually a bid for recognition. Charles punctuated his description of efforts to support his family with a short, shallow sigh at the end of every third or fourth sentence. Exploration brought awareness of his sighing pattern around significant women. The list of its regular recipients included his secretary, his wife, and his mother, who always expressed concern that he was working too hard. Mother's most forceful attention was commanded by worry over Charles' health. She feared he would "work himself to death," as did his father, who died of coronary disease at the age of 42. Charles ceased his sighing when he decided to give up his own feared coronary at the same age.

Signal: Sighing

Style: Noble and harried

Dynamics: Suppressed emotions and desire for recognition

Message: "See how hard I tried."

Coughing

Characteristic coughing or throat-clearing bears attention. Normally, some pattern will become evident in repetitive expressions. The more common theme is some form of inhibition surrounding self-assertion, particularly vocal. Explorations usually reveal significant recognition by formative figures in the person's script for the behavior itself or for what it represents. Woodford, for example, typically began to speak, then stopped and coughed lightly, then started over again. The cough served to erase what had gone before, providing a benchmark for beginning afresh. False starts were not at all uncommon to Woodford, who struggled throughout his life to get things right in order to satisfy a perfectionistic Parent ego state. For seven years he had failed to complete a doctoral dissertation, having begun work on it a number of times, only to abandon efforts and start again. Fear of being caught in a mistake caused him to do the same thing in everyday efforts to express himself to others.

Louise kept a recurrent tickling sensation in her throat, which brought vigorous coughing when she became excited. Constant smoking and an assortment of colds kept her sufficiently congested to produce deep coughing when feelings rose in personal exchange. She grew up with two aunts who died of tuberculosis and possessed many memories of her activities as a child being curtailed against the background of a chorus of coughs.

Jane, on the other hand, characteristically cleared her throat when starting to speak (hugh, ughugh, ghugh, ghM!). This went unattended for several months of weekly treatment until the therapist took note of it one day. Everyone in the group immediately recognized it as her "hallmark" when beginning discussions of her problems with her boy friend or at school in which she was continually treated poorly and misunderstood. Jane, it developed, suffered repeated throat infections as a child which continued into her teen years, when she finally had a belated tonsillectomy. Her throat illnesses brought soup and strokes from mother and a rare interest from her usually inattentive father. When she began clearing her throat in the group, Jane was encouraged to experiment with direct requests for nurture and care; she subsequently got on with numerous activities independently.

Hugh, by way of contrast, never cleared his throat. Others in the group silently wished he would because his "gravelly" voice made them uncomfortable. Finally, George broke the bond of polite tolerance and asked, "Why don't you clear your throat and speak up?" Hugh remembered a number of fights with his older brother in which he was choked. He recalled simply lying there and making his throat and chest tight, afraid to call out because of what would happen if he "ratted" on his assailant. The gravelly voice and tightness in his chest became a landmark of his anxiety attacks, which often produced pains and dizziness through hyperventilation, causing him to fear he would die prematurely. His relief was immediate when he cleared his throat, relaxed with deeper breaths, and declared his fears forthrightly.

Signal: Coughing or throat-clearing

Style: Cautious and inhibited

Dynamics: Fear of self-assertion, particularly vocal

Message: "Pay attention to my suffering."

Yawning

Repetitious yawning is a forceful spontaneous commentary because it is contagious. A number of readers will yawn within 10 seconds after picturing Evelyn starting to talk, stopping to yawn, and continuing. Evelyn usually sounded like a Parent when she spoke of how she should manage her life better. Others tired of listening to her almost immediately. When she explored her yawn, she reported she was thoroughly "bored" with herself. Memories returned of sitting at the table, listening to her mother's lengthy lectures concerning her behavior that she was forbidden to interrupt. Evelyn's contemporary yawns signaled she was going to stop any problem-solving surrounding her recurrent depression, which involved an internal struggle between her demanding Parent ego state and her own bored Child ego state that yearned to go outside and play.

Signal: Yawning

Style: Bored

Dynamics: Adapted Child tuning out a demanding Parent

Message: "Are these lectures compulsory?"

Clicks, Clucks, Tsks, and the Like

Clicking, clucking, pinging, and other sounds made with mouth and tongue often appear at consistently opportune moments in conversation. Ed had repeated difficulties managing employees in his dry goods store. Over and over again, he engaged in unwitting attempts to dominate and control them, while professing to be in his Adult ego state. The source was his father's critical Parent, which Ed detested as a child, now causing him to behave toward others the same way his father had acted toward him. Once some member of the group again confronted Ed with the obvious, he would sit back, shift his head slightly to the side, and make several clucking noises with his tongue. Upon repeating them, Ed identified the sounds excitedly, recalling times when he would attempt some deception of his father, only to be discovered and caught in the end. The same suspense and excited relief at having been exposed accompanied his present transactions in group. The impish quality of deceiving and getting caught is the most common element present in spontaneous commentaries of this type.

Signal: Clicks, clucks, tsks, and the like

Style: Excitement and suspense

Dynamics: Child delight in being exposed

Message: "You caught me again."

Ah . . . aahh-ing

"Ah . . . ah" sounds interspersed throughout speech to fill in silent gaps between words often prove to be significant commentaries:

> Dave: I . . . ah . . . think that . . . ah . . . the most important thing . . . ah . . . is to . . . go through with it . . . ah . . . regardless of the results.

For Dave, repeating his "ah" sounds brought memories of himself as a little boy, bidding for the floor in his large family. When he finally got parental attention, he often "went blank" and couldn't think. This necessitated holding his air time with sounds, lest he lost his turn. Such filler sounds often signal the anxious adapted Child seeking to hold attention while at the same time fearing rejection. Sadly enough, the "ahs" actually bring about what is feared through subjecting listeners to the annoyance of being forced to attend so cumbersome an assortment of speech, hesitant gaps, and noise. The same dynamic in larger measure is present in stuttering. Full attention to what the person is saying, coupled with reassurances which remove the threat of rejection, often elicit an immediate behavioral change to clear Adult statements unmarred by the anxious Child. Sometimes a visual pattern for speaking aids this process, such as encouraging the person to picture a square and speak lines around its perimeter.

Signal: "Ah . . . ahing"

Style: Anxious and hesitant

Dynamics: Fear of rejection

Message: "Don't go away."

Nodding

Head-nodding often signals covert deceptions of oneself or others, not the usual sign of agreement or disagreement. Raphael sat listening to a rather lengthy set of instructions from an older woman across the room, continuously nodding his head, "Yes, I understand." Upon impulse, the therapist asked him what the nod meant. "It means I'm not listening to a thing she is saying," Raphael responded coolly.

"Yes-nodding" often constitutes some similar dismissal, signaling inattention. The likelihood that this is the case increases with the number and intensity of the nods. Adult nods are usually decisive and non-repetitive. Parental nods frequently signal impatience for another to hurry up and finish, so that an individual can make his or her own point. At a slower pace, they may signal approval from a nurturing Parent. Repetitive nodding from the adapted Child signals pseudo-compliance, rather than that a person is listening and understands.

Interestingly, habitual "yes" nodders often possess stiffness in neck and shoulder muscles, and they usually have difficulty saying no. An effective intervention is to encourage them to engage in vigorous negative nodding, while verbally saying no loudly. It is a more natural movement, acquired among our earliest developmental stages to protect our autonomy. Repetition usually makes the person more comfortable, both physically and emotionally, although sometimes a bit dizzy at first.

Covert negative nodding often signals a more basic rejection in an ulterior ego state of what is being affirmed at the social level of discourse. Alicia expressed her willingness to stop the lengthy telephone conversations with her mother which inevitably produced self-doubt and worry over her own abilities. At the same time, she slowly shook her head no from side to side incongruously. When asked to attend the negative movement in her head, she acknowledged two thoughts emerging: "You can never hurt your mother's feelings," and "I can't make it on my own."

Alicia's nonverbal negation of her professed intentions to break off dependency upon her mother revealed two injunctions. The first was easier to address, since it was lodged in her Parent ego state among other moral precepts belonging to the counterscript. The latter revealed a script injunction not to grow up and to remain a little girl. Negative nodding at the covert level often conveys the presence of injunctions forbidding what is declared overtly. Unless the underlying script issues are resolved, predictions that a person's intentions will end in failure can be safely made.

Signal: "Yes" nodding	*Signal:* "No" nodding
Style: Impatience or pseudo-compliance	*Style:* Unspoken negation
Dynamics: Controlling Parent or over-adapted Child	*Dynamics:* Counterinjunction or injunction
Message: "Hurry up and finish."	*Message:* "I can't do what I'm saying."

Gallows Laughter

Gallows laughter is far and away the most important spontaneous commentary of the paralinguistic type. Steiner, Berne, and others have discussed it as a script sign.[1] The distinguishing feature is its inappropriateness. The person laughs at a significant failure which is decidedly not funny. Lance described his elaborate preparations for his annual review at work, which he hoped would be favorable and bring a merited raise. "Once I got in the room," he continued, "everything went blank (ha! ha!) and I couldn't remember a thing." Almost irresistably, others around the circle were enticed to join in, unwittingly tightening the noose of characteristic failure around Lance's neck.

Gallows laughter is distinguished from hearty laughter at the genuinely funny by its shallow, throaty quality, which leads some to describe it as a "witch laugh." When attention is called to it, some clients term it "nervous laughter," or say, "If I didn't laugh, I would cry." The important thing to the script analyst is its repeated occurrence at points where an individual describes the characteristic failure called for by the script. Often this will happen in the first few minutes of the initial interview. The laughter itself seems to preserve the primitive pleasure of an archaic Parent (P_1) at the Child's failure ("Ho! Ho! Ho! He'll never amount to anything!"). It also contains a protective, nurturing quality that appears to have accompanied parenting at the time the injunction was delivered. The intervention of choice with gallows laughter is to explore it for the secret message about the way an individual's life is supposed to go.

Signal: Gallows laughter

Style: Inappropriate

Dynamics: Pleasure of an archaic Parent at the Child's failure

Message: "Isn't it ironical that this always happens?"

VERBALS

Spontaneous commentaries include a number of verbal expressions and habitual phrases which, like paralinguistics, are inserted into the flow of speech, yet add nothing to what is actually being said. Their seemingly habitual repetition leads others to ignore the fact that they appear and disappear with particular ego states. Often they are reliable indicators of what will be the outcome of a series of transactions. When this is the case, they are frequently script signs, too.

"You Know"

"You know" interspersed throughout various units of speech is one of the more common ones. Norbert presented the tape of his work with a trainee in group therapy to a supervisory seminar, discontented with the vague and inconclusive character of their conversation. An excerpt 15 minutes into the discussion of a female patient sounded like this:

> Supervisor: How does she come across to you?
>
> Trainee: She's . . . you know . . . always reserved, and . . . you know . . . never quite sure, you know, of anything, and when somebody tries to . . . you know . . . make contact . . . she doesn't seem to, you know . . .
>
> Supervisor: Yeah . . . yeah . . . Good enough, let's talk about your plans for next week.

Lest the belabored obvious in print deceive the reader, neither the supervisor nor seven colleagues in the room registered any awareness of the "you knows" to this point, even though relistening produced nine of them in one earlier two-minute segment. Most of us "hear them for granted." Once attended, the spontaneous commentary laid bare the ulterior transactional structure of the conversation beneath ostensible Adult data processing about the trainee's work. "You know" constituted a demand from the trainee's Child ego state that his supervisor do the knowing for him, excusing him before the magnitude of his supervisor's superior knowledge and skill from the task of thinking and knowing for himself. Norbert recognized the "yeahs" in his response to mark increasing impatience with the dialogue and was able to interpret the "good enough" to his colleagues as a spontaneous commentary from his own Parent ego state to this effect, "Good enough for now, little boy, but I'm going to expect a lot more than this from you in the future."

The same dynamics we have observed with paralinguistic expressions are present in these verbal ones. Unbound energy from an ulterior ego state protrudes in a characteristic expression or phrase to signal an unacknowledged transactional stance, in this case Child to Parent. If permitted to continue unattended, such dystonic signals will determine the transactional course between the persons involved. Most people know intuitively what the spontaneous commentary conveys. For example, when the trainee listened to the tape of this conversation, he readily identified the type of relationship sought: "The 'you know' means that . . . well, you know what I'm going to say before I say it . . . you know? (Laughter at catching himself) I'm not responsible for knowing things for myself, yet."

Signal: "You know"

Style: Humbled and hesitant

Dynamics: Adapted Child bidding for Parental direction

Message: "Think for me."

"OK?"

Some spontaneous commentaries check out the other person, like "OK?" From the adapted Child they come as bids for approval or permission. Sara, a "professional patient" with two lengthy periods of psychoanalysis, complained that she could not complete things. She dropped out of college to get married. Currently, she could not finish two papers to complete a year of "A"-level work at a nearby university.

> Sara: I had a pretty good week, except that I didn't write the papers, OK? I just lay awake all night thinking about them, OK?
>
> Therapist: No, that's not OK. I don't believe you feel OK when you don't write papers you want to write and lie awake all night thinking about them.

Had the therapist permitted Sara's "OK?s" to go unconfronted, he would have unwittingly given her Child permission to fail. He also would have missed a more important therapeutic task than conveying "understanding and accept-ance"—that of exploring Sara's constant checking-out process to make sure she was "doing all right." Without the sanction of a return signal of approval from a Parent, Sara tended to panic. This panic was magnified when she sat down to write her papers and had to proceed for hours on end without approv-ing responses from her professors. Interestingly, members of her group found the "OK?s" so controlling that several reported they consciously held back solicited approval. "That's what my husband does," reported Sara, "Eventual-ly everybody disapproves and withdraws . . . it's the story of my life."

Spontaneous commentaries of the verbal type evidence the same varied pat-terns as their counterparts among nonverbal signals. They defy universalization of meaning, although every clinician can point to certain common trends among them. Both "You know" and "OK?" can signal the emergence of an ul-terior Parent, making certain that the other is listening and going along with what is being said. A common variation is "Don'tcha' know?" or "Don'tcha' see?" When explored, the ulterior message is literally "Don't know" or "Don't see—let me know and see for you."

Signal: "OK?"	*Signal:* "OK?"
Style: Compliant	*Style:* Dominant
Dynamics: Adapted Child seeking approval or permission	*Dynamics:* Controlling Parent
Message: "Mother, may I?"	*Message:* "Go along with me."

The Subjunctive Mood

Statements cast in the subjunctive mood provide another spontaneous commentary upon adaptations the speaker is making in life. Subjunctives like "would," "should," or "could" frequently belie an ulterior "doubtful mood" shrouded with contingencies that sanction inconclusiveness and inaction. Berne describes "the Berkeley Subjunctive," which is highly developed on college campuses, in classical phrases like "I should, and I would if I could, but . . . ," with variants such as "If only they would, I could . . . ," or "I should, and I probably could, but then they would. . . . "[2] The subjunctive attitude is well formalized in higher education in titles of books, theses, and papers which begin "Toward a Theory of . . . " and never get there. It is interesting that the *Random House Dictionary of the English Language* notes that a proper use of the subjunctive mood "still marks the educated speaker."[3] Its disadvantages are many. As Berne points out, who wants to take an airplane that is "going toward" New York?[4]

In psychotherapy, statements couched in the subjunctive mood signal self-defeating contingencies at the ulterior level. Sentences begin "I would like to . . . " and conclude with the desire for some action ("Say something," "Go somewhere," "Do something," etc.). The proper intervention is to invite the speaker to complete the conditional "if" clause that should follow but normally goes both unexpressed and unacknowledged.

> Everette: I would like to find a way to go back to school.
> Therapist: Will you finish the sentence, "If . . . ?"
> Everette: What do you mean "if . . . ?" Like, if I thought I could borrow the money from my father, and if I thought he really cared, and if I weren't afraid I would flunk out, and if it weren't too late to apply for this fall?

People with banal scripts are accustomed to living in the subjunctive mood ("If only, then I could . . . "). They seldom confront the unvoiced contingencies which reduce their efforts to unfulfilled wishes. Exploration of these contingencies becomes the first order of concern for treatment. People who live in the subjunctive mood search for someone to sanction their inaction. Whatever security this brings is purchased at the everyday price of dissatisfaction and frustration.

Signal: The subjunctive mood

Style: Frustrated

Dynamics: Banal or nonwinning script, forbidding success

Message: "Don't expect me to."

" I Don't Know"

"I don't know" may be an Adult response when information is lacking. Repetitiously interspersed throughout conversation, "I don't know" is a spontaneous commentary of the adapted Child who has learned that not knowing is a good defense against demanding Parents ("Johnny, why did you eat all the cookies?"—"I dunno."). In psychotherapy, "I don't know" frequently signals the fear of asserting thoughts or feelings under threat of punishment. Others who demand or coax something from the person will soon become frustrated. Effective interventions confront the dismissal in "I don't know" without heightening the need to deny knowledge by raising the threat.

> Barbara: I work all day with my husband in his store, and, I don't know, then I come home and prepare dinner while he reads the paper. Then I do the dishes and get the children to bed, and then, I don't know, then he wants to go to bed and have sex.
> Emily: Boy! How do you feel about that?
> Barbara: I don't know . . . I do my best to get along, and then, . . . I don't know.

Invitations to "guess" or "know anyway" miss the necessary task of giving the Child permission to express himself or herself safely without anticipated reprisal. An encouraged repetition of the commentary often helps the client appreciate the transactional value in defending herself by nonthinking and nonaction. For Barbara, who had been in group 12 weeks without knowing much of anything significant about herself, a simple contract to know everything for a short period of time without any commitments brought an immediate and clear change in self-expression:

> Therapist: Barbara, you say "I don't know" a lot. (Laughter, including Barbara's) Will you agree for five minutes to know everything, even if it's wrong? Then, if you want to go back to not knowing, you can still do so.
> Barbara: I have trouble making commitments. (Laughter) (Group laughter) OK, I'll know for five minutes.
> Emily: How do you feel toward your husband?

> Barbara: I hate him. I've never stood up for myself. I don't know . . .
> scratch that, I know I think a lot about divorce, and then I don't let
> myself go any farther for fear I'd never make it on my own. I've
> been angry since we were married. He doesn't know how angry.

Signal: "I don't know."

Style: Mute

Dynamics: Escape, resentment, avoidance

Message: "Name, rank, and serial number."

Hedge Words

Every clinician can compile a long list of hedge words which form spontaneous commentaries in the midst of assertions at another level: "I guess," "maybe," "perhaps," "probably," "kinda," "it could be," etc. "It could be that I'm
angry," said Arlene when asked why she didn't respond to a memo from her
superior requesting information she had already provided. And it could be that
she feels something else. No full commitment to a thought, idea, or feeling is
made when spontaneous commentaries of this type are inserted. Most people
have a clear idea of the function of their hedge words when asked about them.

> Judy: I guess I'm kinda breaking it off with Bob. We just see each other
> occasionally now.
> Therapist: I'm struck by the hedge words in your stentences: "I *guess* I'm
> *kinda* breaking it off. . . ." What's the advantage of sticking those
> in?
> Judy: Well, I suppose . . . (laughter at catching herself). Then you can't
> hang me. It's that trust issue; if I hedge, then you can't hold me to it.
> I didn't really say I was or I wasn't.

Hedge words not only protect the Child with an "out" if confronted; they also
signal a surrender of potency and decisiveness. When the person is encouraged to abandon them, the decks are cleared for definitive thought and action
unmolested by uncertainty. An interesting variation was Arnold's use of "so to
speak," which dotted the answers to questions about his future. "Well, I want to
get my union card, so to speak, and start in some practical job that would use
what I know, so to speak." When asked to explore his "so to speaks," Arnold described three thoughts: a vague sense that he might be reprimanded or "called"

on what he was saying; anticipation of defending himself by denying he meant anything definite since he was using the expression "so to speak"; and excitement at testing how far he could push others who disapprove before they caught him in an unrealistic presentation of his plans. Like so many similar commentaries, his hedge words placed him in touch with a major life drama in which his domineering father systematically discouraged his "idle dreams" from an early age.

Signal: Hedge words like "I guess," "maybe," "could be," etc.

Style: Noncommital

Dynamics: Protection against Parental criticism

Message: "I didn't really say."

"Can't"

"I can't" expresses a more primitive Child defense against Parental demands. "Can't" possesses the added advantage of keeping helpers around to undertake various measures of assistance. "I can't . . . express myself, . . . sleep at night, . . . stop worrying, . . . fight back," etc. is essentially an anal phenomenon developmentally, reminiscent of scenes around the potty chair where one or more helping figures hover above, "trying hard" to encourage movement that just won't come ("Would it help if I ran the water or read to you?").

One common intervention is to ask the person to change "can't" to "won't," which establishes responsibility for the defiant aspects of "being unable." More productive are invitations to explore such other advantages as continued attention and avoidance patterns derived from failures "to perform." Experimentation with options can follow, with prescriptions for immediate action, regardless of how awkward or unsatisfying to the client at first. If "can't" remains "unable," we move on promptly to someone else, inviting the client to engage in chosen channels of self-expression at a time of readiness. The advantages of treating such individuals in a group where we do not have to "finish out the hour" with them are obvious.

Signal: "Can't"

Style: Unable

Dynamics: Anal retentive Child

Message: "No movements for you."

Qualifiers

Characteristic adjectives, adverbs, and conjunctions which reappear in the midst of verbal transactions often provide significant commentaries on how an individual relates to others. Doris remarked to Ann, "I just want to tell you how nice you look." When invited to look at Ann and repeat the phrase "I *just* want to . . ." several times, Doris first gave an Adult analysis: "It's my 'don't get close' injunction, saying 'that's all I want, no more,' controlling the distance between us by setting the limits." Upon repeating the phrase several times more, Doris burst into tears, "It's like 'don't leave me'; I'm not going to ask anything more of you; don't go away." The fear of rejection beneath her habitual qualifier extended her awareness to early scenes with her parents which were formative of her present-day caution. Again, the clinician can expect such commentaries to be unique to each individual's developed pattern of usage. "I *just* want to . . ." for another member of the same group normally prefaced a poorly disguised critical Parent who "just wanted to point out one more thing."

Conjunctions

Conjunctions often reveal the quality and movement of a person's life course. Typically, May began reporting to the group with "and": "*And* I had a bad experience Sunday night . . . *and* I noticed several times I didn't respond when I wanted to say something to George, . . . *and* I felt very insecure several times at school." The "on and on" quality of disjointed, unpleasant experiences linked by the conjunction "and" was characteristic of the way May lived. One unresolved crisis after another was brought to others for parenting. Confronting the pattern represented by "and" becomes more important therapeutically than dealing with any one specific complaint.

"But" is probably the most common conjunction encountered in psychotherapy. The effect of "but" in the middle of a sentence is to cancel one assertive clause by another. "I love her very much," said Robert, "but I hate the things she does to me." Because he loves, he cannot hate; and because he hates, he cannot love. When such statements reoccur, we can count on a pattern of assertion-negation-inaction. The individual engages in circular thinking around a particular preoccupation that blocks any conclusion and often defeats the efforts of others to suggest resolutions ("Yes . . . , but . . ."). The intervention of choice is to ask Robert to change his "but" to an "and," declaring "I love her very much, and I hate the things she does to me." This reframes Robert's emotional reality, permitting ownership of each feeling he has fully, no longer permitting one to negate the other. The difference is between saying, "I have a right hand, but I have a left hand," and saying, "I have a right hand and a left hand and can use them both." Such interventions in our groups are frequently couched in the colloquial phrase "Scratch your *but*."

Questions

Most questions are opinions disguised. An excellent intervention in the treatment room is to encourage clients to change them to assertions. This practice will curtail any number of psychological games like "Stupid," or "Now I've got you, you son of a bitch," or "Gee, you're wonderful, Dr. Murgatroid." It also creates a climate of personal autonomy. Therapists do well to check their own requests for information or activity from clients for similar commentaries from ulterior ego states. The therapist who asks, "Can you do something to make yourself more comfortable?", is vulnerable to the response of "can't" from the client, who will immediately sense the subtle suggestion that he or she may not "be able" to do so. The therapist's ulterior stance is usually rescuer to victim. "Make yourself more comfortable" is a direct, Adult request, free from any discount of another's ability, and crisply invites that person to get on with it.

Declarations of Intent

To the careful listener, the Child ego state more often than not makes some spontaneous commentary ahead of time about how a significant problem will be handled. Even the experienced therapist may "hear them for granted" and permit them to go unattended. When Bert announced to the group he wanted "to bring something up," we could count on a careful, well-thought-out report of some personal affront for which no restitution was possible and, further, that he would make every effort to "keep it up" rather than resolve it. When Joan announced she wanted to do "a little bit of work," she invariably did just that. Nonproductive rehashing of a dilemma always followed Harry's declarations that he "wanted to talk something over with the group." Rachel's intentions to "try to work things out with Bob" predictably ended after much effort with failure. This leads to another well-known clinical axiom: "Try equals fail."

Two special types of declarations are of particular importance to the clinician. The first is of the "honestly" category, marked by phrases like: "To be perfectly frank, . . . ," or "Deep down, I . . . ," or "To tell the truth, . . . ," etc. Interspersed throughout conversation, these commentaries suggest something to the effect that, "although I may not have been completely truthful on occasion before, I am now going to reveal my actual . . . feelings, thoughts, fears, concerns, decisions, or what have you." Invariably, the opposite is the case. Spontaneous commentaries of the "honestly" type usually signal recurrent deception, manipulation, and avoidance.

The other type is characterized by comments like "By the way . . . ," "Oh, I almost forgot . . . ," "I just remembered . . . ," or "That reminds me . . .". Frank described such phrases by the adapted Child as "Pearl Harbors" because they can usually be counted upon to preface the dropping of a bombshell.[5] "By the way . . . " has preceded such announcements as "I can't come back to group any more"; "I lost my job"; "I got married"; or "My wife ran off with another man." The hallmarks of this commentary are surprise (since such major developments have not been discussed before) and inopportune timing in order to create maximum disruption (like the last two minutes of group). It distinguishes a particular species in our area that we came to term "the small-breasted, yellow-bellied, eleventh-hour rat fink," who may announce in the closing moments of a weekend workshop, without warning, that it is so distraught it cannot go home. The advantages in early confrontation, both to the individual's treatment and to the therapist's comfort, are many.

"Like I Say"

On occasion, we encounter an editorial phrase such as "Like I say." Literally, the Child announces: "In situations such as this one, what I have learned to say is. . . ." Following these commentaries, we may anticipate that that person will "read familiar lines" from his or her script. Often it is a repeated slogan, precept, or injunction from the program being lived out. Steve had just cited a series of internal difficulties at the plant where he worked, which now appeared to preclude any chance of advancement. "Like I say," he exclaimed, "there's always something standing in the way." This recurrent state of affairs, which lay at the heart of the program his script called for, is of more importance to his treatment than any of the particulars blocking his success at the moment.

RINGS AND THINGS

Identified Movements during psychotherapy often lead us to rings, lockets, bracelets, key chains, and other articles of significance to the client. A piece of jewelry is touched, fingered, or twisted repeatedly at moments of emotional significance. Rings are particularly important. Often the Child wears them as a secret reminder of destiny. Freud noted the dire consequences to anticipate when someone loses a wedding ring.[6] Among the more significant movements related to script are those the clinician can observe surrounding such artifacts that serve symbolic roles in the life drama.

Rings

Movement behavior surrounding rings is worthy of attending. As Evelyn spoke about unhappiness in her marriage to Bill, she twisted her wedding ring and then began slipping it on and off. Next she moved to a large ring with an inset stone on the third finger of her right hand, and repeated the process. The intervention of choice for the therapist in such cases is to say, "Tell us about your rings."

> Evelyn (surprised): Well . . . , this is my wedding ring. The stone is small. It belonged to Bill's grandmother who insisted he give it to me. She said if I didn't like it I could always give it back (laughs). And this other ring my father had made for me just after my *first* divorce, from George. Daddy brought the stone back from Germany just after the war and gave it to me in a necklace. Then the necklace broke, and just after I got out of the hospital following my breakup with George, he gave me the stone back, set in this ring.

Immediately, the rings organized significant history for Evelyn which impinged upon her present circumstance. When she was five, her father returned from Germany, bringing her the necklace as a gift. It came to represent the role Evelyn played between her parents as a small girl. Just prior to his return, father had "taken up" with a young German girl and refused to accompany mother and daughter back to the States. Evelyn recalled a vivid scene in a German railway station where mother presented her, tearful and distressed, to father as the primary reason he should mend his ways and come home. Several months thereafter, he did so, bearing the gift. The reappearance of the stone in the form of a ring just after she divorced her first husband symbolized the secret pact between father and daughter across the years. Evelyn was to stay depressed and unhappy to keep father around, a task she had faithfully performed through both her marriages. Her selection of men who tended to drink heavily and become abusive only strengthened the primary bond. As she talked, Evelyn became aware of fantasies that her mother would die first, necessitating her return home to care for her aging father.

Often lockets and other artifacts can provide the same symbolism of significant life events. Connie grasped the chain around her neck while speaking of moving out and leaving her roommate. It held a locket, given her by a sister when she was 18. The two were very close. Connie described them as "huddling together to survive the family." Her decision to wear the locket on the day she considered breaking up with her roommate, who occupied a similar slot in her contemporary life, enabled her to place her current feelings within the larger context of her script program.

The cultural significance of giving rings in marriage, graduation, victory (like the Superbowl), and other occasions of passage makes them viable symbols for scripty pacts of all types. One of the most dramatic examples I have seen was a diamond engagement ring worn by Rachel. The ring was given by her grandmother at her death to Rachel's 17-year-old daughter, who wore the ring at the time of her suicide five years before Rachel came for treatment. Rachel had worn her daughter's ring ever since to represent her secret pact never to shed the guilt for her failures as a mother. The therapist does well never to ignore such significant symbols to which Identified Movements of the Child lead. Decisions to change are accompanied by decisions to remove them and get on with life, investing energy elsewhere.

Such symbols can also, on occasion, present the therapist with pleasant news of secret decisions the Child has made for positive change. Bobbie, who thought of herself as the "ugly duckling" in her family and who could never quite grow up, fingered her half-moon crescent ring as she talked about meeting a man and kissing him for the first time. Upon inquiry, she revealed she had bought the ring two weeks before with two purposes in mind. The first was to make her hands look pretty. The second was to remind herself not to bite her fingernails. The ring served to symbolize her decision to shed her "ugly duckling" identity, grow up, and adorn herself as a woman.

Dress

For certain clients, the type of selective symbolism we are considering extends to their whole pattern of dress. It is as if the Child chooses each article of clothing to express a current mood and anticipated developments in script. This is particularly true on days when there is an appointment for therapy. What is worn can serve as a veritable barometer of the life course.

Marge was such an individual. She was locked into a destructive relationship with her husband who drank heavily, disappeared from time to time, and presented her with one disappointment after another. Although Marge was highly verbal, the problem with treating her was that talk about her situation only added to her dilemma, given her penchant for drama and storytelling ("Let me tell you the latest."). She seemed oblivious to any efforts that would address the repetitive pattern in her life course. The therapist decided to interrupt her account of the present crisis to ask her to tell him about what she was wearing today. Without hesitation, Marge responded with the enthusiasm of an eight-year-old at "Show and tell," and with no further prompting revealed the following.

Shoes — "They are brown and earthy because I want to be grounded and stop flying off in every direction."

Green skirt — "The skirt is green because I *am* growing and learning and hopeful for something new in my life."

Red blouse — "That's for my mood . . . I'm angry and determined and I want to stand my ground and be substantial."

Locket — "Rad (husband) gave that to me when we were in Hawaii two years ago. It has pleasant memories that I just don't want to give up. We were happy then."

Brown macrame rope around neck — "This is sort of a . . . (pause), well, it's a rope. And I have a sense of hanging myself as I go on hoping for what isn't, and I know will never be. Not literally, I mean . . . I'd really like to hang him."

Watch, left wrist — "My father gave me this when I went away to school. It's regular and reliable. I could always count on him, provided mother wasn't around."

Engagement ring, third finger, left hand — "This is my engagement ring from Al (first husband). I really don't know why I put it on. I have been thinking a lot about him lately, although we could never go back together. I just can't wear Rad's ring, and I feel naked without one."

Jade ring, third finger, right hand — "Father gave me this after I got my first job. That was the first time I was on my own, and it helped me get over the scare of being independent."

From this, Marge and her therapist were able to discuss the current plan undergirding her life course. She had given her husband Rad enough rope to hang himself, but she was still not through reading all the lines to him that the situation merited. Her reluctance to go ahead and get a divorce was rooted in her fear of being "without a man." This followed from her long-standing dependency upon father. She had still not mastered her decision to stop being his little girl and live an independent life. Shortly thereafter, she did get the divorce, but only after initiating another male relationship equally as unpromising and abusive. She did, however, restrict this to secondary and intermittent periods of excitement while she established her own business on a firm basis for self-support without help from father. Marge and others like her keep reminding me in all my impatience of the meaning of the old phrase, "in my own good time."

Uniforms

It is possible to identify a uniform that goes with the script for many clients. It appears and reappears from time to time in concert with changes the script dictates. Or it is worn constantly in some self-same, uncompromising stance toward life. The uniform itself constitutes what Berne calls the "sweatshirt," which proclaims what the Child wants others to see on the front and conceals the secret ending on the back.[7]

Sometimes there are several uniforms for different occasions or different trends in the script. Trudy presented two distinct dress codes. The first was her "hip" style, which included daytime jeans and boots, nighttime long skirts with dirty blouses, both accompanied with stringy, unkempt hair. When she put on this uniform, young men followed her home from the movies and beat on her door in the middle of the night. In group, she acted "spacey." The second was her "little old lady suit" which appeared from time to time, composed of long black dresses, black hose and shoes, and a shawl around her shoulders. This was literally a security measure, modeled after several "little old aunts" on mother's side of the family who were too old for the dangerous missions undertaken in the first uniform. It represented her anticipated script payoff of a lonely old age. A marked change in dress accompanied her decision to hold a job and create stability in her life.

More frequently, the script uniform is a constant attire expressing an ongoing trend in an individual's life. Frank's "lawyer suit," which he wore to an evening group where others dressed casually, served to mark him off as rigid and properly intellectual. Bill's immaculate dress, careful coordination of subdued colors, and quiet lint-picking presented a flawless front that masked an inward feeling of awkwardness and tendencies to pick at himself mercilessly. "Blue collar" and "white collar" stereotypes in dress frequently accompany banal scripts which call for patterns of working hard and neglecting one's Child ego state. Colorless, unchanging attire can express limitations on feeling and spontaneity created by injunctions like "Don't be close," "Don't be a Child," and "Don't feel."

Once the therapist has learned the pattern of dress which the script dictates, an accurate barometer of its influence is present. Judy, who thought of herself as beautiful but dumb and could never trust men, wore her "Rapo uniform" to group on days that she intended to work. It consisted of a white business suit with a huge split in the skirt that continually exposed her knee and thigh to distracted onlookers whom she accused of not taking her seriously.

Often we deal with actual uniforms of one type or another. There is "the nurse" who manages to show up week after week in uniform. Or the "clerical collar" worn by persons who keep this quiet reminder of their profession present at all times. Usually, these individuals are caretakers who find refuge in their role and are at a loss for individuality and identity apart from it. Occasionally, we may encounter an anti-uniform, which is consistently chosen by persons whose script calls for them to relinquish status and authority. Art was a vivid example. He came to group dressed in combat fatigues, Bermuda shorts, grubby jeans and T-shirts, hunting clothes, and painting clothes which matched his gawky, shy, and unassertive demeanor. "I'd never guess in a million years," observed one group member, "that you are a Colonel in the United States Army."

Paraphernalia

Conspicuously displayed paraphernalia that accompany persons to treatment are often script signs. This includes a list of personal belongings often associated with dress that require considerable effort to ignore. Some brief clinical notes about them are in order.

1) Pockets filled with pencils, pads, and other instruments of trade are usually displayed by persons who have excluding Adult ego states. Their penchant for objectivity and detachment protects them from emotional contact. The bulging left pocket with tools of their profession over the heart may symbolize injunctions against feeling and fear of emotional expressions approaching intimacy.

2) Large key rings are worn by caretakers and rescuers who thrive on responsibility. Characteristically, they had to grow up quickly and provide for the needs of others. They are often workaholics and tend toward depression when "out from under" the continual task of managing things. Earl sat in group, listening to others review their change contracts, jiggling a large ring of keys in his hands. His wife complained that he had not been with the family for two weeks with all the trouble he had at work. When someone called attention to the keys,

Earl held them out, saying, "Do you want the responsibilities that go with them?"

3) Knitting needles and books occasionally come to group, more frequently in extended, marathon settings. They are always significant. Knitters and readers are usually female, busy-bee types, who are devoted to self-improvement and the accomplishment of something worthwhile all the time. Barbara, who read during all breaks in an extended group session, had lived with a sense of being abandoned ever since she was a little girl. When she recreated an early scene at home, she sat alone in the corner, looking at a book while her parents fought bitterly.

4) Assortments of nasal mist, Kleenex, cough drops, inhalers, and other home remedies are not unusual paraphernalia in group. Some people never leave home without them. The only ready source of positive stroking as they grew up may have been near the medicine cabinet. Staying sick keeps someone around.

5) Snackers usually evidence a similar pattern of dependency. Their mothers always sent them to school with a packed lunch. The mother in their head sends them to group the same way. An important distinction lies between the sharers and the privates. Private eaters are isolates and stroke-deprived.

6) Glasses are sometimes significant script paraphernalia. Women who hang them around their necks on a chain or lanyard are "schoolmarm" types. Some people have a sense of hiding behind their glasses, particularly the tinted type. They remove them for spontaneous emotional displays from their free Child.

7) Headbands, auditor's shades, and the like are worn by persons who have a fear of their heads' splitting apart. Often these individuals are noteworthy for their splitting headaches.

8) Cigarettes provide equally important paraphernalia for many people. In such cases, the pattern of reaching for another one bears examination. If we can get beyond denial ("It's time for another"), the individual will usually report an awareness of emotional excitation. The momentary distraction of lighting up and puffing reduces excitement, just as it dulls taste and smell. In many cases, the smoking pattern curtails strong feelings, both positive and negative. This can be observed in the two major "cons" the smoker uses when "trying to quit." Either things are so difficult at the moment that one cigarette won't hurt, or things are so good at the moment that one won't hurt. The more elaborate procedures surrounding pipe-smoking have a time-honored effect in reducing unruly emotional impulses. The ancient tradition of smoking the "peace pipe" preserves the notion that reduced excitement enhances communication and the capacity to engage in difficult negotiations.

Invading the Mundane

A fundamental principle of invading the mundane undergirds all the interventions we make with script signs we have been considering, whether they are sequentia! postures, gestural displays, paralinguistic expressions, or their verbal first cousins, an individual's dress or movements to fiddle with rings and things. Everything that is significant from the past is present in the here and now. What is important about early scenes which shaped decisions about our destiny is the repetitious, seemingly habitual way we recreate them with similar feelings and results over and over again. The type of therapy I am presenting is not so much concerned with hidden traumas or the secrets of an individual's personal closet as it is with the everyday manner in which we perpetuate formative experiences and embellish them with countless nuances across time. The most effective interventions we undertake come through invading the mundane, routine movements and behaviors of our clients. Whatever the value of insight into how they got that way, change is made by altering these precise movements and behaviors in the present through awareness and their own free choice.

REFERENCE NOTES

1. Steiner, C. *Scripts People Live*. New York: Grove Press, 1974, pp. 257, 258. Berne, E. *What Do You Say After You Say Hello?* New York: Grove Press, 1971, pp. 334-337. Steere, D., Freud on the "gallows" transaction. *Transactional Analysis Bulletin, 9*:3-5, 1970.
2. Berne, E. *What Do You Say After You Say Hello?* p. 332.
3. Stein, J., and Urdang, L. (eds.). *The Random House Dictionary of the English Language*. New York: Random House, 1967, p. 1415.
4. Berne, E. *What Do You Say After You Say Hello?* p. 332.
5. Frank, J. S. Adapted child and critical parent. *Transactional Analysis Journal, 4*:8, 1974.
6. Freud, S. The psychopathology of everyday life. In Brill, A. A. (ed.). *The Basic Writings of Sigmund Freud*. New York: The Modern Library, p. 137.
7. Berne, E. *What Do You Say After You Say Hello?* pp. 176-180.

10

Bodily behavior and change

"It is incredible to think, at first," wrote Berne, "that man's fate, all his nobility and all his degradation, is decided by a child no more than six years old, and usually three, but that is what script theory claims."[1] The central decision that governs the script—to be this way and not another—is made too early in life, long before we have all the information and resources we need. It is made with the logic of a small child which remains remote to the kind of contemporary thinking we do as grownups. The notion that one has been scripted to live a certain way always possesses an air of unreality to the Adult. The script exists quietly disguised beneath the routine of denied awareness dictating personal destiny. In psychotherapy, we must encourage the Little Professor in the Child to tell us about it, while the Adult listens and the Parent is forbidden to object.

When we begin to work with persons for specific changes they desire, we are thrust into the task of interfering with behavior patterns of long standing. Sometimes an individual is satisfied through learning to change from a troublesome ego state to a more favorable one in situations that cause difficulty. In such instances, we work toward a *functional change* among that person's existing ego states. More often, there is a desire to alter the troublesome ego state itself in search of more durable well-being. Here we work for a *structural change* within ego states where the life script is vested. Whatever the change, it will be directly observable in the way people live and move and have their being. Functional change is marked by an altered posture, different movement behavior, and the absence of ulterior, dystonic signaling. Structural change is accompanied by the disappearance of script signs.

THE SCRIPTED CHILD

Our earliest thinking, from birth to 18 months according to Piaget, is in the form of sensorimotor schemes.[2] We devise mental processes to make movements, to reach out and grasp things, to put them in our mouth, to crawl, to look at objects and persons, to learn to walk, etc. Our first experience in life is kinesthetic as we master the range of bodily movements necessary to seek and receive care and to move about the world. During this time the child constructs all the cognitive substructures that will serve as a point of departure for later perceptual and intellectual development, together with the elementary affective reactions that inform emotional life. There are no conceptual schemes corresponding to these sensorimotor ones, so they are developed without the benefit of representations common to later thought. If the reader wishes an illlustration, try to explain to someone how you pick up your pencil.

Sensorimotor Schemes

With sensorimotor schemes we begin a lifelong process of adapting to each new situation in life. Adaptation, for Piaget, involves 1) accommodating ourselves to the demands of a new task by developing the skills required to accomplish it, or 2) assimilating new problems within the stock of mechanisms we already possess. We learn to suck, bite and chew to satisfy the demands of hunger. Accommodations may require periods of trial and experimentation, as in learning to walk. But once a scheme becomes well adapted, it no longer poses problems of mastery, and we cease to engage in repetitive, schematic action toward it.

The force of this study supports Piaget's observation that the sensorimotor adaptations of infancy are not replaced by later, more conceptual or cognitive ones. Sensorimotor schemes continue to develop throughout childhood, becoming more adapted and skillful. They persist alongside newer, more intellectual ways of dealing with problems, quite independently. This provides the best explanation for the enduring character of landmarks in bodily behavior which we observe to accompany significant adaptations made by the Child. Recurrent hand-to-mouth gestures, for example, appear in the midst of abstract thinking about situations in adult life. Repetitive gestural and postural displays developed at an earlier age emerge as kinesic markers to similar themes in the present.

Only on occasion do we experience the toilsome process of developing new sensorimotor schemes as adults, when, for example, we learn to drive a car or swing a golf club with accuracy. Even then, learning is not so much a matter of developing new reflexes as it is a process of assimilation in which newly established mechanisms are integrated into existing schemes of movement. Once these behaviors are mastered, they slip quietly from awareness and remain as kinesic skills without conscious attention to specific movements. The remoteness of sensorimotor thinking from ordinary Adult cognition is witnessed in the type of concentration on a whole pattern of movement sought by the professional athlete who must avoid self-defeating awareness of a particular part of his or her body. This accounts for all kinds of mind-emptying techniques, meditation, concentration rituals, superstition, and magical thinking employed to avoid conscious awareness of the elements of a swing, permitting the body to take over and hit the ball. The slumps and errors that accompany conscious correctional thought are well-known.

Piaget describes the process of assimilation during the sensorimotor period (birth to 18 months) in which the infant acquires a whole system of exchanges with others through imitation and the reading of gestural signs.[3] This happens even before the formation of a "self" complementary to and interacting with others. Spontaneous movements made by the child give rise to "reflexive exercises" that are consolidated in schemes through functional exercise. The child first repeats a gesture in response to someone's performing a gesture the child has made. Later, any gesture made by an adult may be imitated, provided that sometime before, this gesture has been made by the child in exercise play. Still later, the child can reproduce models of bodily behavior for the sake of reproduction itself. Then the child becomes able to copy new gestures, but only if they are performed by a visible part of the body. Not until the end of the sensorimotor period is representation in action liberated from the requirements of direct perceptual copy and a new phase of imitating facial movements begun.

In this fashion, the child begins to react to other persons in an increasingly specific manner. Soon a kind of primitive causality is established, linking movement behavior to the responses others make, inasmuch as the child's actions produce pleasure, comfort, pacification, and security. Piaget differs from behaviorists by insisting that a conditioned reflex is never stabilized by the force of its associations alone. The formation of a scheme of assimilation is necessary, in which the result attained satisfies the need inherent in the situation. Although Piaget distinguishes between cognitive and affective aspects of behavior and is primarily interested in the cognitive, he points out that emotions constitute "the energetics of behavior patterns, whose structures correspond to cognitive functions," and "neither one can function without the other."[4] Escalona suggests that what Piaget proposes for cognition is true in all adaptive aspects of mental functioning.[5] The emergence of such functions as communication, modulation of affect, control over excitation, delay, and aspects of identification with others are all the result of a developmental sequence in sensorimotor terms, before they can emerge as ego functions in the narrower sense.

The Pre-operational Period

The script is formed in the Child ego state during what Piaget calls the pre-operational period, roughly from ages two to seven. In the course of the first 18 months, the child has undergone a type of "Copernican revolution" through the discovery of permanent objects, the structures of space and time, and "magical" notions of causality in which the contiguity of two events is sufficient to make them appear causally related. Now as children we regard ourselves as an "object" among other "objects" in a universe made up of permanent objects. This "decentering" of initial experience, in which there was no consciousness of self or boundary between the internal and external world, eventually gives way to seeing other persons as subjects who have their own views to be differentiated from and reconciled to ours, marking entry into a social universe.

The pre-operational period is one of transition from the earlier sensorimotor schemes to cognitive ones. Gradually, we acquire simple sets of operational schemes related by laws of groups or groupings ("These are pencils; those are not"). We learn to talk by imitating sounds and slowly gaining the syntax required for grammatical structures. Language is tied to behavioral schemes. If water is running in the bathroom, "Daddy is shaving." If it runs in the kitchen, "Mommy is cooking."

What is important for our purposes is that sensorimotor structures constitute the source of all later operations of thought. Intelligence proceeds from action as a whole, transforming reality through active operatory assimilation. Perception, for example, develops as a "special case" of sensorimotor activity in which we picture an object mentally in the midst of activities to find or transform it. We learn to talk and gesture to further the completion of tasks in which we are engaged.

What Piaget calls the semiotic (or symbolic) function now appears, and we gain the ability to represent something (an object, event, or conceptual scheme) by means of a signifier. By the second year, the child may engage in representative evocation of an object or event not present. There is deferred imitation which starts after the disappearance of the model, as when a little boy screams and stamps his foot after a playmate does. Symbolic play brings games of pretending to be asleep or putting a stuffed animal to bed, evidencing both imitative gestures and deferred signifiers. By two-and-a-half, the drawing of graphic images is observed as an intermediate stage between play and the formation of mental images. Mental images are the result of internalized imitations evoking sights previously perceived, and then envisaging movements and their results not previously observed. Their prototype is seen neurologically, according to Piaget, when an imagined bodily movement is accompanied by the same pattern of electrical waves, whether cortical (EEG) or muscular (EMG), as the execution of that movement, suggesting that an imagined movement involves a kind of internal sketch of itself.[6] Finally, language is acquired in the context of imitation, constituting the transition between sensorimotor schemes and the level of behavior that is properly called representative. Language permits evocation of events that are not occurring at the time, like a "meow" after the cat has disappeared or a statement that someone "went bye-bye."

With the mastery of deferred imitation, representation is freed from sensorimotor requirements of direct perceptual copy. Symbols become capable of generalization, hence imitation is no longer merely deferred but internalized. Through symbolic play and drawing, this transition from representation in action to representation purely in thought is reinforced. Language finally overlaps the whole process, providing much more effective contact with people than that achieved by mere imitation alone.

The symbolic schemes formed during the pre-operational period are of great importance to later life. Take symbolic play, for example. Children must constantly adapt to the social world of elders whose interests and rules remain external to them and which they understand only slightly. We cannot satisfy affective or intellectual needs through these adaptations. Play is essential to assimilate reality to the self without coercions or sanctions. Through symbolic play, needs for self-expression are met and a system of signifiers constructed, capable of being bent by our own wishes. Exercise play is its most primitive form at the sensorimotor level and is retained in part through the repetition of activities acquired elsewhere for the pure pleasure of it. Symbolic play is an assimilation made possible by a symbolic "language" that is developed by the self and is capable of being modified according to our needs. It fulfills the function of what, for the Adult, would be internal dialogue. Rather than simply recalling an interesting or impressive event, children possess symbols which enable them to relive the event. Affective conflicts appear primarily in symbolic play. A scene at the dinner table may be recreated an hour or two afterward with dolls and brought to a happier solution. Through symbolic play, conflicts are resolved; compensation is made for unsatisfied needs; roles of obedience and authority are inverted, and the self is extended through liberation from the requirements of reality. The semiotic function is put to the particular use of expressing everything in the child's life experience that cannot be formulated and assimilated by language alone.

Piaget notes that many of the symbolic schemes of the pre-operational peri-od remain private, idiosyncratic, and more or less incommunicable. They stand in contrast to verbal schemes which are subject to interpretation, correc-tion, and modification as they are socialized. The schemes of symbolic play, for example, are devised precisely because existing language cannot address the processes they comprehend. Our private symbolic schemes are especially im-portant in our emotional lives and interpersonal relations. The pre-operational period is a perceptual-intuitive period in which we feel our way through to solu-tions without conceptual representations to evaluate how. Conceptual modes of thinking that develop later are by no means superior. In fact, Piaget observes that in such areas of life as the artistic and the socio-emotional, our conceptual understandings often prove so poor that an intellectual approach fails, while a more intuitive approach succeeds.[7] Recognition of the same phenomenon led Berne to describe the Adult (A_1) in the Child as the "Little Professor" who at age four knows more psychiatry than the most learned professor can learn in a life-time.[8]

Much has been written in the literature of developmental psychology about the period we are discussing. Freud saw the development of psychic energy around states of biological excitation in the organism: first, an oral stage; then, an anal stage; then, a phallic stage.[9] In each of these, the child centers growth and interaction with others in activities surrounding the bodily orifice. Erikson characterized each of these stages as formative of lifelong emotional trends in the individual, engendering a sense of basic trust versus mistrust, autonomy versus doubt and shame, and initiative versus guilt.[10] Berne locates the origin of the protocol that governs the life script in the same period.

Concrete and Formal Operations

Whatever the development of our mental picture during the pre-operational period, it is with none of the tools of conceptual thinking we take for granted as adults. Between the ages of seven and 11, we learn to think in *concrete opera-tions*. Cognition becomes focused upon mastering size, orders, numbers, space arrangement, classes and subclasses. Piaget terms these operations "concrete" because they relate directly to objects and not yet to verbally stated hypotheses. Objects are arranged into groupings marked by coherence ("These are boxes"), cloture ("Those are not"), and reversibility ("I had three, but now I have one"). By eight years of age, children can learn the rules of games (like marbles) and submit to them in cooperative play with others. It is a busy period in which Erikson characterizes our developmental task as establish-ing a sense of industry versus inferiority.[11] Our learning remains concrete as we discover the world around ("This is how you add," "Wear your tie," "Behave to get approval"). Conceptually, we master an understanding of relationships among operational groupings like kinfolks and neighbors, Americans and foreigners, the birds and the bees.

Not until after we are 11 do we develop the capacity to engage in what Piaget calls *formal operations.* Formal operations are marked by the ability to understand the laws of causal thinking, to deduce the implications of propositions, and to grasp the principles underlying logical thought. One can now free oneself from the concrete and locate reality within a group of possible transformations. This liberation of thought permits the handling of hypotheses and reasoning with regard to propositions removed from present observation. Whereas concrete operations preserve the immediacy of the situation in which one learns ("Freedom is not being told what to do"), formal operations follow rules of logic and are based upon a growing capacity to think abstractly about concepts and principles ("Freedom of speech involves freedom of the press").

With propositional operations comes the spontaneous development of a questioning or experimental spirit. Reality is no longer considered in its limited and concrete aspects but in terms of some or all of its possible combinations. With formal operations comes the capacity to transcend oneself and address the future. This new perspective poses us with the developmental task Erikson characterizes as achieving a sense of identity (persistent self-sameness) versus confusion.[12] With newfound principles, we may create our own ideals and values and question authorities. Only with the logic of formal operations can one challenge the inconsistency in being beaten as a child for striking a sibling. Not until adolescence does the Adult ego state emerge with the capacity to reflect critically upon our experience. By then, the scripted Child is quietly structuring our experience, with its primitive protocol of private symbolic schemes and archaic logic, in ways remote to our rational awareness.

Memory

When the Adult (A_2 as we have designated it) comes to psychotherapy, it is without effective ways to think about the mental schemes that shape our formative experience. Symbolic schemes are addressed for which the individual has never formed conceptual or rational understanding. As language skills are refined throughout grown-up life, they become progressively detached from the sensorimotor schemes of childhood. Sensorimotor schemes are obliged to follow events without exceeding the speed of action. Verbal patterns, by means of narration and evocation, can represent long chains of actions very rapidly.

Sensorimotor adaptations are limited to immediate space and time, while language enables thought to range over vast stretches of time and space, separating it from the immediacy of action and contact. Sensorimotor intelligence remains embedded in successive (and repetitive) acts, step by step, while language thought can represent simultaneously all the elements of an organized structure. As our proficiency in language grows, we function cognitively with others in ways increasingly removed from our memory of the experiences that shaped our life course in the scripted Child.

Bandler and Grinder have isolated common measures undertaken by successful psychotherapists by examining their use of language in the treatment room.[13] The client begins with a *surface structure* statement of the presenting problem (syntax) which follows particular patterns, forming sentences to describe a *deeper structure* of thinking based upon a *meta-model* of the world constructed from an individual's own unique life experience. Every psychotherapist faces the task of accessing with the client what lies beneath this surface structure of language, filled with generalizations, deletions, and distortions. Take Leta, for example, whom we discussed in Chapter 4 on Interventions. She began with the complaint, "I am flunking out of nursing school because I can't get everything done." Regardless of theoretical perspective, successful therapy takes shape around a conversation that encourages Leta to construct a "fully-formed sentence" about her dilemma. There is the generalization of "everything" to be done that requires exploring. There is the deletion of specific things Leta is doing that result in "flunking." And the notion that she "can't" complete her work is a distortion, because her past grades have been excellent. A "fully-formed sentence in therapy" for Leta might sound something like this:

> When I start to study, I am preoccupied with panic at the thought of returning home to care for my alcoholic father when I finish, so I start distracting myself with errands and conversations with friends, producing failures in my preparation for examinations, which interrupt my plans by causing me not to graduate.

Through repeated use of linguistic skills, the psychotherapist can gain access to the meta-model in the deeper structures of Leta's thought, exposing a pattern of frantic efforts to please demanding authority figures (like father), while denying her own needs and wants. The result is panic and failure, which free her from the obligation to comply ("I can't"). This meta-model which governs her present experience is a relatively enduring pattern of behavior constructed from concrete experiences in her past. Beneath it is the *formative experience* in a series of events which we think of as her *memory*.

Precisely what constitutes memory is a subject of much discussion among developmentalists.[14] For Freud, memories accumulate in the unconscious where they are forgotten and remain ready to be evoked. Janet viewed the act of remembering as a reconstruction comparable to that carried out by a historian through testimony, inferences, and the like. Penfield's experiments on the reactivation of memories by electrical stimulation of the temporal lobes point to a high degree of conservation of the original experience, but numerous observations of the existence of false, but vivid, memories suggest that reconstruction also plays a part.[15]

For Piaget, the memory of a scheme is the scheme itself.[16] What is termed memory, when rid of the remnants of faculty psychology, is the figurative aspect of the system of schemes as a whole, from elementary sensorimotor schemes, in which the figurative aspect is perceptual recognition, to the highest schemes, whose figurative representations exist as pure image-memories. The mental images of the child at the pre-operatory level are almost exclusively static. Not until the stage of concrete operations are children capable of reproducing movements and transformations. Memories always exist in connection with enduring schemes of action, like climbing a tree and falling. Piaget emphasizes the importance of motor or operatory elements at all levels of memory. The image which occurs in image-memory constitutes an internalized imitation, which also includes a motor element of action toward a chosen outcome. The conservation of particular memories can easily be reconciled with elements of reinterpretation and reconstruction within the context of a developing scheme.

When we address the client's life script, we of necessity address an archaic protocol developed in the pre-operatory period. Its mental schemes defy simple conceptualization through formal operations. Elements of memory accompanying its inception consist of fleeting images that are static and laden with private symbolic meaning that has been more or less incommunicable. For this reason, the motor aspects that accompany scripty behavior are invaluable sources of knowledge about its schematic organization. They preserve the movement pattern accompanying the early adaptation to which so much other experience has been added that verbal and visual aspects of memory fail us.

These primitive schemes have the character of what Piaget calls a circular reaction that results when the child's initial efforts at accommodating some new situation are interrupted or incomplete. The child will repeatedly exercise the scheme that has been developed in efforts to complete and master the demands of the situation. The result is a self-reinforcing behavior pattern then generalized through assimilating new situations evidencing similarity, until one loses sight of the original goal or need to be satisfied in repeating the protocol.

Recurrent life problems, such as Leta's difficulties in handling her father's demands, possess the character of circular reactions which must be broken for change to occur. Self-reinforcing repetition of efforts to complete an original task continue in the manner in which it was interrupted, even after the original purpose of the behavior disappears from awareness. This was more evident in Leta's motor behavior surrounding her efforts to deal with her father than in any other aspect of her system of mental representations. As she addressed her father (in the chair), the right side of her body became limp and motionless while she made repetitive, frantic gestures from her left, attempting to placate his demands. The one-sidedness of her movement behavior represented at the sensorimotor level an early decision to abandon autonomous efforts to stand up to him with self-assertiveness and anger. This left her with a one-sided trend toward nurturing and placating significant others. Awareness of the uncompleted task came at the same level of motor experience through elevating and activating movement in her right side, rather than through verbal and visual representations.

If the memory of a scheme is the scheme itself, then the act of remembering is potentially much greater than a simple act of recall. Instead of thinking about formative events, a person can think "from inside" of the schematic process of their formation itself. This is greatly enhanced by adding the dimension of concrete action to the process of remembering, as, for example, encouraging Leta to address her father directly in an empty chair. A dimension of symbolic play from the pre-operational period is added, which is the essence of psychodrama. The child does this naturally, reenacting and reliving events with the potential of bringing about more favorable solutions. In Leta's case, this involved establishing awareness of her suppressed anger and assertiveness through movement play from the right side of her body. It led to experimentation with self-assertion in the safer setting of therapy play, where unresolved situations from the world around can be brought to a more desirable outcome. In such instances, the act of re-membering involves a kind of rejoining of lost parts to a whole pattern of behavior that brings mastery in terms of completion, satiation, and closure.

Memory, then, is accessible to this form of mastery through concrete acts of remembering that involve us in the schemes it represents. And symbolic play by the Child becomes the medium for resolution of the script. Redecision therapy, as we have described it, is predicated upon this phenomenon, namely, the capacity of an individual to cathect the Child ego state and reenter formative scenes with sufficient affect as to relive them in some measure, deciding to do things differently.

The act of re-membering such experiences involves two elements. There must be entry into the formation of the scheme itself through a substantial recovery of the sensory experience surrounding it. The individual must see what he or she was forbidden to see. The individual must feel what he or she wanted to do. The individual must hear or say what went unvoiced. Second, the continuing grip of an unsatisfactory resolution must be broken as the individual addresses it full-grown, with all the present resources that were not available when the initial protocol was formed. What was unsaid can now be said out loud. What went unseen can now be seen clearly, along with all the alternatives that became visible. What the individual was unable to do can now be done to completion and satisfaction. Changing the memory scheme involves changing the structure of the Child ego state. Through such remembering, we change the memory itself.

CHANGE AND MOVEMENT

We are now ready to discuss changes in bodily behavior as they relate to the overall task of achieving the type of changes we seek in psychotherapy. Thus far I have avoided the use of the term *cure*. The word itself falls victim to multiple meanings among its users in the helping professions.[17] These meanings can be sorted easily into two piles. One involves definitions of *cure* as the attainment of a specific change desired by the individual in treatment, expressed in a contract based upon a realistic goal. The other surrounds more general definitions of the word, such as "the reconstruction of personality" or "the achievement of healthy functioning," which are prone to perfectionistic endlessness among therapists who want to cure everybody of everything. Berne used the word liberally to distinguish between therapists who cure their patients and therapists whose patients "make progress."[18] Cure was always specific, whether it be of a sore throat, an irrational fear, the inability to hold a job, or a marital problem. The process of getting well may bring more general change, and Berne could compare cure metaphorically to casting off the frog skin and taking up once more the interrupted development of the prince or princess.[19] But cure itself was always specific, as represented in his well-known analogy of the man with a splinter in his toe who began to limp, tightening leg muscles, back muscles, neck and skull muscles, getting a headache, developing a fever, etc.[20] The effective therapist finds the splinter and removes it.

Specific changes in bodily behavior that accompany cure can be classified into two broad categories. There are changes in movement patterns that accompany a judicious change from one ego state to another. An alteration of postural and gestural displays can be both the means to and the measure of the process of changing from one ego state to another. Since this type of change involves a shift in cathexis among the client's repertoire of existing ego states, it is termed *functional change*. The type of change we have been considering among the pattern of schemes in the scripted Child is of a different order. We term it *structural change* since it represents a reorganization of that ego state itself through redecision and the creation of options within its own boundaries.

Functional Change

Our earliest video research established clearly a person's capacity to interrupt self-defeating cycles of behavior through the concrete act of changing from one ego state to another. Alpha, for example, whom we discussed in Chapter 3, interrupted the process of driving herself into failures and ending up sad and hopeless by becoming aware of her movement behavior, consciously altering her posture to come on Adult. Increased numbers of Identified Movements were evident among subjects in group therapy who were changing in the direction of fulfilling their treatment contracts. There was a measurable redistribution of this movement behavior toward ego states more favorable to their purposes.

Concrete functional change in the way a person invests energy among existing ego states may accompany the structural changes of script redecision, or stand quite independently of them as a result of conscious decisions to abandon game or racket behavior in specific situations. One of the more measurable evidences of functional change is the disappearance of bodily duplicity. Protrusions cease to interrupt the natural flow of existing ego states. Simple divisions give way to a balanced and full expression of movement and affect. Certain patterns of enactment gesturing subside as free movement from denied ego states is permitted and given full sway. Dystonic signals from an ulterior ego state also disappear through conscious acts of attending them and a shifting of cathexis into other ego states of one's choice. Other forms of duplicity such as restraint, attachment, and denial usually require redecision and exploration of options by the scripted Child, as do those signal behaviors that are part of the pattern of script signs.

In clinical practice, there are a number of instances when work for functional change is the treatment of choice, and therapists who do not operate with some concept of the client's changing from one ego state to another are at a decided disadvantage. Depression is one instance. The person who is depressed is not amenable to the normal processes of psychotherapy. Efforts to be supportive and nurturing seldom help and usually result in the client's getting worse and the therapist's becoming depressed, too. The more the depressed person talks, the greater the hopelessness. Before the roots of the problem may be considered, the depression itself must be broken through concrete action.

I learned procedures for breaking depression one night from Emma, who sat

on the couch, her shoulders slumped forward, her brow knit with perpendicular furrows, and her eyes dark and hollow. We tried to conduct group around
her for about 30 minutes until Barbara broke the awkward barrier of Emma's
withdrawal by saying she could not help noticing how "down" she looked.
"Just go on," responded Emma, "I don't feel like working tonight."

With depressed persons, I had always wondered, "How depressed?" The
answers to such a question were always disappointing, nondescript, and singu-
larly unhelpful—"awfully depressed," "terribly depressed," "It's bad." For
some reason that escapes me, I was more resourceful on this particular night
and sought to establish the extent of her depression in the following manner.

> Therapist: Zero is as far down as you have ever been, and ten is as happy
>   as you have ever been. Pick a number to represent where you are.
> Emma: About three.

I have since learned to establish the numerical evaluation of the depression
exactly (2.8? 3.2?). This serves to strengthen the person's commitment to
quantifying experience. All that occurred to me at this point was to establish the
direction in which Emma was moving. When I learned that it was downward,
the opportunity was present to explore her anticipation.

> Therapist: What would have to happen for you to go down to a two?
> Emma: I'd come to group, sit here and say nothing, and leave feeling that
>   nobody could help me.
> Therapist: And from a two down to a one?
> Emma: I'd go home, and nobody would call. I'd be all alone Friday night
>   and have nothing on for the whole weekend. I'd stay in bed and not
>   cook Saturday or Sunday.
> Therapist: And from a one down to a zero?
> Emma: I'd get a call that mother was worse, and I'd know we will never
>   iron out our differences before she dies.

At this point, I was preoccupied with the discovery that we had exposed, step
by step, Emma's plan for a full-blown depression. It was Barbara across the
room who somehow observed the significance of what had happened and interrupted to ask, "What number are you at now?"

"I'm a four," responded Emma dispassionately. The only reason Barbara
could give for her question was that Emma suddenly looked different to her. Of
course, she did. She had made a Trunk Shift and sat up for the first time. Her
head was leveled upon her shoulders, and the thin whine had gone out of her
voice. The theoretical reason did not come until several days later. Since quan-

tifying is an Adult function, Emma had decathected her depressed Child ego state and for 20 seconds transcended her depression to function in her Adult. And if she can do it for 20 seconds, why not two minutes, 20 minutes, two hours? This is the concrete process through which a depression may be broken. Persons who do not knowledgeably or intuitively work with ego-state changes will miss the process of such functional change.

> Therapist: What will have to happen for you to go from a four to a five?
> Emma: I would have to go home and call somebody and have something to do Friday night.
> Therapist: And from a five to a six?
> Emma: I would have to get up Saturday morning and have my hair done and have some plans for the day.
> Therapist: And from a six to a seven?
> Emma: I could call my mother and ask how she is and maybe tell her I'm thinking about her.

That's enough (seven). We don't go for ten and "happy, happy, happy" when breaking a depression. What is important for our purposes is that specific changes in Emma's posture and movement behavior accompany such procedures and can serve as our most reliable indicator that these procedures are being met with success. The numbers and the quantifying are secondary and simply one among any number of procedures that may be undertaken to assist a depressed person to change ego states and assume Adult functions of concrete planning and constructive action. Whatever we do, we must avoid the pitfalls of prolonged discussion of why a person is depressed and must actively cathect the Adult to do something. Those persons who systematically reject such measures and are no longer able to care for themselves may require hospitalization. With pseudo-compliant clients, whose subtle resistance is difficult to determine, bodily behavior provides the most accurate measure of successful intervention.

With other clinical problems, such as acute anxiety, functional change to another ego state permits clients to address an anxiety-producing situation from a different vantage point outside of the existing schemes of the traumatic one. Jill, whom we discussed in Chapter 7, provides a good example. Her anxiety surrounding the memory of being locked in a closet while her parents fought was so great that she responded with panic and pronounced hyperventilation. A change in ego states was effected by encouraging her to switch representational systems (from kinesthetic to visual) and describe a movie of the scene on the wall for everyone to watch.

Sometimes a change in ego states is better undertaken through direct measures which alter bodily posture and induce states of relaxation. Desensitization techniques developed by behavioral therapists that direct clients to visualize a hierarchy of anxiety-producing situations from a state of deep relaxation antithetical to their anxiety operate on this principle. Bob and Mary Goulding report success in treating phobias using the same procedure, particularly when followed immediately by concrete action (like climbing the barn ladder) in the feared situation.[21] Bandler and Grinder have recently described such procedures as a visual/kinesthetic dissociation.[22] Traumatic scenes are visualized in a kinesthetic state different from the one normally accompanying their memory, which, from our perspective, constitutes functional change to a different ego state.

Structural Change

We reserve the term *structural change* to designate basic changes in existing schemes within the scripted Child itself. Cure at this level involves a change in the memory schemes that govern the life course. It is accompanied by a disappearance of script signs that exist as kinesic markers to the formative experiences from which the script protocol was constructed. Numerous examples have been considered in the previous chapters. Recurrent gestural displays of restraint, attachment, or denial give way to Identified Movement of a different kind at points of impasse. Physiological components of the script disappear. Colitis stops; dark cloudy eyes clear; sniffling ceases; skin color evens; muscles that chronically contract in tension relax, and so on.

Again, these bodily behaviors serve both as a means to and a measure of the changes sought in treatment. The exploration of protective postures leads directly to formative scenes where protection became necessary, and experimentation with decidedly different movement in threatening situations serves as evidence of change. Not only do scripted postures preserve the essential response clients made to an injunction; experimentation with polar opposite in posture and gesture points the way to cure. Diminutive posturing gives way to postures that are expansive. Discordant postures indicate movements that reclaim a natural grace and beauty, surrendered at some point in development. Passive posturing suggests the need for energized movement long neglected or forbidden.

Sequences of postural shifting preserve an essential rhythm of movement undergirding the way the script program is lived out. Those who engage in repetitive side-to-side shifting avoid lasting contact with others and evidence change when they make appropriate movements toward others for intimacy and away from others for protection. Forward-backward shifters change when they interrupt their repetitive concert of frustrating effort and surrender, learning to be "forward" and "laid back" with others. Those who shift to side-arrest change by ending their resignation and reaching out to touch and be touched. A similar rhythm of relating is present in gestural displays that serve as script signs. Repetitive hand-to-mouth gestures, for example, point the way to unresolved issues surrounding needs for nurture and care. Gestalt therapists characterize such behaviors as *retroflexion* in which persons do to themselves what they wish to do to others or wish others would do to them.[23] Change involves movement outward into the world around in search of the real thing.

Common to all these changes is an element of mastery in which what was originally a natural striving, interrupted at some point in development, is now recovered and completed. The circular pattern of an unsatisfying scheme governing the script is broken, and optional behaviors become possible through measures that restore functional wholeness. Sensorimotor schemes surrounding the script are especially important because they preserve the formative process of the script protocol in concrete bodily behavior and repetitive sequences of activity. This embodiment in action permits a reentry into the memory scheme itself in a way long lost to fleeting mental images and verbal remnants of a schematic process for which there is no cognitive conceptualization. The result is a change in the memory scheme itself through encouraging the scripted Child ego state to master what the injunction prohibited, in a way that brings satisfaction, completion, and closure.

Those who are familiar with Gestalt therapy will notice this mastery has the character of completing an unfinished Gestalt. Polster likens the innate hunger of the human organism for resolution of that which is unfinished to an apocryphal story attributed to Bach (or Handel? or Haydn?).[24] As Bach readied himself for bed, a friend playing the clavichord downstairs ended the piece abruptly on a dominant chord. In those days, dominant chords were always resolved by the tonic and final chord. The aged maestro tossed sleeplessly in his bed and could not rest until he went downstairs and completed the piece with the necessary tonic chord.

MODELS FOR SCRIPT CURE

Three models for intervention at the level of script cure exist in the literature of transactional analysis. There is the classical model of *permission* advanced by Berne and Claude Steiner.[25] There is the *redecision* model developed by Bob and Mary Goulding, which I have favored throughout this work.[26] And there is the process of *reparenting* practiced by Jacqui Schiff and her associates at the Cathexis Institute.[27] Although they initially appear to be very different, successful interventions with each of these models lend themselves well to the mastery of the memory schemes we have been discussing.

Permission

In the classical approach, Berne and Steiner emphasize what the Child has been told to do by parents and concentrate upon framing permissions to disobey script injunctions. Quite unexplainably, when Berne came to discuss cure at this level, he occupied himself largely with auditory representations of the script. The parental voice was like that of a ventriloquist, taking charge of the person's vocal apparatus. Unless the Adult steps in, the individual follows these instructions, and the Child acts exactly like a ventriloquist's dummy, blindly obeying an injunction as if responding to an electrode. Since the common pathway of the patient's behavior is determined by voices in his head, cure always involves "getting another voice into his head, that of the therapist."[28]

New commands by the therapist constitute specific *permissions* or license to disobey destructive parental directives. Permissions require careful wording to avoid any "legal loopholes" for which the Little Professor in the Child will inevitably search. They must be timed at points of readiness when the client's Child is listening and the therapist has the complete cooperation of the client's Adult. Permission must be delivered with *potency*, because at that moment the therapist is attempting to be more powerful than the client's own parent who delivered the injunction and the client's Child must believe the therapist is powerful enough to offer security in the face of parental wrath. Permission also involves offering the client *protection* during that time when the parental injunction is being disobeyed and the Child often feels alone and terrified and in an existential vacuum. Therapists must make themselves available for support and reassurance during the period when clients are experimenting with alternatives to the old pattern of the script.

Redecision

In the redecision model, clients are encouraged to involve themselves actively in the memory schemes of their scripted Child. Frequently this is an early scene from childhood in which the client had the same problem that is now being presented from contemporary life. The therapist's task is to assist in creating an environment in which the person can cathect this Child ego state and feel intensely the same feelings present in the formative experience. The situation is carefully reconstructed so that it can be experienced vividly in terms of place, participants, and affect. Although it is often a scene from early life preserved through mental images, the Gouldings stress that the same experience is possible with a present scene, a recent scene, an imaginary scene, or some combination thereof.[29] From our perspective in discussing the scripted Child ego state, any significant place of entry into the existing memory scheme of the script protocol will serve to lay it open for intervention and change.

The techniques of redecision therapy are based upon the elements of the *symbolic play* in which the Child engages during the pre-operational period. The scene is reenacted and relived. It is common to encourage some clients to address parental figures in empty chairs, playing everyone's part in the scene. With other clients, visual images of the scene may prove more productive, and the process may be carried through in fantasied interaction. The Gouldings work with a seemingly limitless number of innovative methods that encourage the Child to carry the formative scene through to some more satisfactory solution. When lost in dark places, the Child is supplied with a flashlight. When helpless and disarmed, the Child is provided skills acquired in other areas of experience. When forbidden to act, the Child is given all the opportunities present in the imaginative world of creative play to say or do what was forbidden. All the resources of later life may be brought to bear upon the unsatisfactory memory scheme to bring it to constructive resolution.

Reparenting

The *reparenting* model for script cure was developed by Jacqui Schiff as a method for treating psychosis. It involves a total decathexis of the client's Parent ego state and its replacement with a new, healthy Parent. Its procedures necessitate a supportive external structure for the patient, normally a residential treatment facility. A full regression is encouraged back to the developmental period where growth was interrupted. Schiff believes psychotic persons know cognitively and viscerally what they need to do to get well and will do it in their regressed state if given a supportive environment, permitting them to develop new internal structures and options for behavior. Reparenting constitutes a bold program of intervention involving diapers, bottles, spanking, relearning, and the programming of a new Parent ego state. While psychotic persons are regressed, they are unable to invest energy in their other ego states. Such a full decathexis is not seen among nonpsychotic patients, and reparenting is never undertaken with them. Only temporary and brief regressions are elicited, and the task (distinguished as simply *parenting*) is to fill in the gaps in the extant Parent and relate new Parent messages to all three ego states.

Structural change is sought through reparenting, not only in the Child ego state that is permitted to develop new internal schemes and options for behavior, but also in the Parent ego state that is reconstructed at each step. At first glance, the assumptions of reparenting appear remote to those of classical script cure, yet there are parallels in the role of parenting and the therapist's potence. Berne saw the patient as victimized by parental voices and cure as getting the new voice of the therapist into the patient's head. Schiff sought to dismantle the pathogenic Parent ego state and get a new Schiffian Parent into the client's head. The reparenter accepts a complete investment of transference by actually occupying the Parental role in the client's life, gradually restoring it in the process of "growing up again."[30]

Mastery

Since successful changes have resulted from the use of each of these three models for script cure, I prefer to address whatever curative measures they hold in common rather than to discuss their relative merits. Each in its own way intervenes in the symbolic and sensorimotor schemes of the scripted Child so as to provide what Alexander and French termed a "corrective emotional experience."[31] Permissions are never delivered indiscriminately, but timed exquisitely at moments when the client is deeply involved in the memory scheme governing the script. Such interventions are followed by the period of protection in which the therapist actively supports experimentation in new schematic behaviors by the client outside the old script pattern by virtue of their disobedience of the injunction. A strong element of permission is present in redecision therapy in the way the therapist actively invites a more satisfactory and resourceful response by the client through the elements of symbolic play during reenactment of a formative scene. Reparenting procedures undertake to reconstruct the Parent ego state with a series of permissions during regressions which permit the Child to redo developmental scenes with a more healthy resolution.

What is common to all three models is the mastery of alternatives to those behaviors dictated by the memory scheme of the script itself. Whether this mastery is encouraged through verbal permission and protection, through a structured reenactment of formative scenes, or through controlled regression that permits a measure of "re-living" early development, the aim is the same. Each model seeks to bring to resolution what was initially interrupted, forbidden, or uncompleted. Interventions are designed to break the circular reaction of the memory scheme by changing the scheme itself. Whatever optional behaviors develop in the process are encouraged within the context of cure or change, divesting the original scheme of its energy and grip upon contemporary experience. Three rules of thumb will be helpful for any psychotherapist working with the scripted Child ego state at this level.

1) The mastery of memory schemes from this pre-logical period will often require an action scheme for resolution that is itself *alogical* or appropriate to the symbolic schemes which govern thought for the pre-operational child. Take childhood fears, for example, which by their nature remain private and non-communicable, hence, inaccessible to logical explanation. The problem lies in teaching the child something to do about what is feared. The small boy who fears there is a lion under the bed or in the hallway takes small comfort in being told there is nothing to fear or that lions are kept in cages at the zoo. The sensitive Parent teaches the Child something to do to resolve the problem of the fear, such as assisting in a check under the bed and in the hallway, to buttress verbal reassurance.

Mark at age 37 possessed archaic fears of night noises and irrational worries about being abandoned by others. Within his memory was a mental image from childhood of lying still all night terrified at what appeared to be a huge monster outside his window. His parents told him it was nothing but a crane. Only the next morning did he see that the ominous, shadowy object in the light of day was actually a large piece of machinery pulled into the vacant lot next door. The therapist encouraged Mark to introduce a scheme of concrete action into his memory, visualizing himself getting out of bed, taking a flashlight, going to the door, and seeing the crane for what it was, then returning to his bed and sleeping soundly, having done something about his fear. Similar mastery was encouraged with contemporary night noises and relationships with others, breaking the pattern of waiting long periods in suspense, only to discover later there was nothing to fear.

Imageless fears are even more archaic since they constitute a raw sensori-motor response of panic whose object remains unseen. Charles experienced such a kinesthetic response as he was about to present a paper to a graduate seminar. None of the fearful outcomes he could logically describe merited the reaction. The therapist encouraged Charles to visualize his fear as an object before him. Charles pictured a huge, prickly, white object with sharp points protruding in all directions, shaped somewhat like a Christmas tree. The next step was to find something to do with it. Painstakingly, Charles began crushing the object-fear until it reached the dimensions of a small pile of dust. This he chose to carry physically into the bathroom and flush down the toilet. Often such alogical solutions to prelogical fears provide the Child the necessary action scheme for dealing with them.

2) Mastery of the memory scheme surrounding the script usually entails the successful completion of some initial task that was interrupted or prohibited. Again, the best measure of such a resolution is the appearance of new action schemes or movement behaviors in present situations. Often the archaic feelings which persist unmastered across the years are a mixture of at least two separate emotional displays. The prevailing ambivalence forbids the expression of either to the point of satiation and closure. The archaic feeling usually represents a compromise under a parental injunction forbidding the expression of emotion A and a commensurate encouragement of emotion B. The result is an archaic feeling of AB which has the substitutionary quality which we have noted in our previous discussion of rackets. Although I dislike the term "racket," it does characterize the manipulative way the scripted Child employs an archaic feeling AB to extract strokes from others and avoid responsibility for making feared departures from the narrower perimeters of the script program.

Joan provides an excellent example of the dual character of archaic feelings that sometimes surround the script. She entered treatment with me to rid herself of a sense that there was "something bad wrong deep inside." Joan was tearful throughout the major part of each individual session before she was admitted to group. She cried profusely each time she worked in group, whether over her struggles with her estranged daughter, her quarrels with her ex-husband, or her sense that all her business accomplishments, which were considerable, were unreal and would not last. Joan had a congenitally deformed left hand which was much smaller than her right and without fingers. The most striking feature of her bodily behavior was the manner in which she kept this hand well concealed beneath her right hand, in a pocket, or motionless in her lap. So successful were her efforts that this therapist, who always looks at bodies, did not notice the hand until over halfway through her initial session. Some members of her group had not observed it after five weeks.

Whatever current problem she addressed, Joan consistently reported as she cried that she was both sad and angry. She was sad because things never worked out for her. And although she would acknowledge anger toward her daughter or her ex-husband or her mother, this admission always dissolved into anger toward herself for mistakes and failures with them. Since all of her gestural movements were from her right side, the therapist encouraged her to explore the sense of feeling she had there. It was her familiar sad-angry sensation accompanied by tears. She was then encouraged to explore for the first time the particular sensations that accompanied comparable movement in her left. Joan was immediately angry at the unfairness of her deformity. Extending her left hand into the air in full view, she launched into a tearless tirade against everybody who treated her as different, against school kids who gawked at her misshapen hand, against her mother who taught her to hide it underneath her coat, and finally, against God for failure to create her a whole and unblemished person. The therapist encouraged her to make the rounds of each group member, asserting her angry protest, "Don't you look at me like I'm different." This was followed by genuine sadness at all the pain she had suffered as a child, from which there was a sense of moving relief. Unlike the expressionless flow of tears we had seen before, each feeling received separate display to a point of visible satiation. This mastery of feelings surrounding her deformity was accompanied by an entirely different display of gestural behavior the following week which was now bilateral, using both hands in equal numbers of movements, and her own observation, "I find it difficult to hide my hand anymore."

3) The kind of mastery we have been discussing involves the restoration of natural functioning at the point where it was inhibited or blocked by scripting. Sometimes the exploration of polar opposites in posture or movement at the point of a person's impasse will pave the way for restored functional wholeness when more rational or conceptual approaches fail. The disappearance of the script sign is often facilitated through or accompanied by natural movement behaviors which have long been suppressed. Often some permanent bodily change emerges as a lasting marker to mastery. The individual looks different, feels different, and does things differently. On occasion, these changes happen suddenly and quite apart from the heavier phases of script analysis, as an appropriate landmark to the conclusion of a process of change.

Nan is my favorite clinical example of such restoration of natural bodily functions. A devout member of a religious order, she was also a professionally trained psychologist who worked in a local mental health center. She had done extensive therapy on her script which called for her to deny her own needs in an effort to please significant authorities, going back to both of her parents. This often involved considerable self-sacrifice and the tolerance of others who imposed unreasonable demands upon her. Within the course of personal psychotherapy and intensive training for professional boards, she asserted her right to be herself and live as she chose with profound changes in her own sense of potence. Still, she suffered from recurrent cramps in her right hand which became so severe she had difficulty writing her clinical records.

Nan attributed her "writer's cramp" to her mounting anger toward others who took advantage of her. She described a new assignment in public education she had received at the center where she worked which was in excess of the hours of her contract. She banged her right fist upon the arm of the chair as she declared she already produced more hours of patient care than any other staff member. She ended decisively by stating her freedom from guilt and her resolve to say no when she chose to. During the entire conversation, Nan moved only from the right side of her body. On impulse, this therapist asked her to experiment with movement from her left hand. She began to do so hesitantly, checking her tendencies to return to her right. Then she began to explore broad, sweeping gestures and burst out laughing in delight. Others made remarks about the graceful, free character of her movement, which was immediately accompanied by affective relief, the disappearance of anger, and a rush of plans about how she wanted to do things in her work.

Two days later, quite on impulse, Nan suddenly stopped writing with her right hand, shifted her pen over and began writing with her left. Immediately, the small, pinched, square character of her letters disappeared before the broad, sweeping strokes of her fingers. She wrote with ease at once, without practice or effort, bringing samples of her new handwriting to therapy. It flowed with melodious grace in contrast to the stark and awkward strokes of previous samples. Not only did Nan's writer's cramp disappear, but her newfound ease of movement spread to carry her easily through her professional boards and into the establishment of her own counseling center in a local church.

In Conclusion, Grace

Nan's awkward adaptation to right-handedness serves as a concluding symbol of the suppression of natural ease and gracefulness in any *body*. When anyone—a parent, a teacher, a psychotherapist—fails to recognize the natural rhythm and growth as it unfolds in the development of anybody else, something sacred is violated. At the conclusion of this writing, I am filled with a sense of awe at the marvelous wisdom of our bodies in their innate drive toward health and wholeness. I have long been struck by the relationship between what the theologian calls *grace* and the *grace*-ful expressions of uninhibited movement and growth we can encourage among people of all ages. In its most profound sense, grace is a gift freely given by the Creator. Our task as creatures is not so much one of learning how to get it or receive it; rather it is one of discovering what we have already been given, opening ourselves to where it has already begun to lead, and gracefully accepting the full lines of our being that are constantly seeking expression and completion.

Such a gift presents itself to me as I sit here working on this concluding section in the cabin behind my house. As I look out the window, my 14-year-old son, Tevis, is lofting field goals high onto the garage roof beside my window, with two footballs and a kicking tee. He delights in my watching and calls for me to applaud the next kick. And I delight in watching him—until the thought occurs to me that he is kicking in the general direction of the window out of which I am looking. Without thinking, I go out and issue what I intend to be a Parental word of caution, "Tevis, sooner or later you are going to kick one through this window."

Yes, I said it. Even after years of working with injunctions and writing a book about them, that is exactly what I said. As predicted, the next kick sailed disastrously close to the window, although, before my unwitting command, he had not kicked a ball within ten yards. And while I was writing the paragraphs above about the incident, two other kicks bounced off the cabin wall outside, although he had previously kicked for half an hour without coming near.

Such is the power of injunctions with significant others. And this power persists within an injunctive relationship so as to interfere with efforts toward mastery way beyond the formative years we have been discussing. How can my fearful expectations so influence that delicate confluence of sensorimotor schemes that govern my son's kicking that he can so accurately miss according to my unwitting command? Perhaps we hypnotize our children with such unintended suggestions formed from our anticipation of feared consequences. And they obey our expectations as secret commands. Now my fantasies grow. Were I in the NFL defending against a last-second field goal, I would stop the arm-waving and distracting, station the most formidible Parent-beaked linebacker squarely before the kicker, and have him say, "Watch your tendency to shag it to the right."

What is this power of expectations in the hands of a potent therapist? What is it in the hands of a potent parent? In mine, now? I look at the window, and my values race before me. What is the cost of a pane or two? Besides, the large bush in front masks at least half its surface. I get up and go outside and tell Tevis *he can't damage the window* because the bush in front would probably break the impact of any ball that comes toward it. The thumps upon my cabin wall promptly cease. My son is free to return to the graceful mastery of the art of place kicking unmolested by the secret commands of my fears. There is genuine cause for hope in the world.

REFERENCE NOTES

1. Berne, E. *What Do You Say After You Say Hello?* New York: Grove Press, 1971, p. 53.
2. See Piaget, J., & Inhelder, B. *The Psychology of the Child.* New York: Basic Books, 1969. Also, Piaget, J. *The Origins of Intelligence in Children.* New York: International Universities Press, 1952. Piaget, J. *The Construction of Reality in the Child.* New York: Basic Books, 1954. Piaget, J. *Play, Dreams, and Imitation in Childhood.* New York: W. W. Norton, 1951.

3. Piaget, J., & Inhelder, B., op. cit., pp. 24-27, 54-56.
4. Ibid., p. 114.
5. Escalona, S. Patterns of infantile experience and the developmental process. In R. Eisaler, et al. (Eds.), *The Psychoanalytic Study of the Child* (Vol. 18). New York: International Universities Press, 1963, pp. 198, 199.
6. Piaget, J., & Inhelder, B., op. cit., p. 68.
7. See Baldwin, A. L. *Theories of Child Development*. New York: John Wiley & Sons, 1967, p. 230.
8. Berne, E., op cit., p. 104.
9. Freud, S. Three contributions to the theory of sex. In A. A. Brill (Ed.), *The Basic Writings of Sigmund Freud*. New York: The Modern Library, 1938, pp. 580-603.
10. Erikson, E. H. Identity and the life cycle. *New York Psychological Issues*, Vol. I, No. 1. Monograph. New York: International Universities Press, 1959.
11. Ibid.
12. Ibid.
13. Bandler, R., & Grinder, J. *The Structure of Magic*, I. Palo Alto, CA: Science and Behavior Books, 1975.
14. An excellent summary is found in Bartlett, F. C. *Remembering*. Cambridge: Cambridge University Press, 1932.
15. Penfield, W., & Jasper, H. *Epilepsy and the Functional Anatomy of the Brain*. Boston: Little, Brown & Co., 1954, pp. 127-147.
16. Piaget, J., & Inhelder, B., op. cit., p. 81.
17. See, for example, the special issue on "cure," *Transactional Analysis Journal, 10*:96-153, 1980.
18. Berne, E. Away from a theory of the impact of interpersonal interaction on non-verbal participation. *Transactional Analysis Journal, 1*:6-13, 1971.
19. Berne, E. *Principles of Group Treatment*. New York: Oxford University Press, 1966, p. 290.
20. Berne, E. Away from a theory of the impact of interpersonal interaction on non-verbal participation. *Transactional Analysis Journal, 1*:11, 12, 1971.
21. Goulding, M. M., & Goulding, R. L. *Changing Lives Through Redecision Therapy*. New York: Brunner/Mazel, 1979, pp. 258-279.
22. Bandler, R., & Grinder, J. *Frogs into Princes*. Moab, Utah: Real People Press, 1979, pp. 79-136.
23. Polster, E., & Polster, M. P. *Gestalt Therapy Integrated*. New York: Brunner/Mazel, 1973, pp. 82-89.
24. Ibid., p. 36.
25. See Berne, E. *What Do You Say After You Say Hello?* pp. 123-125, 371-376. Steiner, C. *Scripts People Live*. New York: Grove Press, 1974, pp. 258-269.
26. Goulding, M. M., & Goulding, R. L., op. cit.
27. Schiff, J. L. *Cathexis Reader*. New York: Harper & Row, 1975.
28. Berne, E. *What Do You Say After You Say Hello?* p. 369.
29. Goulding, M. M., & Goulding, R. L., op. cit., p. 185.
30. Schiff, J. L., op. cit., p. 102.
31. Alexander, F., & French, T. *Psychoanalytic Theory*. New York: Ronald Press, 1946.

Index

301